DESIRE, DISCORD AND DEATH

APPROACHES TO ANCIENT NEAR EASTERN MYTH

ASOR Books Volume 8

Victor Matthews, editor

Billie Jean Collins
ASOR Director of Publications

DESIRE, DISCORD AND DEATH

APPROACHES TO ANCIENT NEAR EASTERN MYTH

by

Neal Walls

American Schools of Oriental Research • Boston, MA

DESIRE, DISCORD AND DEATH

APPROACHES TO ANCIENT NEAR EASTERN MYTH

Cover art: Cylinder seal from Susa inscribed with the name of worshiper of Nergal. Photo courtesy of the Louvre Museum. Cover design by Monica McLeod.

Library of Congress Cataloging-in-Publication Data

Walls, Neal H., 1962-
Desire, discord, and death : approaches to ancient Near Eastern myth / by Neal Walls.
p. cm. -- (ASOR books ; v. 8)
Includes bibliographical references and indexes.
ISBN 0-89757-056-1 -- ISBN 0-89757-055-3 (pbk.)
1. Mythology--Middle East. 2. Middle East--Literatures--History and crticism. 3. Death in literature. 4. Desire in literature. I. Title. II. Series.
BL1060 .W34 2001
291.1'3'09394--dc21

2001003236

Contents

Abbreviations

ABD .... *The Anchor Bible Dictionary*, ed. David Noel Freedman (New York: Doubleday, 1992)
AHw .... Wolfram von Soden, *Akkadisches Handwörterbuch* (Wiesbaden: Harrassowitz, 1965-81)
AOAT .... Alter Orient und Altes Testament
CAD .... *The Assyrian Dictionary of the University of Chicago* (Chicago: University of Chicago, 1956–)
CANE .... *Civilizations of the Ancient Near East*, ed. Jack M. Sasson (New York: Charles Scribner's Sons, 1995)
DDD .... *Dictionary of Deities and Demons in the Bible*, eds. Karel van der Torrn, Bob Becking, and Pieter W. van der Horst, 2nd ed. (Leiden: Brill, 1999)
GAG .... Wolfram von Soden, *Grundriss der akkadischen Grammatik,* 3rd ed. Analecta Orientalia 33 (Rome: Pontificium Institutum Biblicum, 1995)
HR .... *History of Religions*
HSM .... Harvard Semitic Monographs
JBL .... *Journal of Biblical Literature*
JCS .... *Journal of Cuneiform Studies*
JEA .... *Journal of Egyptian Archaeology*
JNES .... *Journal of Near Eastern Studies*
LÄ .... *Lexikon der Ägyptologie*, eds. W. Helck and W. Westendorf (Wiesbaden: Harrassowitz, 1972–)
OBO .... Orbis biblicus et orientalis
RlA .... *Reallexikon der Assyriologie*, eds. E. Ebeling et al. (Berlin: de Gruyter & Co., 1932–)
TUAT .... *Texte aus der Umwelt des Alten Testaments*, ed. Otto Kaiser (Gütersloh: Gütersloher Verlagshaus, 1982–)
UBL .... Ugaritisch-Biblische Literatur
UF .... *Ugarit-Forschungen*
ZA .... *Zeitschrift für Assyriologie*

Acknowledgments

I would like to thank numerous friends and colleagues who aided and abet-ted me in the production of this book with their many acts of kindness. These include, among others, David Casson, Amy Cottrill, David Garber, Brad Kelle, Jacqueline Lapsley, Brian Mahan, Victor Matthews, Dan Mathewson, and Tim Sandoval. I am especially grateful to Billie Jean Collins, Jerry Cooper, Chip Dobbs-Allsopp, and Carol Newsom for their wise advice and continued encouragement, and to my research assistant, Katherine Logan, for her many hours of labor on this project.

Support for the research and writing of this book was provided by generous grants from the Wabash Center for Teaching and Learning in Theology and Religion and the University Research Committee of Emory University.

INTRODUCTION
Hidden Riches in Secret Places

The prophet Isaiah ben Amoz proclaimed an ominous fate for the glorious city that once dominated the ancient Near East:

And Babylon, the glory of kingdoms,
  the proud splendor of the Chaldeans,
will be like Sodom and Gomorrah
  when God overthrew them.
Nevermore shall it be inhabited,
  nor settled through all the ages.
No Arab will pitch his tent there,
  no shepherd will rest flocks there.
But wild animals will rest there,
  in houses filled with howling creatures.
Ostriches will reside there,
  and there will satyrs dance.
Hyenas will howl within its fortresses,
  and jackals, in the pleasure-palaces.
(Isaiah 13:19–22)[1]

Isaiah's prophetic oracle of Babylon's abandonment foresaw the great city's utter desolation from ancient times to the present. Like Akkad and Nineveh before her, Babylon would eventually succumb to the relentless forces of change and decay. While Babylon's memory survived in the Christian and Muslim worlds as a symbol of pagan excess, much of her actual splendor lay forgotten, buried under the drifting soil of the Mesopotamian plain. The teeming metropolis ruled by Hammurapi (c. 1792–1750 BCE) and Nebuchadrezzar (604–562 BCE) was reduced to a heap of ruins on the distant horizon. Yet, as the Sufi mystic Rumi wrote, "Where there is ruin, there is hope for treasure."[2] This hope was fulfilled by modern archaeologists who in the nineteenth century began to excavate the sites of Babylon, Nineveh, and other ancient Near Eastern cities from Mesopotamia to Egypt. The archives of cuneiform and Egyptian texts that they brought to light after two thousand years of entombment include treasures of world literature. Indeed, these literary texts are among the "treasures of darkness and hidden riches in secret places" that Isaiah so long ago promised to Cyrus, the Persian conqueror of Babylon (Isaiah 45:3).[3]

Ancient Near Eastern literature may lack the poetic grace of Homeric metaphors or the delightful expression of Norse kennings, but it possesses its own stark beauty and poetic charm. Some ancient poems sing in sonorous voices of primordial events or serenade us with lovely songs of the splendor of the gods. Other texts, however, are not so beautiful; their ideologies of conquest and oppression are distasteful to contemporary readers. Sometimes the words of the story lay heavy upon the page, obscure and unintelligible. Perhaps the narrative lacks artistry; perhaps we are simply unable to perceive it. As our western eyes are unaccustomed to reading cuneiform and hieroglyphic scripts, so our modern ears are not attuned to the rhetorical forms of this alien and exotic literature. Our hearts are not always warmed by the ancients' concerns nor our minds enlightened by their insights. In general, our interests and obsessions are different from theirs. No matter: the allure of ancient voices compels us to meditate upon their sacred literature and listen attentively to their myths repeated from the dawn of civilization.

Ancient Near Eastern mythology offers its readers fantastic accounts of the birth of the gods and the creation of the world, the flood and its few survivors, the mount of the gods' assembly, and the gloomy underworld of departed shades. Composed in hieroglyphic characters on papyrus scrolls or inscribed on clay tablets in cuneiform signs, the world's earliest literature records the myths of Ishtar and Gilgamesh, Isis and Osiris, Horus and Seth, and Nergal and Ereshkigal, to name but a few. These narratives construct elaborate scenarios of divine conflicts on the Nile's African shores, heroic journeys across Asian landscapes, and Netherworld itineraries for the restless dead. The mythological imagination and literary subtlety displayed by this early literature deserve greater acclaim and deeper appreciation than generally accorded by scholars of comparative myth or Near Eastern studies. Many riches still remain hidden in these texts.

In an effort to display the literary art and poetic vision of ancient Near Eastern mythology, this collection of essays uses contemporary methods of literary analysis to explore the interrelated themes of desire, divine conflict, and death's realm in selected mythological narratives. Common to all chapters is the theme of erotic desire—its various manifestations, the conflicts it produces, and its symbolic association with death. The book's first chapter, informed by queer theory, traces the poetic construction of desire in the Gilgamesh epic's extended meditation upon love and death. The second chapter uses a Freudian lens to interpret the bizarre sexual symbolism and competing desires of Horus and Seth in "The Contendings of Horus and Seth." The entwined themes of desire, discord, and death most fully converge in the third chapter, "Desire in Death's Realm," about the stormy romance of Nergal and Ereshkigal, the fearsome rulers of the Netherworld. This chapter applies a feminist theory of power to the analysis of trickery, sex, and violence in the two versions of "Nergal and Ereshkigal." Thus, the first and third essays explicitly focus on erotic desire and death; the second and third essays more closely examine the relationship between desire and divine discord. All three chapters portray the driving force of passion for these mythic characters. Ontologically significant and viscerally powerful, sex and death are standard fare for mythological speculation and thus provide an appropriate focus for our interpretive venture. It should be no surprise that contemporary readers also share a persistent fascination with these dominant themes of world mythology.

METHODS AND APPROACHES

As the literary remains of long-dead civilizations, ancient Near Eastern mythological texts have been orphaned by time. The tablets and scrolls rest on museum shelves in distant archaeological collections, forever separated from the ancient world that produced them. The interpreter of ancient Near Eastern myth must often be more anthropologist than literary critic, but we would-be ethnographers are bereft of native informants and living traditions to aid in our analyses and interpretations. We lack the intimate cultural and religious knowledge to fully contextualize the mythological narratives. Instead of hearing the myths chanted by priests or performed in public festivals, we must be content with the small fraction of ancient mythology that was recorded by the scribal elite in highly literary form and fortuitously recovered by archaeologists. Bridging the gap between ancient texts and contemporary readers requires a careful discipline as well as a certain amount of imagination. Interpreters of ancient Near Eastern mythological literature must therefore be especially vigilant in examining our own theoretical assumptions and hermeneutical practices. This kind of methodological conscientiousness, unfortunately, has not always been observed in the analysis of mythological narratives.

For most of the twentieth century, the traditional curriculum of Near Eastern studies emphasized the technical methods of archaeology, history, and philology but neglected the fields of anthropology, comparative religion, and literary theory. As a result, Near Eastern scholars were often unfamiliar with current methods in the academic study of myth. Many scholars adopted out-dated interpretive approaches, such as euhemerism, nature-myth, or myth-ritual approaches; others adopted overly romantic perspectives toward the ancient world and attributed a prelogical, mythopoeic mentality to practitioners of ancient "fertility religions" (see Kirk 1970:1–42, 84–90; Rogerson 1974; Oden 1992). While earlier generations of Near Eastern scholars did brilliant work in philology, history, and the production of critical editions, they did not always have the same high standards or appropriate methods for sensitive interpretations of mythological literature. Recently, however, scholars have begun to cross disciplinary lines in order to apply contemporary forms of literary and symbolic criticism to the world's oldest mythology. Indeed, the need for scholars of ancient Near Eastern literatures to break out of their self-imposed isolation and engage critical literary theory is now openly acknowledged within the guild.[4]

A necessary prerequisite for contemporary interpretation of ancient mythological literature is an appreciation of myth as a complex, multivalent form of symbolic discourse that cannot be reduced to a particular form, function, or mentality.[5] As a complex of symbols developed into narrative form (Ricoeur 1969:18), myth is a dynamic vehicle of thought that points to and generates meanings beyond its literal subjects. Following Paul Ricoeur (1969:3–18), I understand symbols to be expressive as well as referential forms of signification (cf. Bynum 1986). Instead of merely referring to previously established social meanings, symbols create the possibility of new meanings; symbols "give rise to thought," to use Ricoeur's evocative phrase. Symbols provoke spontaneous leaps of imagination in the minds of their audience through the cognitive functions of analogy and association. Since the symbol's meaning is not inherent in the object itself, the symbol may signify any of a matrix of associated meanings. In turn, the symbol integrates and condenses within itself the full matrix of possible meanings. Symbols are therefore multivalent and polysemic in that they have the ability to express different meanings in different contexts (see Turner 1967:45–52). Because of this symbolic overdetermination, myths produce a surplus of meaning that is exploited by an audience in its apprehension of the narrative. Instead of clearly expressing one particular meaning, myths generate multiple and diverse interpretations.

Symbolic interpretation in its native context, therefore, is not simply the process of decoding or assigning cultural values to symbols; rather, interpretation is a mental improvisation based upon culturally implicit knowledge to explain the hidden, implied levels of signification beyond a symbol's literal referent (see Sperber 1975:xi). Caroline Walker Bynum (1986:9) explains that for Ricoeur, "meaning is not so much imparted as appropriated in a dialectical process" between the symbol and the user, and so individual users may appropriate the symbol in widely different ways. Meaning is thus always an interpretive rather than normative function. Symbolic condensation allows for a host of potential responses by the user, depending on which symbolic associations are actuated in a particular context. Furthermore, by pointing beyond ordinary experience, symbols can transmute as well as reflect social reality. Myths may therefore work to reinforce, invert, or subvert social practices and ideologies. This dynamic quality means that myths do not necessarily portray actual social practice and ideology in an accurate fashion. Likened to a chameleon by Wendy Doniger (1998:100), myths have an uncanny aptitude for reinterpretation and adaptation to new contexts because of their inherently malleable character (see Doniger 1998:79–107).

The recognition of myth's multivalent and multifunctional character highlights our limitations in fully understanding ancient Near Eastern mythology. We cannot explain the social function of ancient myths and we lack the implicit cultural knowledge of native interpretations. However, thanks to the work of scribal authors and compilers, contemporary readers can constructively engage the literary and symbolic complexity of ancient mythological literature. Indeed, the incorporation of living myth into poetic narrative results in highly elaborate symbolic expressions of cultural and ontological significance. The literary sophistication of Near Eastern literature is such that the texts encompass multiple perspectives, sustain unresolved ambiguity and paradox, and remain open to a variety of meanings. The mythological texts' multivalent symbolism, surplus of meaning, and narrative polyphony therefore allow for multiple and conflicting interpretations by different readers, both ancient and modern. Thus, the hermeneutical challenge to contemporary readers of Near Eastern mythology is to apprehend ancient cultural codes and meanings as fully as possible, at the same time that we appropriate the texts in our own postmodern frames of reference. The best way to meet this challenge, in my opinion, is to approach the texts from a variety of critical perspectives and to apply multiple forms of literary analysis.

A methodological pluralism offers a refreshing alternative to monolithic or universalistic theories that attempt to subjugate all mythological discourse under a single functional rubric (see Kirk 1974:38–91; Oden 1987:40–91). As Laurie Patton and Wendy Doniger explain in their introduction to *Myth and Method* (1996:1–2), scholars of myth no longer hold out much hope for a unifying theory of myth or a universalistic method of interpretation to unlock all of myth's secrets. Lacking Ariadne's thread to mark the one safe passage out of the symbolic labyrinth, scholars have turned to a variety of critical methods for new approaches to mythological narratives (see Edmunds 1990; Patton and Doniger 1996). Indeed, a variety of interpretations is necessary to match the variety of ways that myths work; the multivalent and multifunctional quality of myth cannot be exhausted by any one interpretive approach. Commenting on literary theory in general, Eve Kosofsky Sedgwick (1997:9) explains that a critical method offers one way (among others) of "seeking, finding, and organizing knowledge" from within a text. The application of literary theory to seek, find, and organize knowledge recognizes that the questions one asks of a text determine the answers one finds. Other methods will seek out and organize other forms of knowledge from the same text. The text has many things to tell us, but we can often apprehend only one message at a time. Indeed, a critical method is analogous to a diagnostic medical procedure that tests or explores one system of the body while ignoring other systems within the organic whole.[6] The text remains the same, but our perception of its features changes based upon our perspective. Again, the answers we get (and the interpretations we construct) depend entirely upon the questions we ask (and the methods we apply).

In summary, the complexity of mythological literature compels me to employ a complex set of methods in order to exploit more fully the surplus of meanings produced by ancient Near Eastern mythological narratives. I apply a variety of methods in order to explore the texts as examples of sophisticated literature and symbolic discourse, to unpack their poetics, and to emphasize literary features not adequately appreciated by previous interpreters. I borrow this idea from literary criticism, that perspective from psychoanalysis, and the other notion from ideological criticism in order to offer new readings of very ancient myths. These contemporary reading strategies ask new questions of both the reader and the text and so open up new vistas of meaning; they cast a new light on the ancient texts and illumine neglected facets of their discourse. These methodological approaches are meant to expand rather than challenge the traditional repertoire of scholarly tools for the analysis of ancient Near Eastern texts. Although the ancient texts are most fully understood within their original cultural and historical contexts, contemporary readers may profitably engage contemporary critical theories when interpreting the ancient world. These essays are therefore meant to be constructively provocative in order to stimulate further hermeneutical conversations. In the end, I hope to foster a greater appreciation of the literary artistry and symbolic complexity of these mythological texts; to convey to other Near Eastern scholars the importance of contemporary methods; and to generate a wider awareness of ancient Near Eastern myths among scholars of comparative mythology.

NOTES

[1]All translations, unless otherwise noted, are the author's.

[2]The quote is from Lamott (1999:76), who appears to paraphrase Barks's translation of Rumi's *Mathnawi* IV, 2540-59 (Barks and Green 1997:69).

[3]Jacobsen (1976) alludes to this verse in the title of his culminating study of Mesopotamian mythology, *Treasures of Darkness*.

[4]See Harris 1990:219; Jones 1993; Ray 1996; and Michalowski 1996, among others. Leick (1998:198) writes for Assyriologists: "I feel very strongly that unless we take steps to break free from the confines of scholasticism that so restrict and intellectually isolate our discipline, there is a real danger that this solipsism will lead to further alienation not only from popular culture but from other academic disciplines too. A reorientation toward greater interdisciplinary work, a willingness to engage in current debates… are vital." Egyptologists have also been adopting a more conscientiously methodological approach to their literary sources (see Loprieno 1996a; 1996b).

[5]Myth may be oral or written, prose or poetry, primitive or postmodern; myth is multivalent as well as multifunctional. On the study of myth in general, see Dundes (1984), Doty (1986), Strenski (1987), Oden (1992), Dubuisson (1993), Patton and Doniger (1996), Doniger (1998), and Segal (1980; 1999).

[6]I thank Max Miller for this analogy. See also Doniger (1998:7–25), who artfully explores the analogy of using microscopes and telescopes in examining myth.

CHAPTER 1

The Allure of Gilgamesh: The Construction of Desire in the Epic of Gilgamesh

INTRODUCTION

The Native American writer Sherman Alexie (1993:145–46) tells the story of a Spokane Indian named Victor who brought an old, weather-beaten piano onto the reservation. One day he sat down and pounded out an impromptu rendition of a piece by Béla Bartók. “In the long silence after Victor finished his piece, after the beautiful dissonance and implied survival, the Spokane Indians wept, stunned by this strange and familiar music. ‘Well,’ Lester FallsApart said. ‘It ain’t Hank Williams but I know what it means.’” Contemporary readers may be similarly stunned by the strange and familiar *Epic of Gilgamesh*, a poetic narrative full of the “beautiful dissonance and implied survival” of human existence. Like Lester, we know what it means. It is not as familiar as the music we hear on the radio but we nevertheless anticipate the melody before it arrives; we hear the exotic harmonies before they are voiced. We recognize themes and motifs that express our own awareness of mortality and the struggle against oblivion. This ancient text surprises us with its familiarity and relevance as we discover in Gilgamesh a kindred spirit who rages against the “dying of the light” and howls at the injustice of human finitude. Like Native Americans who share a common vision with the Hungarian Bartók, postmodern Americans of various identities may unexpectantly recognize themselves in the ancient Akkadian poetry of Gilgamesh.

The artistry of the Gilgamesh epic traverses historical and cultural boundaries to raise perennial questions about the meaning of life, the mystery of love, the fragility of desire, and the relentlessness of the grave. These poignant themes resonate in the human heart, whether ancient, modern, or even postmodern. Indeed, the narrative of Gilgamesh's journeys provides an uncanny correspondence to Annie Dillard's (1989:72) literary quest when she asks: "Why are we reading, if not in hope of beauty laid bare, life heightened and its deepest mystery probed?" The timeless quality of the Gilgamesh epic derives from its wrestling with similar ideas. In his search for wisdom, Gilgamesh probes the deepest mysteries as he descends into the Abyss, journeys to the edge of the world, and brings back secrets from before the Flood. He is a king, as well as a hero, whose epic feats and majestic buildings have never been equaled. Yet, the epic's conclusion is not the satisfaction gained by great accomplishments so much as their ultimate futility.

The strange yet familiar poetry thus beckons us to engage in interpretation, to distill some purpose from the chaos of events, and to form some conclusion about the meaning of human existence. We are told that Gilgamesh eventually attains wisdom, but we are left without a definitive accounting of its substance. There is no moral to the tale than can be captured in a pithy aphorism or summarized in a didactic proverb. Multiple voices compete for our allegiance as each expresses a worthy goal of human endeavor: heroic deeds, monumental building, erotic indulgence, or the establishment of a familial lineage.[1] Indeed, like other literary classics, the epic's subtle intentions and supple narrative allow for divergent and conflicting interpretations of its ideological perspective. The text uses the grandeur of its settings—on the edge of the world, in the mountains of darkness, before the cave of Humbaba—and fantastic episodes of sex and violence, catastrophic disaster, and visitations from the Netherworld to distract the reader from a simplistic solution to the enigma of human consciousness. Yet, as Dillard surely knows, these mysteries are questions to be explored rather than answers to be found. Rather than resolve the ambiguities, therefore, the epic text negotiates between divergent perspectives as it leads the reader through a labyrinth of possibilities in the search for meaning and significance.

Such richly textured narrative requires an equally complex set of interpretative approaches to appreciate fully its nuanced themes. Once the necessary text-critical and philological work has been done, contemporary methods of literary and ideological criticism may elicit from the text its more subtle charms and clever rhetoric. Thus, through a close reading of episodes that depict the inciting of passion and other forms of erotic investment, this chapter traces the literary discourse of erotic attraction and the poetics of desire through the epic text.[2] In particular, I will apply the hermeneutics of queer theory to examine the use of homoerotic imagery within the text's construction of desire. This erotic focus must not be confused with the epic's more comprehensive concerns with life, death, and the meaning of human existence; yet, what is closer to the human heart than the enduring quest for love and the contemplation of ardent yearning for another person? As an exploration of the Gilgamesh epic's poetics of desire, this chapter necessarily concentrates on Tablets I and II—where the allure of Gilgamesh, Shamhat, and Enkidu is described—and Tablet VI, where Ishtar attempts to seduce the triumphant king. The analysis of the heroes' erotic relationship also draws from Gilgamesh's mournful elegies in the epic's latter half, where the theme of desire is replaced by motifs of death and decay.

The principal witnesses to the ancient Akkadian text of the Gilgamesh epic are tablets of an Old Babylonian (hereafter OB) version and Neo-Assyrian copies of an edition attributed to the priest Sin-leqe-unnini and written in the Standard Babylonian literary dialect.[3] Copies of this latter version, hereafter called the Standard Babylonian or SB edition, were discovered in the ruins of Asshurbanipal's seventh-century BCE library at Nineveh. They provide the basic source for the twelve-tablet compilation now called the *Epic of Gilgamesh*.[4] Reliable English translations of the Gilgamesh epic include those by Stephanie Dalley (1989:39–153), Maureen Kovacs (1989), and Andrew George (1999) (cf. Bottéro 1992a; Hecker 1994; Tournay and Shaffer 1994). My analysis follows the SB version, although the OB text is occasionally used to restore lines lost from the SB when they appear to be parallel accounts.[5]

The Construction of Desire: Queering Gilgamesh

Contemporary methods of literary and ideological criticism often require the reader to put aside social and cultural presuppositions in order to consider a text from a particular, non-traditional perspective. Ideological criticism employs strategies of interpretation that challenge dominant political, social, and cultural practices and structures, including gender roles and sexual identities. These hermeneutical methods aid in identifying and exploring cultural assumptions and ideological agendas within both ancient texts and their contemporary interpretations. Especially pervasive among the ideological presumptions of the modern West is heterosexism, which attributes to authors and literary characters a consistent and normative heterosexual experience. In fact, most interpreters uncritically assume a natural and normative heterosexuality as they imaginatively reconstruct the worldview of ancient Near Eastern literature. Yet, just as readers may recognize themselves in the existential struggles of Gilgamesh, many gay men recognize homoerotic desire in the affairs of Gilgamesh and Enkidu. Along with ambiguous descriptions of love and devotion between the heroes, Gilgamesh's dreams of embacing and caressing Enkidu "like a wife" (see I 229–72) are especially suggestive of a sexual relationship. Indeed, the regularity with which readers of diverse identities now conclude that the two heroes are lovers rather than platonic friends invites a more detailed analysis of homoeroticism in the ancient epic.[6] Previous scholars have certainly acknowledged the possibly homosexual nature of the heroes' relationship (e.g., Doty 1993:73–85), but none has carefully analyzed the poetic and literary techniques that foster this ideological reading. None has explored the ways in which the text generates its own discourse of sexuality. In response, this chapter will examine how erotic desire is rhetorically constructed and literarily represented within the Akkadian text and then attempt to situate hom-eroticism within the epic's larger discourse of desire.

Following the example of David Halperin and other classicists who explore the discourse of sexuality in ancient Greece, my analysis is predicated upon the Foucauldian understanding that sexuality and erotic desire are cultural constructs rather than natural or instinctual phenomena.[7] Jeffrey Henderson (1988:1250) explains: "Sexuality is that complex of reactions, interpretations, definitions, prohibitions, and norms that is created and maintained by a given culture in response to the fact of the two biological sexes." Rather than a natural condition or inherent, personal attribute, sexuality is a socially constructed category, a cultural product, analogous to formal dances and table manners. Cultures produce compulsory models of gender and sexuality, which are then internalized by their members as normative, natural, and self-explanatory. Thus, even the conceptualization, experience, and expression of sexual drives and erotic responses are determined by cultural categories. Subjective desire and erotic object-choice are similarly encompassed by this constructionist theory of sexual experience. The very content of sexuality—what qualifies as sexual behavior—is culturally relative, as well.[8] There is therefore no normative or natural form of sexual expression from which all others deviate; rather, deviation and perversion are merely social tags placed upon certain behaviors.

A constructionist approach to the study of sexuality defends against the uncritical attribution of contemporary models of sexual experience to an ancient discourse of sexuality. It undermines the cultural assumptions of modern sexual identities and requires one to consider an expanded range of erotic experience. The difficulties of identifying and analyzing a poetics of desire in ancient Akkadian literature call for a nuanced hermeneutics, which we find in the recent applications of queer theory to literary analysis.[9] An heir to deconstruction, queer theory challenges normative, heterosexist assumptions by destabilizing gender and sexual categories and emphasizing their artificial qualities as cultural constructs. By problematizing the identification of persons based solely upon the objects of erotic attraction, queer theory actually deprives sexuality of its metonymic power to catalogue people according to seemingly clinical distinctions of gay, straight, or bisexual. In contrast to the traditional categories of sexual identity in the modern West, queer theory seeks a more nuanced erotics that perceives a fuller spectrum and appreciates a broader continuum of sexual experience. It promotes the understanding of "sexuality as pleasurable and relational, rather than as procreative or as an index of status" (Jagose 1996:41). Queer theory further deconstructs the artificial dichotomy between erotic and platonic forms of desire, a feature that is especially significant in analyzing a literary text's poetics of desire. Thus, rather than accept the modern ideology of obligatory heterosexuality, this chapter views the *Epic of Gilgamesh* through the lens of queer theory in order to achieve a sharper focus on the text's discourse of sexuality and poetics of desire.

There is no Akkadian or Sumerian word for "homosexual" and thus no Mesopotamian conception of the personal or public identity in the modern sense. Contemporary readers force ancient literary characters into anachronistic sexual and social identities by classifying them with modern labels such as homosexual, heterosexual, gay, or bisexual. The hermeneutics of queer theory should restrain us from asking the sophomoric question, "Were they really gay?", as though there were some transhistorical essence to homosexuality shared by ancient and postmodern cultures (see Halperin 1990:41–53). The phrase "same-sex love" is more appropriate for the intense friendship of Gilgamesh and Enkidu since it describes a strong emotional bond without evoking anachronistic images. This more ambiguous phrase also has the advantage of encompassing a wide range of sexual behaviors and non-sexual affection. It effectively expands the notion of sexuality from an exclusive focus on genital contact to a broader range of expressions of affection and intimacy between members of the same sex (see Frantzen 1998:1, 68). In an early application of queer theory, Eve Kosofsky Sedgwick (1985:1–2) introduced the useful phrase "male homosocial desire" to denote the continuum of same-sex male love and the proclivity for male companionship. Sedgwick (1985:2) further defines desire as an affective force—like the psychoanalytic term "libido"—that draws and holds people together in various kinds of relationship. I will also use desire or eros to connote a potentially wide range of interpersonal attraction, from sexual passion to platonic friendship, in my analysis of the Gilgamesh epic.[10] Joan Westenholz similarly argues that there is no distinction in ancient Mesopotamian literature between platonic love and erotic desire. Westenholz (1992:381) writes that "love the emotion and sexuality the physical attraction that occurs between two individuals (gender distinction not being particularly important) were not perceived as two separate forces." The ancient Mesopotamian perspective on familial love and sexual arousal as two facets of the same driving power is represented by the use of the verb *râmu* to mean "to make love" as commonly as it refers to platonic or familial love.[11] Thus, we may appreciate the literary portrayal of the intense, homosocial companionship of

Gilgamesh and Enkidu—sexually realized or not—without classifying it with contemporary social identities.

Given the lack of the sexual category, it is not surprising that several recent studies of "homosexuality" in ancient Mesopotamia have been able to reach only meager historical conclusions, often based upon arguments from silence.[12] Apart from the Gilgamesh epic, the assembled evidence for consensual, male homosexual behavior in ancient Mesopotamia seems limited to two possible references in the Middle Assyrian law codes, a few protases in omen collections, and vague references to cult actors who may or may not be eunuchs and/or homosexual prostitutes.[13] Although Bottéro and Petschow (1975) conclude that the two Middle Assyrian laws address only male homosexual prostitution and rape, W. G. Lambert (1992:146–47) holds that the laws are express condemnations of male homosexuality in general. Jean Bottéro (1992b:191) argues, to the contrary, that male homosexuality was of a "perfectly natural character" in ancient Mesopotamia. He (1992b:191) writes, "There is nothing that allows us to think that these homosexual relations were condemned in the least, or even simply considered to be, as such, more ignominious than heterosexual relations, or that they would be discouraged." Although Bottéro (1992b:193) may go too far in his depiction of unrestricted "free love" in ancient Mesopotamia, his wider perspective reminds us of our limited knowledge of ancient sexual ideology. In fact, apart from the inference that there was a certain dishonor and loss of masculine status in being the recipient of anal intercourse, there is very little we know for certain about ancient Mesopotamian attitudes towards male-male sexual practices. Sexual relations were apparently not imagined as reciprocal acts between social equals but, like ancient Greek sexual ideology, as inherently unequal relationships with active and passive, dominant and submissive roles. This implicit power dynamic complicates the description of same-sex relationships between consenting adult males of similar status. There are so few references to male-male sexual behavior in cuneiform sources that we cannot determine if it was strictly prohibited, socially acknowledged, or generally ignored in the various cultures of ancient Mesopotamia.[14] While our ignorance hinders our ability to appreciate the Gilgamesh epic's subtle uses of sexual categories and cultural assumptions, it also forces us to consider a wide array of ideological perspectives in exploring the text's discourse of sexuality.

In examining homoeroticism in the *Epic of Gilgamesh* we must also acknowledge that the epic's discourse of sexuality originates among the privileged, male elites of the scribal tradition. As frequently observed (e.g., Richlin 1993:523), the acts of reading and writing are thoroughly male practices throughout much of human history. This is especially true in ancient Mesopotamia. Piotr Michalowski (1996:192) explains that the symbolic system of cuneiform texts "has to be seen as part of the ideological indoctrination of future bureaucrats, not necessarily as part of a unified world view that permeated all of Mesopotamian society." Moreover, in contrast to other epic traditions performed by bards and singers, the opening column of the Gilgamesh epic (I 11–26) intentionally directs itself with imperative verbs to the solitary male reader (Moran 1995:2331). The Gilgamesh epic thus explicitly locates the discourse of wisdom among a literate, elite male audience. Wisdom is defined and legitimated by the king and scribes in order to persuade other males in a form of ideological procreation. In a similar way, the literary construction of allure and desire is defined by a masculine perspective as the reader is aligned with the narrator's own androcentric focus (cf. Harris 1990:220). The text constructs a poetics of desire through its manipulation of the male reader's desirous gaze. The employment of homoerotic images within this inherently masculine context is worthy of note since exclusively homosocial men can be seen to embody the epitome of androcentric culture and values. Indeed, some cultural critics argue that male homosexuality is the logical extreme of both misogyny and patriarchal ideology.[15]

Finally, in tracing the poetics of desire through the *Epic of Gilgamesh*, my application of queer theory will emphasize erotic desire and sexual object-choice rather than the social location of same-sex love or gender identity (cf. Richlin 1993). My purpose in putting aside heterosexist assumptions is not because a queer reading will result in a more plausible cultural context for the story but because it highlights neglected facets of the text; it listens for a voice in tension with or subversive to the traditional interpretive perspective. Queer theory recognizes that narrative, as a form of discourse, both constitutes and contests its own meaning. Indeed, one should expect a multivalent and polyphonous work of poetic art such as the Gilgamesh epic to generate divergent and competing readings, of "giving rise to thought" rather than advocating predetermined or propagandistic conclusions. In addition to being an increasingly important form of ideological criticism in itself, queer theory provides an appropriate method to analyze the poetics of desire in this ancient Akkadian text because both the theory and the text effectively deconstruct the modern Western dichotomies of sexual/platonic love and hetero-/homo-eroticism.

The following presentation assumes the reader's familiarity with the basic plot of the Gilgamesh epic and so does not summarize or follow the narrative progression from scene to scene. Instead, my analysis begins with the rhetorical presentation of heterosexual desire in the depictions of Enkidu's erotic encounter with Shamhat in Tablet I and Gilgamesh's denial of Ishtar's marriage proposal in Tablet VI. We then return to the epic's beginning for a detailed examination of homoeroticism and heroic love throughout the epic narrative. I hope that this presentation will aid the reader in tracing the text's discourse of desire as it weaves a complicated web of allusions and interplay over the epic's twelve tablets.

THE EROTIC GILGAMESH

Wielding a broad erotic vocabulary in the text's opening columns, the epic narrator inscribes a poetics of desire upon the alluring body of Gilgamesh. The text celebrates the semi-divine king's charms and authoritatively establishes his erotic appeal by proclaiming, "His body is glorious...his delights are complete...he is most handsome" (*šaruḫ lāššu...gitmālu lalêšu...dummuq*; I 49–51, restored by George 1999:3). Shamhat the courtesan similarly praises him as "virile" (*balta*; I 220) and "splendid in manhood" (*eṭlūta bani*; I 219).[16] As the embodiment of sexual appeal (*kuzbu*), Shamhat judiciously applies the same term to Gilgamesh when she concludes that his "entire body is adorned with seductive allure" (*zu᾿᾿una kuzba kalu zumrīšu*; I 220).[17] Irene Winter (1996:14) describes the enticing power of *kuzbu*, "seductive allure," as more than just a passive attribute; it is an energy that emanates from the possessor to arouse the observer, "like some sort of pheromone." As a normative category of Mesopotamian sexual discourse, *kuzbu* should inflame desire in the receptive beholder. The text's application of this term to Gilgamesh thus identifies the king as an appropriate object of erotic desire as it defines and reinforces the ideal of masculine beauty. In describing the *kuzbu* of Gilgamesh, the epic narrator invites the reader to participate in an appreciation of masculine allure. The text's eroticization of Gilgamesh subtly manipulates the reader, regardless of sex or gender, to acknowledge the male body of Gilgamesh as attractive, beautiful, and a delight to the senses.[18]

The Prostitute and the Primal Man: Inciting Desire

In a subtle and sophisticated play of words and images, the poetic narrative continues its construction of desire through the marginal characters of a prostitute and a primal man. While the epic's introduction of Gilgamesh provides a vocabulary of allure, this scene of primal sexuality establishes the characteristics of attraction and sexual response along the gendered lines of female enticement and male aggression. A woman, defined exclusively by her erotic appeal and sexual availability, is engaged expressly to arouse and manipulate desire in the wild man as a means to his humanization. This depiction of male response to feminine allure appears to reflect the traditional Mesopotamian ideology of gender and desire as it presents masculine sexuality in its most raw and natural form.[19] Such an extreme scenario exemplifies the tension between nature and culture, the beastly and the civilized, in the construct of human sexuality. The poet works with these themes to produce a nuanced portrayal of erotic desire in Shamhat's seduction of Enkidu, the epic's only explicit depiction of sexual intercourse.

While the urban prostitute will eventually civilize the wild man and introduce him to the pleasures of Uruk, Enkidu enters the narrative as a wild, feral being, a primal man who knows nothing of human society. Created deep in the heart of the wilderness, he runs with the herds in a state of animal innocence. The description of Enkidu "eating grass with the gazelles" and "enjoying the waters" with the herds (I 93, 95) suggests a peaceful and idyllic existence among the animals, but Enkidu is really a dangerous predator (*eṭla šaggāšâ*; I 162), an experienced fighter (III 8), and a threat to even the lions of the wild (II 207).[20] The goddess Aruru creates his body at the command of Anu to be a wild man (*lullû*) and a warrior (*qurādu*), with a dash of the war god in his nature (*kiṣir Ninurta*) (I 86–87). He is endowed by the gods with extraordinary strength as a match for the rampaging king of Uruk. The trapper describes him as "mightiest in the land" and, foreshadowing Gilgamesh's dream, "as powerful as a meteorite" (I 107–8). The text especially emphasizes Enkidu's hairiness—"His entire body is thickly coated with hair" (I 88)—and poetically describes him as "dressed like Sumuqan," the god of wild animals (i.e., naked and hirsute) (I 92). Following the celebration of Gilgamesh's seductive allure in the previous column, the physical description of Enkidu as a ferocious, hairy beast makes him all the more frightening and repulsive: a brutish Neanderthal to Gilgamesh's elegant hero.

Enkidu's savage appearance as he jostles with the animals at the watering hole is indicated by the trapper's terrified reaction. Dismayed and distraught (I 99–104), the trapper turns to his father, who tells him to procure the services of Shamhat from Gilgamesh. Although Enkidu is too intelligent for the trapper's usual pits and snares, he can be lured and captured by the bait of a prostitute's body. Shamhat is directed to initiate him into the erotic pleasures of human sexuality, which will cause the animals to shun him. Exactly how sexual experience will alienate him from the wild animals is left unexplained but the narrative makes use of this assumption in depicting Enkidu's transformation from beastly to human identity.[21] The employment of a whore to humanize the wild man may surprise modern readers who enshrine romantic love but deem the portrayal of anonymous sexual coupling as pornographic and dehumanizing. Benjamin Foster (1987:22), however, explains the civilizing role of sex in this episode by emphasizing its initiatory function. As a basic form of human knowledge, sexual experience transforms Enkidu from an animal to a human being.

The narrative introduces Shamhat as a stock character, "Shamhat the prostitute" (*ḫarīmtu šamḫat*; e.g., I 145), whose name and occupation associate her with the erotic arts of seduction and pleasure.[22] Her name means something like "voluptuous one," based on the verb *šamāḫu*, "to grow abundantly, thrive, attain extraordinary beauty."

The plural form *šamḫātu* designates prostitutes or courtesans as a group in the Gilgamesh epic (I 213; VI 162).[23] Contrary to Lambert's (1992:128) opinion that *šamḫat* simply means "prostitute," the consistent use of the term in the absolute form makes it more likely that this was her name, even if a transparent "professional" one. She thus has a certain individuality within her stock role that will be developed as the narrative progresses. Bell (1994) reminds us that the cultural construction of "prostitute" varies significantly from street walkers to aristocratic courtesans. It is quite difficult to reconstruct with any nuance the prostitute's actual status within the Mesopotamian moral order and social ideology. Modern generalizations are rendered suspect by the temporal range and cultural diversity of ancient Mesopotamian societies, as well as the different genres of cuneiform literature from which data must be gathered (e.g., legal codes, literary texts, omens, and proverbs). Lambert (1992:132–33), however, surveys the available cuneiform sources and finds no evidence for any moral condemnation of the institution as a whole. He (1992:128) concludes that the Gilgamesh epic shares the perspective of other Mesopotamian texts that prostitution is one of the original arts of civilization handed down by the gods and is thus not subject to moral critique. Rivkah Harris (1990:222, n. 14) similarly states that the Akkadian title *ḫarīmtu*, "prostitute," is a "non-judgmental term for a woman who uses her sexuality to support herself" (cf. *CAD* s. v.). Shamhat's title of prostitute thus identifies her as a member of a legalized profession without necessarily casting aspersions on her personal character.

Shamhat is often called a "temple prostitute" in secondary literature, but there is little evidence of her cultic function.[24] Although prostitutes were devotees of the goddess Ishtar, who describes herself seated outside the tavern as a "loving prostitute" (*ḫarīmtum rāʾimtum anāku*; see *CAD* 6:101), the nature of their association with the goddess remains unclear. In a flight of rhetoric, Lambert (1992:135, 143) declares that the sexual act was itself sacramental and so "all prostitution was regarded as a sacrament" of the goddess Ishtar. While perhaps accurate in one sense, Lambert's words obscure the distinction between the romantic notion of a secular profession's divine patron and routinized cultic sex as part of formal worship. In fact, the patriarchal social patterns of ancient

Mesopotamia and the androcentric perspective of its literature result in the prostitute's ambiguous social status in cuneiform sources, including the Gilgamesh epic. The curses of Enkidu reflect the fact that even though their profession was not subject to moral condemnation prostitutes were often socially marginal women. Prostitutes are presented as thoroughly alluring and associated with the goddess Ishtar in cuneiform literature, yet their function was to service male clients rather than to exalt feminine sexuality. Far from a priestess with sacred status, Shamhat embodies the masculine exploitation of feminine sexuality that leaves her vulnerable to male aggression and violence.

Hence, Shamhat is initially treated as an object more than a person, a sexually available female body manipulated by men for their own purposes. No concern is expressed for her person, her desire, or even her safety as she is passed like a possession from Gilgamesh to the trapper, and then set out in the wilderness to bait the hunter's snare. She is a female body for hire who silently obeys her employer's directions. Marcel Detienne (1979:25) points out that wilderness scenes often "compose a masculine landscape from which the woman/wife is radically absent; so, too, are excluded the sociopolitical values that define the proper use of the female body." Shamhat's social marginality as a prostitute excludes her from the category of "wife," and Enkidu is naturally unconcerned with "sociocultural" values or practices; he will react on a purely animal level to what he perceives to be the "proper use of the female body"—"the task of woman" in the Akkadian idiom (*šipir sinništi*).

In ironic contrast with the trapper's admission that he is too terrified to approach the wild man (I 139), Shamhat is instructed to show no fear. She should "strip off her clothes and reveal her voluptuousness" (*lišḫuṭ lubūšīšā-ma liptâ kuzubša*; I 147).[25] The trapper more explicitly prompts her to "uncradle your bosom" (*rummî kirimmīki*; I 163) and "reveal your vulva," (*ūrki petê-ma*; I 164); the narrator adds, "she unfastened her loincloth and revealed her vulva" (*urtammi…dīdāša ūrša ipte*; I 171–72). Shamhat here embodies the masculine exploitation of feminine sexuality in its most blatant form. The hunter has set out to trap a ferocious beast and he does so by baiting the snare with a prostitute's alluring body. While contemporary deer hunters use doe's scent to lure bucks into range, the *Epic of Gilgamesh* employs the trope of vision—the masculine gaze—to elicit male desire. It may be a truism that men's sexual response is geared primarily towards sight, yet the characterization is appropriate to this scene. In fact, the common presumption throughout the narrative has been that the wild man "will see her and so draw near to her" (*immaršī-ma iṭeḫḫâ ana šâši*; e.g., I 148), as though he would have no defense or self-restraint against the sight of the nude Shamhat.

The irresistible allure of the naked female body has a long history in Mesopotamian literature, beginning with the Sumerian myths of Enki and Enlil. The phallic sexuality of these lusty young gods is portrayed in their aggressive rape of various goddesses, often encountered when bathing (see Cooper 1989; 1997; Leick 1994:21–54). This theme also appears in the Late Assyrian version of "Nergal and Ereshkigal," where the sight of the nude Ereshkigal finally compels Nergal to make love to the goddess of the Netherworld even though it may mean his incarceration there (see Leick 1994:249–53 with references). Like Shamhat's seduction of Enkidu, the sight of a nude female incites an overwhelming desire in each of these mythic traditions. Even a bovine female—a cow!—can sexually arouse a Mesopotamian god if she possesses "an attractive shape" (*binûtam kazbat*), as the incantation "A Cow of Sîn" succinctly reports: "Sîn saw her and so loved her" (*īmuršī-ma Sîn irāmši*) (see Veldhuis 1991:8 and passim). Once again, it is the inherent *kuzbu* of the visual object that provokes the male sexual response.

Similarly, Shamhat's brazen display of her sexual charms incites desire in the wild man. Such provocative entrapment may cast Shamhat herself as a kind of hunter. Detienne (1979:39–40) notes the Greek image of the courtesan as a panther who tracks and ensnares her prey using "her woman's body, beautiful and yearned for." Shamhat, however, is not the aggressor in the Gilgamesh epic; she is not a deceitful hooker soliciting a client for her own gain. Shamhat is only the lure used by the trapper to entice the wild man, a pawn in this contest between men. Her erotic allure (*kuzbu*) is powerful in its attraction, but it is nonetheless only an invitation, an availability, rather than a coercive force. Desire, like beauty, remains in the eye of the beholder. Shamhat is complicit in that a skillful seductress may knowingly incite and then manipulate male desire, but the emphasis in the Gilgamesh epic remains on the courtesan's alluring quality rather than her predatory ability.[26] Shamhat disrobes and offers her body for the wild man's exploitation, but he must approach her and initiate sexual contact. (Shamhat's passive role will be countered by the more rapacious image of Ishtar in a later scene of erotic attraction.) The trope of the masculine gaze is thus used to good effect in portraying Enkidu's sexual aggression. As Ann Guinan (1998:42) points out, the act of seeing is charged with a power dynamic in Akkadian literature because seeing is an act of taking: "Power is wielded by the subject who looks at another. To be the object of a look makes one vulnerable and exposed." Guinan's (1998:42) analysis of the sexual omens concludes that the male gaze upon a woman is auspicious because it is "based on the proper relationship between male subject and female object" in Mesopotamian ideology. The Gilgamesh epic begins to construct a poetics of desire in its utilization of the masculine gaze—Enkidu's and the reader's—upon Shamhat's nude body and the exploitation of her allure by Enkidu's approach.

The poetic depiction of their sexual intercourse is abrupt and explicit (I 172–77):

ūrša iptē-ma kuzubša ilqe,	She revealed her vulva and he possessed her charms,
ul išḫut ilteqe napīssu,	She did not fear (but) took (to herself) his virility.
lubūšīša umaṣṣī-ma elīša iṣlal,	She spread out her garment and he lay upon her;
īpussū-ma lullâ šipir sinnište,	She performed for the wild man the task of a woman.
dādūšu iḫbubū eli ṣērīša,	His passions embraced (and enveloped) her:
6 urrī 7 mūšī Enkidu tebī-ma šamḫat irḫi	For six days and seven nights Enkidu was aroused and copulated with Shamhat.

Jerrold Cooper (1997:92) describes this scene as a "male fantasy of sexual initiation" in which Shamhat simply spreads her legs to be mounted by Enkidu, who behaves like a bull in rut. There is no foreplay or erotic dialogue and the woman's compliance with masculine lust is simply assumed as the action moves directly to genital intercourse. The scene's poetic vocabulary is sexually explicit without being erotic in character. The first line is literally "she opened her vulva and he took her *kuzbu*," where *kuzbu* is a euphemism for her vulva or sexual vigor rather than the more abstract "allure, charm." Compare a bilingual text describing "a young man who has not (yet) obtained sexual satisfaction in his wife's embrace," or more literally, "a young man who has not touched the *kuzbu* in his wife's lap" (*eṭlu ša ina sūn aššatīšu kuzub lā ilputu*) (*CAD* 8:614).[27] Similarly, line 173 states that "she took his life-breath," where *napīšu* is the breath of life and a euphemism for virility.[28] The line hints at the depletion of his sexual energy by the woman as a parallel to his active exploitation of her sexuality. Finally, the sexual objectification of Shamhat (and all women) is reflected in the use of the phrase "the task of woman" to refer to heterosexual intercourse.

Enkidu and his passions are the subjects of the active, transitive verbs in the next two lines (176–77). The plural noun *dādū* means "lovemaking, passion" but the verb *ḫabābu*, also used to describe Gilgamesh's amorous actions to the meteorite in his dream, is difficult to translate. The phrase *dādūšu iḫbubū eli ṣērīša* (I 176) is often rendered as "his passions caressed her" but the verb may refer to sounds rather than touching.[29] If the attempt is to describe the throaty sounds of lovemaking, then Kovacs (1989:9) offers a nice translation in "His lust groaned over her." The sexual connotation of the verb (in the D-stem) is clear in ancient potency incantations in which a woman commands, "Get an erection, make love to me! ... Get an erection, embrace me!" (*tibâ rāmanni ... tibâ ḫubbibanni*) (14:7–8 in Biggs 1967:33) and "Embrace me!... copulate with me!" (*ḫubbibanni...ritkabanni*) (13:46–47 in Biggs 1967: 31). Whatever its literal meaning, however, the connotation of *ḫabābu* is clearly sexual (Parpola 1997:126; see Tigay 1982:274). The explicit quality of this passage continues in line 177: Enkidu has an erection (*tebi*, the same verb as in the potency incantations) and copulates (*irḫi*) with Shamhat for seven days. A more Anglo-Saxon translation of *reḫû* would use a transitive verb that requires no preposition and connotes the male's active penetration and the female's passive receptivity. Cooper's (1996) choice of "inseminate" also provides a clear and more literal reading.[30] The duration of Enkidu's copulation and excitation, in contrast to the more episodic quality of normal male sexual response, is an example of his super-human appetites and capacities.

The sexually explicit but non-erotic quality of this passage distinguishes it from Sumerian and Akkadian genres of erotic literature, where greater emphasis is given to the figurative and allusive expression of desire (see Westenholz 1995). The symbolism of fruit and gardens, common in erotic poetry, is also missing in this scene of primal sex. The emphasis on Shamhat's nudity and her physical attributes also distinguishes this scene from Akkadian erotica, which usually locates feminine beauty in jewelry and adornments as symbols of allure, fertility, love, and marriage (Westenholz 1992:387). Of course, the prostitute's seduction of the wild man has nothing to do with love and marriage and so the depiction is appropriately natural and wild. Cooper (1997:90) characterizes male sexuality "as ruled by a phallic teleology with implications of conquest and undertones of potential violence." Gwendolyn Leick (1994:50) contrasts this with the "female voice, which exults in the verbalization of emotional and sensual desire" in ancient erotic literature. Thus, in contrast to the lyricism of pleasant dialogue, garden and jewelry imagery, and the slow build-up towards mutual satisfaction, this episode is closer to the Sumerian mythic tradition of phallic, masculine sexuality and its emphasis on quick penetration and male orgasm with no concern for female pleasure. In presenting the female body as merely an object of male sexual exploitation, the Akkadian poet neatly portrays the encounter between the wild man and the prostitute as a scene of bestial mating rather than refined eroticism.

Enkidu's indifference to his mate once he is satisfied is equally uncivilized (I 178–181):

ultu išbû lalâšu	When he was sated with her delights,
pānīšu ištakan ana ṣēri būlīšu	He turned his gaze towards his herd.

īmurāšū-ma Enkidu irappudā ṣabâtu	The gazelles saw Enkidu and started to run;
būl ṣēri ittesi ina zumrīšu	The wild herd fled from his body.

The idiom "to set the face" (*pānī šakānu*) usually connotes a decision or intention and in line 179 it signals the shift in Enkidu's attention from Shamhat to his herd. The literary theme of vision thus continues with Enkidu looking with desire upon the animals as they look upon him with fear and revulsion. Previously, humans saw Enkidu in his pristine animal form and were repulsed by his savage appearance. He, however, was attracted by the sight of Shamhat's exposed female body. Through sexual contact with her, Enkidu has somehow been transformed into a body whose sight is now repellent to the herd. Yet rather than repeat the previous phrase, "his herd will spurn him" (*inakkiršu būlšu*) (e.g., I 149), the poet chooses the feminine plural "gazelles" (*ṣabâtu*) as the subject of feminine plural verbs in line 180. Although the text does not imply Enkidu's previous sexual experience with the animals, the reference to the gazelles fleeing his body subtly conveys his new potential for sexual aggression.[31] The animals understand before Enkidu does that his animal innocence has been forfeited by his contact with the human female.

The corruption of Enkidu's pristine animal form through sexual knowledge has both physical and intellectual components. One result of Enkidu's marathon lovemaking with Shamhat is a reduction of his strength and physical ability. The narrative voice provides an explanation for the perceived change in Enkidu's status. The obscure, poetic vocabulary and textual variants preclude a definitive translation, but the general implication seems clear enough (I 182–85):

ultaḫḫi Enkidu ullula pagaršu	Enkidu had corrupted his pure body,
ittazizzā birkāšu ša illikā būlšu	His legs, which used to run with his herd, stood still.
umtaṭṭu Enkidu ul kī ša pāni lasāmšu	Enkidu was weakened and could not run as before,

u šū išīḫ-ma rapaš ḫasīsa	But he had grown in broad wisdom.

Line 182 is the most difficult to establish since the three available texts are in disagreement.[32] I prefer to read *ultaḫḫi* and derive it from *šuḫḫû*, "to ruin, destroy," with wordplay on its alternate meaning, "to have illicit sex."[33] The parallel verb in line 184, a (passive) Dt-stem *umtaṭṭu*, "he was weakened," helps clarify the overall sense of the passage (*CAD* 10/1:434–35). This meaning is also reflected by Enkidu's deathbed curses upon Shamhat (VII 100–129) in which he vehemently accuses her of corrupting him: "Because me, the innocent, you weakened! Yes me, the innocent, you weakened in my wilderness!" (*aššu yâši ella tušemṭînni u yâši ella tušemṭînni ina ṣērīya*) (VII 128–29).[34] These verses reiterate the corruption of Enkidu's pristine form and perhaps supplement I 173, *ilteqe napīssu,* "she took (to herself) his virility."

Enkidu's weakness is more than postcoital lassitude; he has been fundamentally transformed by his encounter with Shamhat. Enkidu's initiation into human contact signals his transition from an animal to a human, from innocence to sexual knowledge, from ignorance to "broad wisdom." Scholars have of course pointed out the parallels of Shamhat and Eve in "seducing" Enkidu and Adam, respectively, and providing them with humanizing knowledge (e.g., Bailey 1970). The transformative power of sexual knowledge is thoroughly explored in the history of exegesis of Genesis 3. The force of sexual arousal, both edifying and destructive, is also described in OB incantations that attempt to control its overwhelming power:

uzzum illaka rīmāniš	Passion comes over me like a wild bull,
ištanaḫḫiṭam kalbāniš	It keeps springing at me like a hound;
kīma nēšim ezzi alākam	Like a lion it is fierce in its onslaught,
kīma barbarim mali libbātim	Like a wolf it is full of fury![35]

Other incantations describe passion as a wolf, "tireless in running" (*lakāta mād*), and a dog, "long of leg, swift in running" (*urruk birkāšu aruḫ lasāmam*), phrases reminiscent of Enkidu's legs (*birkāšu*) that could no longer run (*lasāmu*) with the herds (I 183–84).[36] The shared vocabulary and theme of passion suggest a literary relation between these incantations and the Gilgamesh epic's depiction of Enkidu's depletion. Ironically, Enkidu's surrender to animalistic passion costs him his animalistic prowess. When Enkidu springs up (reading *ultaḫḫiṭ* in I 182), he is bereft of the passion that is likened to a springing dog (*ištanaḫḫiṭam*). Whether or not there is any literary influence, the depiction of passion as an overwhelming, animalistic force in Akkadian literature is relevant to the discourse of sexuality in the Gilgamesh epic. Finally, Enkidu's depletion at Shamhat's hands is not a negative portrayal of her seductive role. While Ishtar may turn men into animals through her aggressive sexuality, Shamhat represents the positive development of an animal into a human.

Abandoned by his herd, exhausted by a week-long orgy of sexual indulgence, Enkidu returns to sit at Shamhat's feet. In contrast to his previous, lustful gaze upon her body, he now casts his attentive gaze upon her face (*inaṭṭala pānīša*; I 187) and opens his ears to her instruction. Shamhat speaks her first words in the epic in order to tempt Enkidu to return to Uruk with her. She recognizes a beauty, or at least rustic charm, in the subdued barbarian at her feet and says, "You are handsome, Enkidu, you have become like a god! Why should you run the steppes with the wild animals?" (*damqāta Enkidu kī ili tabašši ammīni itti namaššê tarappuda ṣērī*; I 190–91). I interpret the attribution of divinity as hyperbole, meant to contrast Enkidu's previously repulsive appearance and ferocious animal identity with his newly acquired humanity; Enkidu is godlike in his human potential. With further education in proper attire, food, and drink, he will become thoroughly civilized (see Moran 1991). The hidden agenda in Shamhat's praise, however, is eventually disclosed (I 192–95):

> Come, I will lead you to Uruk the Sheepfold,
> to the holy temple, the dwelling of Anu and Ishtar,
> where Gilgamesh is perfect in strength,
> and like a wild bull lords his superiority over the people.

Shamhat cleverly entices Enkidu to the urban center of civilization while also introducing Gilgamesh as a rival to his own strength. Her wise words strike a chord in Enkidu and "he yearns for one who knows his heart, a friend" (*mudû libbašu iše*ʾʾ*â ibra*; I 197).[37] Enkidu here perceives that neither an animal nor Shamhat can be a truly suitable companion; he will continue to have sex with her (I 279) but she is not one who can understand his warrior's heart. Enkidu, with his first spoken words, agrees to accompany Shamhat to Uruk. But in a move still reminiscent of the wild—like one bull challenging another for ascendancy in the herd—Enkidu states his intentions to challenge Gilgamesh rather than befriend him: "I will contend with him!" (*anāku lugrīšum-ma*). Enkidu will proclaim in Uruk, "I am the mightiest!" (*anākū-mi dannu*) (I 203–4).

Shamhat counters Enkidu's aggression with a sensuous description of Uruk's urban pleasures and festivities. She says, "And there are courtesans, most shapely of figure, adorned with seductive allure and full of joy!" (*u šamḫāti šūsum-ma binûtu kuzba zu*ʾʾ*una malâ rīšātum*; I 213–14) (see *CAD* 17/3:375–76). Shamhat continues to describe the equally alluring body of Gilgamesh (I 219–20) and his dreams of Enkidu's arrival (I 228–77) discussed below. It is fitting that Shamhat's advocacy for Uruk takes such an erotic and sensual form meant to incite masculine desire. As a representative of civilization who is identified with the natural functions of sex, Shamhat is a most appropriate guide for Enkidu's conversion from wild man to urban citizen. Harris (1990:222–24) skillfully describes Shamhat's role as an intermediary between nature and culture, as she cites Sherry Ortner on the symbolic role of females: like many female characters, Shamhat is depicted as "one of culture's crucial agencies for the conversion of nature into culture, especially with reference to the socialization of children" (Ortner 1974:84). After initiating Enkidu into humanity through sex, Shamhat continues to play a traditional female role in educating the wild man. In a maternal function, Shamhat teaches Enkidu the childhood lessons of proper eating, drinking, and dressing himself. Harris (1990:224) states that Shamhat, like the wise Ninsun, "speaks in proverbial language and is a woman of wise counsel" (*milkum ša sinništum imtaqut ana libbīšu*; OBP ii 25). Certainly, she is eloquent and persuasive in telling Enkidu of Uruk's erotic attractions.

Shamhat's success as both a seductress and pedagogue is seen in the extent of Enkidu's acculturation. In contrast to his previous defense of the wild animals against the hunter's traps, he now guards the sleeping shepherds, chasing off wolves and lions (II 50). He will later experience city life and association with the King of Uruk, the apotheosis of civilization. Enkidu enters the narrative as a hairy savage in the wild, but he will enter Uruk as a handsome and civilized man. Shamhat's tutelage has transformed him into an alluring presence of his own, discussed further below. Although the SB narration is lost, the OB edition describes the culmination of Enkidu's humanity by stressing his physical appearance (OBP iii 22–27; see Tigay 1982:277):

ultappit malî	He groomed (his) matted hair,
šuʾʾuram pagaršu	So hairy was his body;
šamnam iptaššaš-ma	He anointed himself with oil (and so)
awīliš īwi	He turned into a human;
ilbaš libšam	He put on a garment,
kīma muti ibašši	He looked just like a groom.

Foster (1987:29) notes the wedding imagery of this scene along with Enkidu's role as a true shepherd protecting the flock, in contrast to Gilgamesh's poor shepherding of Uruk's population. It is soon after this point in the narrative that Enkidu encounters the caterer on his way to Uruk and receives the news of Gilgamesh's mistreatment of the brides. Enkidu's transformation is complete as his outrage motivates him to become a champion of the cultural institution of marriage.

In her provocative book on the prostitute body, Shannon Bell (1994:2) strives to "displace the more traditional linkage of the contemporary prostitute to the profane, diseased, and excluded female body of the nineteenth century, foregrounding instead its lineage to the ancient sexual, sacred, healing female body."[38] While Harris (1990) argues that Shamhat's positive portrayal is actually an inversion of the prostitute's social status in ancient Mesopotamia, Bell chooses to read against the grain as a postmodern challenge to the dominant political discourse on prostitution. Whatever its value in other contexts, Bell's image is not inappropriate for Shamhat's portrayal in the *Epic of Gilgamesh*. Shamhat enters the narrative as an objectified female body, but she proves herself to be an agent for knowledge and culture. The epic presents the prostitute as a benevolent and maternal woman rather than the deceitful, lustful whore common to literary characterization. Her sexual function is not simply a base or vulgar expression of humanity's bestial nature but a cultured expression of the erotic arts, necessary for humanity and enriching to Enkidu. Bell (1994:13) quotes Michel Foucault (1978:61) on the erotic arts of ancient Greece: "In Greece, truth and sex were linked, in the form of pedagogy, by the transmission of precious knowledge from one body to another; sex served as a medium for initiations into learning." Like the role of Diotima as Socrates' teacher in erotics (see Halperin 1990:113–51), Shamhat enlightens Enkidu concerning his true nature. As her student, Enkidu receives first sexual and then cultural knowledge from Shamhat. Enkidu pours himself (*reḫû*) and his vitality (*napīšu*) into Shamhat, and in return she gives him his humanity.

The narration of Enkidu's seduction shows no attention to feminine pleasure because it presents the female body as merely an object of masculine desire. As the narrative progresses, however, it attributes to Shamhat an increasing subjectivity, as evidenced by her speech and interactions with Enkidu. After she tells him of Gilgamesh's dreams, Enkidu and Shamhat again have sex, yet here the poet uses the phrase *urtammū kilallān*, "the couple made love to each other" (I 279). Unlike other Akkadian verbs that denote copulation (e.g., *garāšu*, *nâku*, *reḫû*, *šuḫḫû*), *râmu* is not restricted to a male subject. The poet's choice of the Dt-stem conjugation in its reciprocal sense emphasizes the mutuality of the actions and the equality of both characters, male and female, as verbal subjects. Enkidu is no longer the rutting bull who abruptly mounts the passive female; Enkidu now knows eroticism, perhaps even affection (*urtammū*, "they made love"), in contrast to his original beastly mating (*irḫi*, "he inseminated"). With this one verb the text subtly introduces the possibility of feminine sexual subjectivity, foreshadowing Ishtar's more fully libidinal character in Tablet VI. Harris (1990) associates Shamhat's positive portrayal with her maternal function, yet the prostitute consistently plays an erotic role as Enkidu continues to enjoy her pleasures—and her instruction in erotics—until he arrives in the city and meets Gilgamesh face to face.[39]

Shamhat is a powerful symbol that mediates between nature and culture; there is, however, much ambiguity in her intermediary role. She is a highly cultured representative of her indulgent civilization, yet it is only in the wilderness, sitting with the marginally human Enkidu, that Shamhat attains her own voice. She becomes an eloquent teacher to Enkidu and plays a maternal role within the shepherds' camp, but once she returns to her city she will be deprived of her newly discovered subjectivity. In fact, once they enter Uruk, she is never again allowed to speak in the extant SB text.[40] The reader is thus reminded of the original purpose of Shamhat's seduction: to humanize the wild man who was sent in order to distract Gilgamesh from his oppression of Uruk's citizens. Shamhat is a useful tool for initiating men into proper male company, but she will be discarded as soon as Enkidu meets Gilgamesh. As noted above, Shamhat is not a suitable candidate for social companionship and so is forgotten until Enkidu reflects upon his life in Tablet VII. Bell's image of the "philosopher/whore" has heuristic value in identifying the multiple roles played by Shamhat in Enkidu's acculturation, but this image should not obscure the social reality of prostitutes as liminal women in ancient Mesopotamia. Shamhat's silence is thus explained by the patriarchal perspective that defines her existence and against which Bell is agitating. Ninsun and other women will have much to contribute throughout the rest of the text, but Shamhat is a prostitute, "the other of the other" in Bell's (1994:2) phrase, the other even within the categorical other of "woman." The prostitute will be further stigmatized and separated from proper female society in Enkidu's curse: "May she not dwell in the young women's banquet house" (VII 106; reading with Lambert 1992:129–30). As an inherently marginal social body she is in opposition to the wife and mother of patriarchal culture, who are disempowered but respected.[41]

With bitter irony, Shamhat's reversion to her original depiction as the archetypal prostitute is completed by the curses of Enkidu. His ungrateful treatment of the woman who initiated him into humanity, educated him in cultural practices, and led him to Uruk shows his own adoption of patriarchal ideology and the denial of female agency. Enkidu's curses describe the prostitute's social alienation and destine her to be an object of male violence (VII 100–129): "May ruins be the place where you lie.... May drunk and sober strike your cheek!" (following Lambert 1992:129–30). Shamash, the god of justice, reminds Enkidu of her important role in introducing him to bread, beer, clothes, and Gilgamesh (VII 130–36), and so Enkidu relents in his hostility towards her by also providing blessings (VII 151–61). His blessings, however, consist only in establishing the efficacy of her seductive allure and her receptivity to male sexual aggression. Like his curses, Enkidu's benediction reduces Shamhat to the dehumanized status of an alluring female body whose sexual availability will be exploited by men. She is introduced in the text as an objectified body for hire, and so will she exit the text after Enkidu's ungracious sentencing.

Finally, the lack of concern with female sexual pleasure in Enkidu's seduction can be attributed to the masculine perspective of the text and its objectification of the female body, but the lack of attention to pregnancy and procreation throughout the epic requires further comment. Halperin (1990:140–41) notes the patriarchal tendency to see women's sexuality as a function of reproduction rather than of desire: women are denied, in his words, an "autonomous domain of desire, a subjectivity of one's own." Bell (1994:22) also describes the theme of woman as reproductive body in Western tradition, what she calls the "discourse of the womb," in which the female procreative ability seemingly negates the possibility of sexual pleasure; the maternal function precludes erotic desire. With the obvious exception of Ishtar's libidinous character, the SB Gilgamesh epic similarly deprives its female characters of sexual desire.[42] What is more striking, however, is that male sexual desire does not result in impregnation as evidence of male fertility. As Cooper (1989) and Leick (1994:50) have argued, the Sumerian myths of Enki and Enlil always associate male ejaculation with pregnancy as a sign of the efficient, fertilizing powers of the divine phallus. The focus on masculine desire in the Gilgamesh epic, however, apparently excludes reference to sex as a means of procreation; sex is depicted here only as pleasurable genital activity.

Foster (1987:22) argues that the Gilgamesh epic implicitly denounces such unproductive heterosexuality, symbolized by prostitution, while it advocates the proper channeling of sexual energies in the marriage bed to produce children.[43] We will return to this theme below, but for now it is sufficient to note the sterile eroticism of the prostitute's allure and its contrast with the maternal symbolism of women's procreative ability. Although the SB Gilgamesh epic is relentlessly patriarchal and androcentric, it ignores that most patriarchal of concerns, progeny and male lineage, until its final tablet. This lack of interest in women's procreative function betrays an obsession with male desire, erotic and otherwise, in this masculine epic.

The Gaze of Ishtar: Denying Desire

Like Shamhat's seduction of Enkidu, Ishtar's temptation of Gilgamesh in Tablet VI presents fundamental elements of the text's discourse of sexuality as it plays on the themes of gender and desire, attraction and response.[44] In contrast to Shamhat's intentional arousal of the wild man's passion, the allure of Gilgamesh inadvertently attracts Ishtar's libidinous gaze. Ishtar inverts the patriarchal exploitation of Shamhat by forcing Gilgamesh into a passive role as the erotic object of her aggressive feminine desire, symbolized by her desirous gaze.

The scene opens with a description of Gilgamesh bathing after his triumphal return from the Cedar Mountains (VI 1–5):

imsi malêšu ubbib tillēšu	He washed his matted hair and cleaned his gear,
unassis qimmassu elu ṣērīšu	He shook out his locks over his back.
iddi maršūtīšu ittalbiša zakûtīšu	He cast aside his dirty (attire) and was dressed in his clean (garments).
aṣâti ittaḫlipam-ma rakis aguḫḫa	He was clothed in robes, tied with a sash,
Gilgamesh agāšu ītepram-ma	And then Gilgamesh put on his crown.

As noted above, the bathing scene is an erotically charged motif throughout ancient Near Eastern literature, including myths of Enki, Enlil, Ereshkigal, and the Egyptian goddess Hathor, as well as the biblical story of David and Bathsheba. In each of these examples, however, it is the nude female who attracts the male gaze, as Shamhat catches Enkidu's eye by the water hole. The epic of Gilgamesh plays on this type-scene by switching the roles of male and female, with the bathing king attracting the amorous attention of the goddess Ishtar. Clean, luxuriant hair is a natural symbol of seductive allure, just as filthy and matted hair is a metonym for a repulsive appearance (i.e., XI 246). In the OB edition of Enkidu's acculturation quoted above, Enkidu "became human" (*awīliš īwi*) when "he had groomed his matted hair" (*ultappit malî*); and "he appeared just like a groom" (*kīma muti ibašši*) once he put on a garment (OBP iii 22–27). Likewise, Gilgamesh is depicted washing his matted hair (*malû*), putting on a clean robe, and then receiving an invitation to become a groom (*mutu*). The reference to Gilgamesh shaking out his flowing locks (*unassis qimmassu*) alludes to one of Enkidu's blessings on Shamhat, that even at a distance her ardent suitor will "shake out his locks" for her (*linassisa qimmassu*; VII 155). The gesture has sensual and erotic connotations and Ishtar reacts accordingly. The *aguḫḫu* is a sash or belt that is associated with both warriors and erotic charm; Ishtar herself is called "Mistress of 'fruit' and sashes," *bēlet inbī u aguḫḫī* (see Lambert 1982:29; *CAD* s.v.), in which "fruit" is a euphemism for sexual appeal. The reference to the *aguḫḫu* further alludes to Enkidu's blessing on Shamhat that soldiers will be quick to undo their belts for her (VII 156). These symbolic associations and literary allusions are used by the poet to construct a scene fraught with sexual possibilities.

The goddess Ishtar responds to the luxurious portrayal of the king with her openly desirous gaze and the verbalization of her passion (VI 6–9):

ana dumqi ša Gilgāmeš īnā ittašši rubûtu Ištar	Princess Ishtar gazed with desire upon the beauty of Gilgamesh.

alkam-ma Gilgāmeš lu ḫā᾿ir atta	"Come to me, Gilgamesh, (for) you are a lover!
inbīka yâši qâšu qīšam-ma	Give, O give me freely of your 'fruit'!
atta lū mutī-ma anāku lū aššatka	You be my husband and I will be your wife!"

The narrator's confirmation of Gilgamesh's attractiveness (*dumqu*) in line 6 makes the absence of any description of Ishtar's allure even more conspicuous. "Fruit," *inbū*, is a common figurative expression for sexual appeal and vigor in Akkadian erotic literature, apparently based on the metaphor of fruit's luscious qualities (see Lambert 1987b:27–31). The word *ḫā᾿iru* denotes a lover, groom, or the husband of a *ḫīrtu*-wife of equal status. Ishtar follows her opening lines with a list of impressive gifts for her intended groom.

Shamhat's encounter with Enkidu established the erotic theme of feminine allure and masculine response, and Ishtar's attempted seduction of Gilgamesh provides variations on that theme. Like a jazz musician improvising on a melodic riff, this scene of sexual tension and erotic conflict takes the original theme and transforms it, syncopating its rhythm to create something innovative yet still related to the original motif. Among the twists and turns of its thematic variation, Ishtar's proposition inverts numerous elements of Shamhat's seduction of Enkidu. In Tablet I, a nude prostitute silently attracts the gaze of a wild man of the steppe who responds with sexual arousal. Here, a goddess spies upon the royal body of an urban king, engages him in poetic dialogue, proposes marriage, and is rudely rebuffed. Shamhat transforms the animalistic Enkidu into a civilized human while Ishtar would reduce her human lovers to actual animals. The previous episode constructs a poetics of desire based on the compulsory heterosexuality and androcentric focus of its patriarchal culture, in which Enkidu's phallic drive is satisfied by his penetration of the female sexual object. Ishtar voices a countertheme of feminine desire that challenges the patriarchal emphasis on both womb and phallus yet retains its compulsory heterosexual perspective. The epic's nuanced presentation incorporates these thematic variations without resolving the ambiguities and tensions of its sexual discourse.

Ishtar introduces the feminine sexual subject to the epic, the libidinal rather than maternal female who, in Bell's (1994:9–10, 20–22) terms, privileges the clitoris over the womb. Like Shamhat and other prostitutes of Uruk, Ishtar embodies feminine sexuality in opposition to the androcentric motif of woman as reproductive body. Yet, in its objectification of women as wombs for male reproduction, patriarchal culture subsequently tends to deny women a share in erotic desire. Thus, Shamhat and her erotic colleagues are objectified by patriarchal control and their sexual allure is exploited by male desire. They remain objects of phallic sexuality rather than subjects of their own erotic desires. The goddess Ishtar, however, seizes the subjective role for herself and demands her own sexual gratification. Bell (1994:20) refers to the "radical excess" of sexual pleasure associated with the clitoris since, unlike male ejaculation, female orgasm has no necessary function in the mechanics of procreation (cf. Halperin 1990:142). By her own indulgent eroticism, insatiable libido, and insistence on feminine pleasure, the goddess Ishtar opposes the objectification of females as either maternal wombs or sexual objects.[45] As the list of her discarded lovers will show, Ishtar's active erotic agency leads her to exploit masculine sexuality according to her own pleasures just as males (including Enkidu and Gilgamesh) exploit feminine sexuality in their phallic teleology.[46]

Ishtar's embodiment of feminine sexuality makes her a common protagonist in the Sumerian and Akkadian love lyrics and erotic dialogues (see Westenholz 1995). Her expressions of passionate longing for her lover and hymns to her vulva provide a useful background for her role as seductress in Tablet VI of Gilgamesh. Leick (1994:125–26) summarizes the gendered roles of Sumerian courtly love poetry, noting that the woman often addresses her husband with an emphasis on feminine sexual pleasure.[47] Cooper (1997:94–96) demonstrates that the feminine voice of the Sumerian love songs represents a romanticized erotic fantasy, full of sensuous desire and extended foreplay, which enjoys the security of marriage while suppressing its most negative consequences for women, such as pregnancy, childbirth, childcare, and male sexual aggression. Like modern romance novels, the love songs focus on emotional and sensual desire while avoiding coarse or explicit sexual descriptions. These songs thus celebrate the joys of courtship and sexual awakening without reference to maternal responsibilities in a patriarchal society. Similarly in her proposal, Ishtar uses no coarse or explicit description of sexual organs or intercourse, she adopts the poetic reference to Gilgamesh's sexuality as "fruit" (*inbū*), and she invokes the security of marriage with two terms that could denote a husband or groom (*ḫāʾiru, mutu*) and her own willingness to be a "wife" (*aššatu*). Although Leick (1994:258) calls this speech "an odd mixture of a harlot's proposition and an actual marriage proposal," there is actually nothing in her words that is vulgar or objectionable, apart from the fact that the dialogue is initiated by a female rather than a male. On a superficial level, Ishtar's relatively restrained proposal is consistent with her traditional role as the voice of feminine sexual desire. As his devastating response shows, however, Gilgamesh sees through the outward propriety of her offer to its hidden dangers. Foster's (1987:34–36) analysis of Ishtar's speech also uncovers more subtle clues to her undesirable character, as he notes the poet's unflattering use of grammatical features to convey the intensity of her passions.

In his elaborate rejection speech, Gilgamesh ridicules Ishtar's proposal of marriage by repeating a litany of her unfaithfulness to previous husbands and lovers.[48] He concludes the list with the story of her attempted seduction of Ishullanu: "You loved (*tarāmī-ma*) Ishullanu, your father's date gardener" (VI 64). Gilgamesh's account of Ishtar's lascivious attempt to bed the gardener belies the thin veneer of her more refined words to the king (VI 67–69):

īnā tattaššîšum-ma tattalkīššu	You gazed with desire upon him and then approached him:
išullānīya kiššūtaki ī-nīkul	"O, my Ishullanu, let us enjoy your strength!
qātka šūṣâm-ma luput ḫurdatni	Stretch forth your hand and stroke our vulva!"[49]

By quoting her lewd come-on to Ishullanu, Gilgamesh unmasks the coquettish Ishtar as a wanton seductress rather than a respectable bride. Ishtar's ambiguous phrase *kiššūtaki i-nīkul*, "let us enjoy your strength," obscures the danger of the verb *akālu*, "to eat, consume."

Foster's (1987:35) clever translation—"let us have a taste of your manliness!"—more clearly expresses the wordplay in this dialogue, but Ishtar's coy suggestion is actually a veiled threat to utterly consume, not just taste, Ishullanu's virility. Ishullanu appreciates the ambiguity of *akālu* and puns on it in his short reply with references to eating bread (*ākul ša akkalu akal*...; VI 72–73). Furthermore, Ishullanu's retort deftly juxtaposes the maternal and erotic images of women: the mother/wife provides nourishing bread while Ishtar abandons her lovers to obscenities, curses, and winter exposure. The maternal symbolism of familial love, procreation, and generational continuity contrasts with Ishtar's "love," which is reflected in her lovers' fates as isolating, destructive, and deadly (cf. Foster 1987:36). Gilgamesh is thus able to demonstrate the duplicity of her proposal through his recitation of her unfaithfulness to past lovers.

The text poetically conveys Ishtar's aggressive sexuality through her predatory gaze and the kindling of her own desire. In contrast to the passive display of Shamhat's charms to arouse Enkidu, Ishtar actively initiates her encounters with Gilgamesh and Ishullanu by looking, approaching, and speaking. She does not attempt to entice the men with her seductive feminine allure but instead takes the active courtship role of the male. Ishtar is thus implicitly compared with the beastly Enkidu in her sexual response to visual stimuli. In fact, Ishtar's aggressive sexuality is neatly encapsulated by the trope of her desirous gaze, a trope employed to introduce both of her attempted seductions in this episode (*īnā ittašši* and *īnā tattaššîšum*). Guinan's (1998) work with the Mesopotamian sexual omens noted above, shows the symbolic power of the gaze as control over an object. Although a male looking upon a female is auspicious and consistent with androcentric ideology, the female gaze symbolically depletes the male because he loses control as the object of the feminine subject.[50] Guinan (1998:44) explains the omens' discourse of masculine hegemony in their ideology of competitive domination and subjugation: "Questions of power, gender and sexuality become questions of masculine agency and social identity." Thus, the objectification of a male results in the loss of his virility and manhood. The assertion of female sexuality to initiate sexual intercourse is even more of a threat to male health and competitive power, according to Guinan (1998:43). Harris (1990:227) similarly concludes that Gilgamesh's insulting rejection of Ishtar may be based upon her usurpation of the masculine role in proposing and offering gifts. Ishtar has symbolically "unmanned" him by casting him in the feminine role, and so Gilgamesh reproaches her for her insult to him. In this way Gilgamesh forcefully wrests control of the situation from the aggressive goddess and maintains his masculine identity.[51]

Foster (1987:36) describes the narrative's unmistakable contrast between Shamhat and Ishtar by noting that the prostitute is alluring, eloquent, and successful in her humanization of Enkidu, while Ishtar is unappealing, speaks poorly, and fails in her seduction. An additional contrast between the two females, however, is Ishtar's sexual subjectivity and Shamhat's objectification. While Shamhat was successful in her seduction, she does not attain a fully subjective sexual character; she remains the erotic object of Enkidu's desire, with perhaps a brief experience as an equal partner in the shepherds' hut (*urtammū kilallān*; I 279). A rare example of a libidinal female subject who seduces a male in Akkadian mythological literature is Ereshkigal, Queen of the Netherworld, in the first-millennium version of her myth. The dark goddess's erotic subjectivity is reflected by her exclamation when she realizes that her lover, Nergal or Erra, has escaped from her bed: "Erra, my delightful lover! I was not sated with his delights when he left me!" (*Erra ḫāmeru lalêya ul ašbâ lalâšu ittalkanni*; iv 53′–54′) (Gurney 1960:120; cf. Hunger 1976:17). Among other clues to her sexual agency, Ereshkigal is the mutual subject (*kilallān*) of verbs for embracing and going to bed (see Gurney 1960:126). Yet even as a libidinal female seeking her own erotic pleasure, Ereshkigal does not attempt to seduce her lover through speaking words, bribing him with gifts, or approaching him to initiate sex. Ereshkigal simply allows him to see her nude body while bathing (*zumurša uštabarrā-ma*; iii 62′), thereby inciting his desire and provoking his initiation of sexual contact, whereupon they go passionately off to bed for seven days.[52] Ishtar, however, takes the masculine role in gazing with desire upon the body of Gilgamesh instead of using her feminine allure to attract his gaze and arouse his desire. In this way Ishtar's lustful gaze symbolizes her sexual aggression and contrasts with other females' use of erotic appeal.

The epic poet thus portrays the goddess as a failed and inept seductress, unable to stir the passions of Gilgamesh.

Many Assyriologists interpret Ishtar's predatory sexuality as inherently threatening to males and conclude that Gilgamesh's rejection of her proposal is necessary to retain his masculinity, if not his very life (e.g., Abusch 1986; Lambert 1987a:42; Harris 1990:227; Leick 1994:262; Cooper 1997:93). These scholars often agree that Gilgamesh's sin is not his rebuffing of Ishtar's advances but the hubris he demonstrates in his excessive derision of the goddess. In a detailed analysis of Ishtar's proposal and her luxurious gifts, Tzvi Abusch (1986:148–61) uncovers not merely a symbolic threat to Gilgamesh's masculinity but a veiled description of actual death, entombment, and descent to the Netherworld. Abusch argues that Ishtar is actually offering Gilgamesh a role as a ruler in the Netherworld rather than the blessings of an earthly reign. Since Gilgamesh was in fact the Netherworld judge of shades in Mesopotamian tradition, the epic's audiences would have recognized his divine function in Ishtar's allusive descriptions of her marriage gifts.[53] Abusch (1986:157) explains that the inherent ambiguity of her proposal rests upon the similarities of wedding and funeral imagery and the multivalence of their shared symbolism. Gilgamesh is not deceived by Ishtar's duplicitous offer, however, and so rejects her deadly invitation.[54] His insults and abusive recitation of her rejected lovers simply demonstrate Gilgamesh's detection of her ruse in promising love when she really offers death (see Abusch 1986:173–79). Abusch's analysis of the symbolism and literary allusions of this episode provides numerous insights for its interpretation, especially concerning nuptial and funereal references. Yet to conclude that Ishtar's proposal is only an invitation to join the denizens of the Netherworld is reductive of the complex symbolism that Abusch is so careful to establish. As a warrior and erotic female, Ishtar embodies the tensions between sexuality and death. Her proposal is fraught with danger and allusions to the realm of the dead, but it is nonetheless a sexual proposition that one would expect the arrogant hero to accept. Since Gilgamesh and Ishtar's erotically charged skirmish plays upon the symbolic relationship of sex and death, there is no need to resolve the symbolic ambiguities in one direction or the other. In fact, one might assume that the heroic

Gilgamesh would accept her erotic offer even with its lethal risks, since he so cavalierly disregards the threat of death earlier in the epic.

Other scholars, often in sympathy with Abusch's approach, interpret Gilgamesh's rejection of Ishtar as evidence of his ethical or philosophical transformation from his earlier lustful and vulgar character (Held 1983; Foster 1987; Leick 1994:263; Nissinen 1998:23–24, 145; cf. Parpola 1993:192–94). Based upon Platonic philosophical categories, these interpretations explain Gilgamesh's denial of the erotic goddess as symbolic of his transcendence of base sensuality to the higher pursuit of virtue and heroic asceticism, an ethical progression from physical lust to his celibate alliance with Enkidu. As Benjamin Ray (1996:311–13) points out, however, Gilgamesh's reaction to Enkidu's death clearly demonstrates his raging egocentrism and psychological imbalance at this point in the epic. His morbid attachment to Enkidu's body rather than some platonic ideal of friendship is especially telling. Whatever his eventual attainment of virtue or self-transcending knowledge, Gilgamesh remains a passionate and self-absorbed character throughout this episode of the epic, and probably throughout his search for Utnapishtim.

Finally, some Assyriologists place Ishtar's proposal within the context of the Sumerian sacred marriage rite (e.g., Vanstiphout 1990), in which case Gilgamesh's refusal of her proposal is a dereliction of his royal duties. Instead of depicting Ishtar's dangerous sexuality as a threat to one man's masculinity, this interpretative approach places greater emphasis on Gilgamesh's kingly responsibility, as the representative of his people, to pleasure the city goddess and procure her blessings for his reign. The episode does foreground Gilgamesh's royalty by its description of him donning the crown in the line immediately prior to Ishtar's approach (VI 5).[55] Gilgamesh's bathing and dress might suggest his preparations for a ritualized sexual encounter, even though Akkadian love lyrics usually portray the woman in such preparations. There are, however, no other indications of a ritual context for this scene.[56] In fact, the ritual celebration of the sacred marriage remains obscure and contested among Assyriologists. Cooper (1993) summarizes recent discussion of the Mesopotamian sacred marriage, or *hieros gamos*, with its depiction of the sexual union of the king and a goddess. The oldest evidence suggests a special (but not unique) association of this ritual with Inana and the king of Uruk (Cooper 1993:82–83). The royal epithet "beloved spouse of Inana" is attested in Early Dynastic and Ur III—Isin period sources (c. 2400–1800 BCE), although the only explicit descriptions of a human king copulating with Inana are from two kings of the Ur III and Isin periods (Shulgi, c. 2050 and Iddindagan, c. 1950 BCE) (Cooper 1993:82–85). Sumerian legends of Enmerkar, king of Uruk c. 2800 BCE, describe Inana choosing him for her holy loins; and a hymn to Inana quotes her reference to Shulgi touching "my pure vulva" (Cooper 1993:82–83, 85, n. 22). Cooper (1993:89–92) explains that the sacred marriage was a means for the king to gain legitimacy, to regulate relations between humans and deities, and to reaffirm the king's and his people's obligations to the gods. The sacred marriage therefore has more to do with the legitimization of the king than alleged fertility issues. As a king of Uruk, Gilgamesh should indeed have been the "beloved spouse of Inana," according to Sumerian tradition. Thus, the composers and audiences of the Gilgamesh epic could have assumed that the ancient Sumerian king participated in the sacred marriage rite with Inana, even though there is no evidence for the celebration of such a rite after the early OB period.[57]

Abusch (1986:157, n. 35) provides a balanced perspective on this issue when he writes, "While it would be a mistake to dissociate our text completely from the sacred marriage, we should also not overestimate the latter's importance." He argues that the poet employs the motif of the sacred marriage tradition without necessarily referring to an actual religious ritual.[58] Thus, one need not establish a ritual context to appreciate the general association of Inana-Ishtar with the kings of Uruk, if only as a literary fiction. Like Abusch's own funereal interpretation of Ishtar's proposal, the sacred marriage tradition illuminates aspects of the text without exhausting its symbolism or resolving its ambiguities. Interpreters may recognize the sacred marriage symbolism without assuming the actual performance of the ritual as the scene's setting. Along similar interpretive lines, Leick (1994:260) states that Ishtar's promised gifts may be taken at face value since "they merely reiterate the gods' blessing for the ruler and his superiority in all spheres of life."

Ishtar approaches Gilgamesh with a valid proposal, perhaps even a legal formula ("You be my husband and I will be your wife!") (see Abusch 1986:148–49). Gilgamesh, however, rebuffs her with direct insults and folkloristic references to her rejected lovers; he ignores her "marriage" to previous Sumerian kings, such as Enmerkar (see Cooper 1993:82–83), and her blessings on their reigns. If this is the correct scenario, then Gilgamesh's review of her jilted lovers is not only out of place, it manifests a stunning hubris and profound disregard for the citizens of his realm. Ishtar is strongly associated with kings from Sargonic through Neo-Assyrian times, according to Harris (1991:270–71), who states, "When Ishtar turns away from a dynasty, ruin and devastation inevitably follow." Gilgamesh here represents the selfish hero at the height of his arrogance rather than the good shepherd who would sacrifice himself for his flock. Even if Ishtar's proposal is divorced from the sacred marriage rite, Gilgamesh's insolence towards Uruk's patron goddess is inherently unworthy of the king. What would motivate Gilgamesh to risk Ishtar's mercurial temperament with his gratuitous insults?

Gilgamesh's rejection of Ishtar is actually an interpretive crux in most commentaries on the epic since readers must explain the hero's reaction in accordance with their own hermeneutical approaches.[59] In fact, the only reason Gilgamesh provides for rejecting Ishtar's proposal in the extant text is the inconstant nature of her love. Although textual gaps remain, Gilgamesh begins his list of her abandoned lovers with the question, "Which of your bridegrooms endured forever?" (VI 42, following George 1999:49), and he concludes his diatribe with a parting accusation: "And now me? You would love me and treat me like them!" (VI 79). Gilgamesh rebuffs Ishtar for her disloyalty and fickle passion, even though he knows from his own recounting of Ishuallu's predicament that rejecting her will lead to her hostility (Abusch 1986:171–72). Gilgamesh's scorn and derision demonstrate his fearlessness and contempt for the capricious goddess, but they do not explain the motivation for his vehemence. Indeed, the complexities of Ishtar's proposal and Gilgamesh's refusal cannot be resolved without a comprehensive interpretation of the epic and its relation to other traditions within Mesopotamian mythology. Yet, although aspects of this episode remain abstruse to Assyriologists, I doubt that we are missing some key piece of evidence that would cinch the interpretation in one way or the other. The poetic text's inherent ambiguity, multivalent symbolism, and narrative polyphony allow for multiple interpretations of this scene. This is especially true concerning Gilgamesh's unexpressed, interior motivations in rejecting Ishtar's love. All interpreters privilege certain assumptions to achieve a consistent reading of the text. Therefore, rather than offer a definitive solution to the literary puzzle, the present analysis merely applies a queer hermeneutic to trace the configurations of desire in this finely textured epic poem.

A hermeneutics of desire suggests that the most significant aspect of Ishtar's failed seduction is the epic's shocking lack of reference to her own erotic allure. Ancient audiences would certainly have been familiar with the literary tradition of narratives and hymns to Ishtar's powerful sex appeal, and so it is striking that the poet whose erotic vocabulary describes the various charms of Shamhat, Gilgamesh, Enkidu, and Uruk's prostitutes does not spare a single adjective to acknowledge the allure of Ishtar, the divine mistress of eroticism. Her allure is under erasure. Commentators who emphasize Ishtar's fatal beauty as she entices her victims with irresistible charms therefore presume too much in their reading of this text. The mystery is not that Gilgamesh rejects Ishtar's erotic proposition, but that the narrator does not convey her allure for him (or the reader) to appreciate. The narrator's intentional omission of Ishtar's appeal (i.e., *kuzbu*) is consistent with Gilgamesh's own lack of expressed desire, as the text provides no hint of his need for self-restraint in resisting her charms. In fact, Gilgamesh's rhetorical speech reflects the cool retorts of an older schoolboy, adept at the art of verbal sparring (Foster 1987:35), instead of a man beset by passionate longing, struggling to resist the powerful allure of the lethal goddess. The conclusion that Ishtar is simply not desirable to Gilgamesh is therefore most compelling. Certainly, the epic's recounting of Ishtar's failure to seduce an impudent mortal—on two separate occasions—is an outrageous affront to her divine dignity since, by any objective measure, Ishtar is charged with seductive allure in Mesopotamian tradition. Erotic desire, however, is not an objective force whose quality can be measured or mandated. On the contrary, passion is a thoroughly subjective phenomenon that arises in response to the perception of erotic stimuli. As noted above, desire, like beauty, is ultimately in the eye of the beholder, and here the narrator has manipulated the reader's desirous gaze with his subtle technique to discount the beauty of Ishtar. Gilgamesh, the narrator tells us, has a beautiful body and is decked in robes with a sash and crown, but Ishtar is denied even one adjective to convey her appeal.

Gilgamesh's absence of desire for Ishtar, a thoroughly desirable object in other contexts, requires further explanation. Interpreters who stress Gilgamesh's moral or philosophical development explain the heroes' rejection of (heterosexual) passion based upon their transcendence of erotic desire through their higher fraternal love (e.g., Foster 1987:22; Leick 1994:268). The epic's narrator is therefore said to neglect Ishtar's erotic appeal in order to promote the values of heroic asceticism. This perspective may be supported by the recent analysis of the Mesopotamian omen series by Guinan (1998:43), who concludes that in the sexual omens "masculine power expresses itself as disavowal and withdrawal from erotic interactions with women." Guinan explains (1998:40): "The omens oppose the male public persona and male/female eroticism in such a way that the denial of one is the assertion of the other." The rigorous control of male sexuality is auspicious because heterosexual relations are understood to deprive males of their power and social status. Gilgamesh's refusal of Ishtar's proposition could thus represent a heroic ideal of celibacy. The sexual omens, however, undermine this conclusion since they also provide auspicious meanings for male homosexual behavior.[60] Hence, rather than assume that the heroes' rejection of sexual involvement with women is an ascetic denial of sexuality in general, a queer hermeneutics can contend that their exclusionary, homosocial companionship is indicative of homoerotic desire. As foreseen in his dreams, Gilgamesh will love Enkidu and caress him like a wife. Ishtar's proposal of marriage thus presents Gilgamesh with a choice between the hero's homosocial adventures with Enkidu and a royal existence as the goddess's spouse.[61] Ishtar attempts to reduce him to an object of her libidinal desire, but Gilgamesh's denial of the goddess privileges masculine appeal and the desire for male companionship. The heroes' mutual devotion obviates any further consideration of feminine allure in the SB epic text. The heroic rejection of women for the manly life of comrades is therefore easily read as code for same-sex male love rather than celibacy.

A further, more sophisticated, indication of Gilgamesh's homoerotic desire may be intimated in his rhetorical enumeration of Ishtar's jilted lovers. Harris (1991:272) perceptively observes that Ishtar's choice of erotic partners—Tammuz, the allallu-bird, the lion, the horse, the shepherd, and Ishullanu—confuses the boundaries between gods, humans, and animals, while the range of her animal consorts—bird, wild, domestic—further communicates the boundlessness of her passions. What interpreters have not sufficiently considered, however, is Gilgamesh's own rhetorical goal in offering these literary allusions in his eloquent rejection speech.[62] Ishtar's erotic encounters with a variety of animals symbolize her ambiguous and boundary-crossing character, yet they also introduce the possibility of unprecedented sexual pairings. In her desire for diverse partners, Ishtar expands the scope of potential erotic objects. Even if used as negative charters, the divine actualization of such unconventional couplings subversively endorses and legitimates other "unnatural" sexual associations. Barry Weller (1997:243) treats a similar theme in White's Aurthurian fantasies, where Merlin magically transforms the future king into different animals as part of his schooling. Weller argues that "what Aurthur's excursions into the animal kingdom offer him is an open-ended variety of erotic connections..., with the corollary that no single ordering of human affairs is right or final." Gilgamesh may similarly appropriate the example of Ishtar's crossing of sexual boundaries to convey his own susceptibility to an unconventional and socially unsanctioned passion. Gilgamesh's litany of Ishtar's lovers forcefully demonstrates that conventional boundaries and categories in a culture's construction of desire do not matter in erotic attraction. Love, or lust, is sparked by a mysterious but overpowering attraction that does not always conform to traditional models of sexuality. Desire cannot be tamed or restrained, or even defined in some instances. Ishtar's examples of erotic excess demonstrate the instability of cultural categories of erotic desire; in fact, the goddess actively destabilizes the normative (and thus repressive) categories of her culture's discourse of sexuality, thereby fulfilling in herself one of the main goals of queer theory.

The most conspicuous absence from the list of Ishtar's erotic objects is of course the feminine. The thorough disregard for lesbian desire in Akkadian literature suggests not the absence of female homosexuality in ancient Mesopotamia (cp. Lambert 1992:146) but the ignorance and neglect of its existence among the androcentric world of the scribes, as though patriarchal ideology could not conceive of woman-to-woman erotic desire.[63] Ishtar's purpose in gathering Uruk's courtesans and female sex workers around herself in the epic's one episode of female homosociality is not for feminine solidarity but to lament the slain Bull's amputated "haunch" (*imittu*; VI 163), possibly a phallic euphemism. In constructing a poetics of desire, the Gilgamesh epic eventually considers divine-human, divine-animal, and human-animal engagements, as well as both masculine and feminine heterosexual aggression. The expanse of erotic possibilities offered by Ishtar suggests virtually every sexual permutation of divine, human, and animal categories except the homosexual—the very subject explicitly introduced by Gilgamesh's dreams of Enkidu. In this episode, however, the homoerotic alternative is but tenuously conveyed through Gilgamesh's rhetorical strategy, as though it were too far outside of the dominant discourse to receive a fair hearing. Indeed, the general avoidance of homosexual love in cuneiform sources suggests that it must remain the "love which dare not speak its name" in ancient Mesopotamian texts. The implication, however, is clear. In his irresistible love for Enkidu, Gilgamesh transgresses the heterosexual boundary to engage the homoerotic possibility with his divinely ordained companion. Gilgamesh's listing of Ishtar's animal affairs may therefore be a subtle defense of his own unconventional liaison with Enkidu. Ishtar's various forms of unorthodox sexuality provide the context for the heroes' own illicit love, at the same time that her caprice and faithlessness contrast with their loyalty and devotion.

In conclusion, Ishtar's attempted seduction of Gilgamesh in Tablet VI stresses Ishtar's sexual subjectivity in appropriating the masculine gaze and approaching Gilgamesh to initiate a sexual encounter, yet this emphasis does not sufficiently explain the text's utter disregard for Ishtar's own seductive allure. Gilgamesh's absence of desire for Ishtar may represent various ideas, including the invalidation of feminine sexual agency by androcentric ideology;

the rejection of sterile eroticism in preference for procreation in marriage; and the homoerotic rejection of heterosexual attraction. A queer reading can account for Gilgamesh's lack of response to Ishtar's provocation by positing his lack of desire for the goddess and his inability to reciprocate her ardor. Ishtar's vision of Gilgamesh inflames her passion for the king but his gaze upon her does not spark his own desire. The vehemence of his scorn may result from his complete disinterest in—or repugnance at—her erotic proposition, as well as a recognition of her deceptive words. In contrast to their previous exploitation of heterosexual relations, neither Gilgamesh nor Enkidu exhibits any desire for women after their meeting. This suggests that their erotic drives are fulfilled in each other, as Gilgamesh's dreams portend, rather than the sublimation of their erotic drive in heroic adventures. Thus, Gilgamesh's rejection of Ishtar's desire allows him to continue his exclusive friendship with the loyal Enkidu, just as it allows him to retain his masculine identity instead of submitting to her controlling power. The integrity of the heroes' relationship is contrasted with the treachery of Ishtar's love as Gilgamesh implicitly denies the validity of female sexual subjectivity and erotic desire.

Commentators often conclude that the *Epic of Gilgamesh* promotes the cause of reproductive sex within marriage in opposition to sterile eroticism (e.g., Foster 1987). This utilitarian discourse of sexuality, with its teleology of procreation, is symbolized by the maternal womb as the locus of desire, the center of most significant activity that motivates sexual behavior. The courtesan Shamhat represents a competing image of sexuality that identifies masculine desire and feminine appeal as the constituent elements of human sexuality. Her encounter with Enkidu challenges the more conservative definition of sex as only a means of procreation but pushes the boundaries no further than to recognize masculine erotic desire, whose phallic teleology is realized by the penetration of a feminine sexual object. This construct focuses on appetite and pleasure rather than procreation, with the masculine drive's locus of desire symbolized by the phallus. Ishtar introduces a third construct that promotes feminine sexual pleasure, symbolized by the clitoris (in Akkadian terms, the vulva). Ishtar voices a counter-theme of feminine desire, opposing the patriarchal emphasis on both womb and phallus, in order to advance the possibility of female sexual gratification. Yet even the polymorphous desires of Ishtar are constrained by the limits of a compulsorily heterosexual perspective. The womb, phallus, and clitoris thus symbolize three focal points of sexual discourse. The Gilgamesh epic, however, moves beyond these three loci of desire to envision a wider expanse of erotic potential by introducing the additional variable of objects of desire. The volatile combination of sexual subjects and (unpredictable) erotic objects thus allows for unprecedented permutations on the theme of desire within the text's construction of sexuality.

Heroic Love: Requiting Desire

While the erotic relationships of Ishtar and Shamhat reflect a strictly heterosexual discourse of sexuality, the companionship of Gilgamesh and Enkidu is more ambiguous in its eroticism. Commentators debate the sexual or fraternal character of their friendship but no one denies the intensity of their loyalty and devotion to each other.[64] This devotion manifests a desire for each other's company that is properly called erotic even if nonsexual. Enkidu's complete disregard for Shamhat after encountering the king indicates that his passion for Gilgamesh is more powerful than his attraction to the prostitute's erotic charms. Indeed, Enkidu's physical lust for Shamhat's body is merely his apprenticeship to desire before accepting his true vocation in loving Gilgamesh.

We must return to the epic's opening columns for the description of Gilgamesh's lonely existence as the semi-divine king of Uruk. Like a wild bull rather than a gentle shepherd, Gilgamesh exhausts his subjects with his rampaging exuberance and monumental building activities. He harries the young men with violent games and harasses the young women with sexual demands. The text pointedly describes the plight of the city's women (I 62–64, restored; cf. I 74–76):

ul umaššar Gilgāmeš batulta ana ḫāʾirīša	Gilgamesh released no maiden to her bridegroom.
mārat qurādi ḫīrat eṭli	The warrior's daughter, the young man's bride,

tazzimtašina išmû ilānū	To their lament the gods paid heed.

The women's complaint is clarified by the parallel OB text, broken in SB, when a caterer on his way to a wedding informs Enkidu of Gilgamesh's exercise of the "right of first night" (*ius primae noctis*) with Uruk's brides. Gilgamesh "copulates with the intended wife; He first, the husband afterwards" (*aššat šimtim iraḫḫi šū pānānum-ma mutum warkānu*; OBP iv 25–27).[65] Although there is no historical evidence for this practice in ancient Mesopotamia, the caterer affirms that Gilgamesh has a divinely sanctioned right to the brides (OBP iv 28–30). This exploitation of his subjects is likely a historical fiction by the epic poets to emphasize Gilgamesh's insatiable sexual appetite as well as his poor shepherding of his flock, and Enkidu's outrage at Gilgamesh's practice probably reflects an ancient repugnance at such royal impropriety. While some commentators believe that the king's erotic energies were directed towards the young men as well as the young women of Uruk (e.g., Bailey 1976:446–47), the text does not confirm this reading. Gilgamesh's frenetic state is actually the result of his adherence to a hypermasculine social script; he is "compulsively masculine," to borrow Philip Slater's (1968:339, 377) phrase, in his ostentatious display of stereotypically male behavior, including monumental building, aggressive competitive sports, and excessive heterosexual indulgence. Even though successful by the terms of patriarchal ideology, Gilgamesh does not find satisfaction or fulfillment in his many achievements.[66]

The citizens of Uruk pray for relief from their oppressive king and his boundless energies. In response, the gods commission Aruru to create the ferocious Enkidu as Gilgamesh's equal and rival: "Let him be a match for the storm of his heart. Let them contend with each other so that Uruk may be relieved!" (*ana ūm libbīšu lū mašil ištannanū-ma Uruk lištapšiḫ*; I 80–81). Enkidu fulfills his destined role when, hearing of Gilgamesh and his tyranny, he wishes to challenge the legendary hero. The wild man tells Shamhat that he will confront Gilgamesh with his superior strength (I 203–5):

anāku lugrīšum-ma danniš	I will contend with him and

luqabbi	challenge him!
luṣarriḫ ina libbi Uruk anākū-mi dannu	I will cry out in the midst of Uruk, "I am the mightiest!"
lūrum-ma šīmātu unakker	I will arrive and change the customs.

Yet even here, when Enkidu is most belligerent towards Gilgamesh, the epic narrator subtly introduces the erotic force of the heroes' fated attraction by revealing Enkidu's prior, unspoken reaction to hearing of Gilgamesh: "He yearned for one who will know his heart, a friend" (*mudû libbašu iše’’â ibra*; I 197). The narrator thus subverts Enkidu's aggressive speech by revealing his conflicted motivations in approaching Gilgamesh. Rejected by the animals and finding no lasting or appropriate companion in Shamhat, Enkidu realizes his need for a true friend and partner. His heroic nature compels him toward masculine competition, but Enkidu is also destined to love the mighty king of Uruk.

Although he does not know it, Enkidu was specifically designed as a match for Gilgamesh's passions and appetites, "the storm of his heart" (*ūm libbīšu*; I 80) in the Akkadian idiom. Gilgamesh has the young men of Uruk to bully but no real friend, partner, or equal (*ibru*, *tappû*, *tamīlu*; e.g., VII 136–37) until the arrival of Enkidu. He lacks a suitable comrade with whom to expend his heroic energies in epic adventures. Like the wild man who yearns for someone to know his heart (I 197), Gilgamesh longs for someone who will understand his super-human capacities when he says, "May I acquire a friend as a counselor!" (*ibri māliku anāku lurši*; II 273). Contrary to the biblical account of the solitary Adam, it is not a wife that will ease Gilgamesh's loneliness and be a "companion appropriate for him" (Gen 2:18). Instead, the epic casts Gilgamesh's soul-mate as another male, a wild man to exhaust his energies and distract him from his oppression of Uruk's citizens. The text conveys the heroes' competitive friendship through verbs that mean "to contend with each other" (*šitannunu* in I 81 and *gerû* in I 203) and the Št-stem verb *šutamḫuru*, which connotes both "to make equal" and "to make rival" (*CAD* 10/1:51, 70).[67] The text plays with these verbal nuances to describe the men as equals who spur each other on to heroic deeds. Yet, in addition to being a companion and rival for the semi-divine king, Enkidu is an erotic trap to ensnare Gilgamesh. Enkidu is sent by the gods at the people's request to distract Gilgamesh from his intolerable behavior, just as Shamhat is sent by the king at the trapper's request to domesticate Enkidu. In each case the means of entrapment is erotic desire, as I will argue.

Although the narrator has previously established the allure of Gilgamesh, Enkidu first learns of Uruk's king through Shamhat's seductive speech. In contrast to his attraction to the woman through his masculine gaze, it is by hearing that Enkidu is initially drawn to Gilgamesh. Shamhat purposefully incites Enkidu's desire through her sensual description of Uruk's enticing prostitutes: "And there are courtesans, most shapely of figure, adorned with seductive charm and full of joy!" (*u šamḫāti šūsum-ma binûtu kuzba zu᾽᾽una malâ rīšātum*; I 213–14). She then artfully draws Enkidu's attention from female sexual objects to the masculine allure of Gilgamesh. Playing upon the trope of the masculine gaze, she says, "I will show you Gilgamesh" (*lukallimka Gilgāmeš*; I 217). Shamhat urges Enkidu to appreciate the seductive appeal of the royal body for himself (I 218–20):

amur šâšu uṭul pānīšu	Look at him, gaze upon his face:
eṭlūta bani balta īši	splendid in manhood, dignified is he.
zu᾽᾽una kuzba kalu zumrīšu	His entire body is adorned with seductive allure!

Rather than simply communicate her own desire for the beautiful male form, Shamhat invites Enkidu to participate in the cathexis of Gilgamesh's charm. Using sensual language appropriate for any desirable object, she eroticizes the masculine body by equating its seductive allure (*zu᾽᾽una kuzba*; I 220) with the enticing bodies of Uruk's prostitutes (*kuzba zu᾽᾽una*; I 214). Enkidu may think that he is going to confront Gilgamesh, but Shamhat's description of the king conveys to the audience that Gilgamesh is himself an erotic object worthy of Enkidu's desire. Shamhat's manipulation of Enkidu's erotic gaze in this passage signals the text's movement from the theme of feminine appeal to its preoccupation with masculine allure.

Shamhat gives Enkidu no chance to respond to her eroticization of the masculine body as she launches immediately into the subject of Gilgamesh's dreams of Enkidu—dreams that emphasize the power of Gilgamesh's yearning for a companion and the intensity of his fore-ordained attraction to Enkidu. Still playing on the trope of the erotic gaze, Shamhat tells Enkidu that even before he came from the mountains, Gilgamesh "was seeing dreams of you" (*inaṭṭala šunātīka*; I 227). In the ancient world as now, dreams are a most suitable vehicle for sexual subjects (see Butler 1998; Oppenheim 1956). One need not be a Freudian to appreciate the importance of dreams as expressions of unconscious or latent desires, and Gilgamesh's dreams barely sublimate their homoerotic content. In relating his dream of Enkidu's arrival in the form of a meteorite, Gilgamesh avoids the trope of masculine gaze to focus instead on emotional attachment. Gilgamesh claims, "I loved it and embraced (and caressed) it like a wife" (*arāmšū-ma kī aššate elīšu aḫbub*; I 239). The text employs the same verb (*ḫabābu*) that earlier describes Enkidu's passions flowing over Shamhat as they copulate (I 176) (see note 29). In direct contrast to Enkidu's beastly approach to Shamhat, Gilgamesh's dreams of Enkidu include the tender caressing or murmurings of a loving couple (see *AHw* 1:301; cf. *CAD* 6:2). Lambert (1992:156, n. 31) observes that the common phrase to depict sexual pleasure is "to love a woman" rather than "to love a wife," and he suggests that the image here refers to the steadfastness of marital love rather than its sexual component. This passage uses a simile (*kī aššate*, "like a wife") rather than Lambert's idiom, however, and the verb *ḫabābu* clearly carries a sexual meaning. Furthermore, the multivalence of this symbolism obviates the need to choose between the sexual and marital metaphors as though they were mutually exclusive. Even those scholars who wish to emphasize the superiority of celibate friendship to sexual intimacy acknowledge that the text applies explicitly sexual metaphors to describe the heroes' relationship (e.g., Halperin 1990:81; Van Nortwick 1992:17–18).

Ninsun's interpretations of the images in her son's dreams further imply a sexual component to the heroes' companionship.

Ninsun identifies the meteorite of Gilgamesh's first dream as a warrior companion: "A mighty comrade will come to you, one who will save a friend" (I 250). She proclaims, "You will love him and embrace him like a wife" (*tarâmšū-ma kī aššati elīšu taḫbubu*; I 253). Her interpretation of the second dream is even clearer in stating that Gilgamesh will be sexually intimate with another man (I 267–70):

mārī ḫaṣṣinnu ša tāmuru amīlu	My son, the ax you saw is a man.
tarâmšū-ma kī aššate elīšu taḫabbub	You will love him and embrace him like a wife.
u anāku ultamaḫḫaršu ittīka	And I myself will make him equal to you.
illakakkum-ma dannu tappû mušēzib ibri	A mighty comrade will come to you, one who will save a friend.

Gilgamesh responds enthusiastically to the announcement of a new comrade while ignoring the overtly sexual content of Ninsun's interpretation (I 274–76):

...ina pî Enlil māliki rabî limqutam-ma	...According to the command of the great counselor Enlil, may it befall me!
ibri māliku anāku lurši	May I acquire a friend as a counselor!
luršī-ma ibri mālika anāku	A friend as a counselor may indeed I acquire!

Although it remains possible that it is Gilgamesh who is "like a wife" in embracing Enkidu, the simile more likely refers to Enkidu as the object of Gilgamesh's embrace: "I embraced him as (though he were) a wife." This feminine portrayal of Enkidu has received much attention from commentators, who routinely note that the epic depicts Enkidu with long hair "like a woman" (I 89) and dressed in women's clothing when he enters the shepherds' camp (OBP ii 27–28). Later in the epic, Gilgamesh will veil the dead Enkidu's face "like a bride" (VIII 58), further suggesting the conjugal nature of the heroes' relationship. More subtle homosexual innuendoes in Gilgamesh's dreams have been detected by Anne Draffkorn Kilmer (1982), who notes the puns between the dream symbols of Enkidu, *kiṣru* and *ḫaṣṣinnu*, and the cultic functionaries *kezru* and *assinnu*, possibly male homosexual prostitutes in the service of Ishtar.[68] These puns symbolically cast Enkidu into an emasculated or feminine role as the recipient of male sexual aggression according to traditional heterosexual ideology (see Leick 1994:266–68; Doty 1993:81). Conversely, Gilgamesh takes on feminine imagery when he mourns bitterly for Enkidu like a "mourner-woman" (*lallarītu*; VIII 44) and a lioness deprived of her cubs (VIII 60).

Interpreters often argue that one of the two heroes must be the feminine counterpart to the other's masculine character. Thomas Van Nortwick (1992:18), for example, holds that Enkidu symbolizes the feminine forces of nature to supplement Gilgamesh's overbearing masculinity, while Leick (1994:268) argues that the urban Gilgamesh has a feminine persona, in contrast to Enkidu's wild, "phallic masculinity." In fact, both of the heroes are overtly masculine according to traditional and ancient standards of gender in their courage, strength, combativeness, and sense of honor (see Gleason 1990; Loraux 1990; cf. Asher-Greve 1998). Neither hero demonstrates signs of feminine gender, although some feminine images are applied to each of them. The attempt to force one of the heroes into a feminine role is reminiscent of the homophobic question concerning a gay couple: "Which one wears the dress?" In a more constructive move, Foster (1987:33) notes the unity of the heroes achieved by their "near perfect similarity." Although Foster argues against any sexual component to the men's relationship, he is right to emphasize the common heroic identity of Gilgamesh and Enkidu. Martti Nissinen (1998:24) also observes that the warriors' similarity allows for a shared experience that is unavailable to a heterosexual couple bound by the social structures of patriarchal society. Thus, the epic's use of marital and gendered imagery to describe the heroes' intense relationship may be an attempt to depict the unorthodox relationship between two warriors who love each other as male-identifying men. Their intimate bonds of loyalty are likened to those of a married couple, while their passionate devotion is described with images that blur the distinction between platonic and sexual love. The rhetorical function of this poetic equivocation is best exploited by queer literary methods that discern and disclose the homoerotic elements of Gilgamesh and Enkidu's homosocial relationship.

In contrast to its glorification of Gilgamesh's physique, the SB epic is restrained in its descriptions of Enkidu's charms, only once noting the beauty of his body in the narrative voice (*bani* [*lāššu*]; II 88, restored). Shamhat, however, tells Enkidu that he is indeed handsome (*damqāta*, I 190), and the shepherds who gather around him exclaim (II 32–33), "This fellow, how similar to Gilgamesh is his body: a towering body, glorious as a battlement!" (*eṭlum ana Gilgāmeš kī mašil lānu, lānu šīḫi naburriš šarḫu*) (cf. II 132–34). The text further applies the adjective *šarḫu*, "glorious," to the body of Gilgamesh (*šaruḫ lāššu*, I 49), a galloping stallion (VI 20), and Gilgamesh's self-exaltation after killing the Bull of Heaven:

mannum-ma bani ina eṭlūtim	Who is most splendid among young men?
mannum-ma šaruḫ ina zikkarī	Who is most glorious among males? (VI 176–77)

Gilgamesh identifies himself as the most splendid among young men (VI 178), but the subject of VI 179 is broken and may identify either Gilgamesh or Enkidu as the most glorious among males. Enkidu therefore shares with Gilgamesh this masculine and militaristic attribute (*šarḫu*) at least once and perhaps three times in the SB epic. Upon his arrival in Uruk, the young men gather around Enkidu and "kiss his feet like a little baby" (*kī šerri laʾî unaššaqū šēpīšu*; II 87; cf. I 238), an act that conveys their delight in his charming form.[69] The SB narrative of Enkidu's entrance to Uruk is otherwise fragmentary, but the parallel OB text quotes the people, saying, "In build he is the image of Gilgamesh, but shorter in stature and bigger of bone" *(ana-mi Gilgāmeš mašil padattam lānam šapil eṣemtam pukkul*; OBP v 10–12). The OB narrator further describes Enkidu as "the youth whose appearance is fair, an equal set up for the god-like Gilgamesh" (*eṭlim ša išaru zīmūšu ana Gilgāmeš kīma ilim šakiššum meḫrum*; OBP v 20–22, cf. II 88–90). In fact, it seems that Enkidu's similarity to Gilgamesh is the most common and highest praise for his physical charm in the OB and SB epics. Tablet I defines the standard for masculine allure with the ideal body of Gilgamesh, and so Enkidu is appealing to the extent that he reflects Gilgamesh's qualities. Gilgamesh's love for Enkidu can therefore be likened to the gaze of Narcissus or the love of the mirror's reflection. Gilgamesh responds to that in Enkidu which is most like himself; the only man worthy of the king's respect and devotion is the one who reifies his own strengths and beauty. Jean-Pierre Vernant (1990:472) explains that love of the mirror's reflection naturally results in homoeroticism, "the most beautiful love" in some ancient Greek sources that celebrate the virtues of manhood.[70]

In keeping with their hypermasculine identities, Gilgamesh's first encounter with Enkidu takes the form of a wrestling match outside the door of a bridal chamber. Scholars have proposed various events as the setting for this athletic contest—including Gilgamesh's own wedding, a sacred marriage rite, and a secular orgy—but Gilgamesh's attempted exercise of the "right of first night" remains the most plausible explanation for this episode (see Bailey 1976:443; Tigay 1982:176; Foster 1987:30–31; and Jacobsen 1990:237). Enkidu is the unlikely champion of civil marriage as he prevents Gilgamesh from interfering with the bridal couple's consummation of their union. The SB text describes the two heroes' confrontation with the reciprocal (Gt) verbs *iṣṣabtū* and *ittegrû*, "they grasped each other, they fought each other" (II 93–94). The SB epic breaks off after another line and we must rely upon the parallel OB account, which adds, "They grasped each other like wrestlers, they bent down" (*iṣṣabtū-ma kīma lēʾīm ilūdū*; OBP vi 11–12).[71] The intimate bodily contact of wrestling, the implied grunts and groans of physical exertion, and the threshold symbolism of the doorway all contribute to the scene's sexual symbolism. The bridal chamber provides an erotically charged setting for their tussle, while the walls' shaking and shuddering during their struggle is suggestive as well (II 95). Leick (1994:266) points out the euphemistic implications of grappling, bending down, sudden weakness, and tenderness. The wrestling match is not overtly sexual, of course, but it serves as a transparent metaphor for a male sexual experience of struggle and dominance, climax and relaxation.

Furthermore, Gilgamesh's combative introduction to Enkidu has numerous literary parallels to Enkidu's passionate encounter with Shamhat. Enkidu does not address the king as he obstructs the door to the bridal chamber with his foot; he positions his body to be seen by Gilgamesh, parallel to Shamhat's intentional display of her body in the wilderness. Gilgamesh approaches Enkidu and engages in a wrestler's hold, similar to Enkidu's approach and embrace of Shamhat. In each encounter, the aggressor is eventually drained of his energies and breaks away from the embrace: "(Gilgamesh's) passion subsided and he turned away" (*ipšiḫ uzzašu-ma inēʾ irassu*; OBP vi 21–22), with wordplay on *uzzu*, which can denote either anger or sexual arousal as in the OB love incantations quoted above. Enkidu then addresses Gilgamesh in admiration of his royal superiority, just as Shamhat initiates a conversation with Enkidu concerning his beauty and god-like humanity. The remaining text of Enkidu's conversation with Gilgamesh is unfortunately lost or fragmentary in all versions, but the OB Yale tablet apparently concludes the scene with the narrator's remark, "They kissed each other and formed a friendship" (*ittašqū-ma īpušū ruʾūtam*; OBY i 19–20). The wedding scene thus concludes with the union of two grooms but no bride.

Having earned a mutual respect through their physical struggle, Gilgamesh and Enkidu become inseparable companions, a theme not uncommon in tales of heroic adventure. Even though the text is broken, commentators unanimously conclude that Gilgamesh is sufficiently enchanted by his new friend that he forsakes his night with the bride.[72] When the SB text resumes (II 132), Gilgamesh is praising Enkidu's strength and beauty as he introduces him to his mother. In fact, neither of the heroes will display the slightest interest in heterosexual activities after this episode. The heroes' complete disregard for women as erotic objects stands in stark contrast with their previous exploitation of feminine sexuality. In fact, the text leaves the reader with only negative images of heterosexual desire in Enkidu's animalistic attraction to the nude prostitute and Ishtar's fickle passions. Shamhat's "love" is merely the erotic technique of the professional sex-worker, while Ishtar's libidinal passion is deadly and dehumanizing. Gilgamesh's sexual appropriation of Uruk's brides is equally selfish and pointless in light of his authentic and requited love for Enkidu. The shallow heterosexual relationships of Enkidu and Gilgamesh thus serve by contrast to emphasize the emotional commitment, passion, and fulfillment of their exclusively male relationship. Whether sexual or not, their erotic attachment to each other is powerful and profound.

Enkidu responds to Gilgamesh's affection with intense loyalty and devotion. Brought to tears by his friend's impetuous decision to challenge Humbaba and cut down the cedar forest (e.g., II 156), Enkidu nevertheless accompanies and protects Gilgamesh in his grandious scheme to win eternal fame. Devotion to Gilgamesh apparently drives Enkidu to unprecedented heights of hubris in his malevolence towards Ishtar, whose frustrated desire for Gilgamesh compels her to send the Bull of Heaven against Uruk. After the two heroes slay the divine Bull, Enkidu viciously hurls the Bull's haunch or thigh (*imittu*; *CAD* s.v. and 17/1:193) at the distraught goddess and threatens her with uncharacteristic vehemence: "And to you too would I do the same if I could catch you! I would drape his guts over your arms!" (VI 158–60). Ishtar gathers courtesans and prostitutes (*kezrētu*, *šamḫātu*, and *ḫarīmātu*; VI 161–62) to mourn the Bull's thigh, likely a phallic euphemism. Enkidu's unexplained rancor against the goddess casts him in the guise of a jealous lover, lashing out against his romantic rival with vulgar gestures and venomous insults. Although the text does not explore the motivation for Enkidu's insolence, a queer hermeneutic can plausibly identify his rivalry with Ishtar for Gilgamesh's affection as the source of Enkidu's bitterness. Just as Gilgamesh scorns Ishtar's proposal, Enkidu's emotional outburst and spiteful abuse demonstrate his own defiance of the goddess of heterosexual eroticism. His passion for Gilgamesh, as well as a latent fear of being replaced by a divine wife, drives Enkidu to mock the power of Ishtar.

Enkidu's devotion to Gilgamesh is further expressed when, hearing of his fated demise, he seems more concerned with his separation from Gilgamesh than his own death. In a Hittite paraphrase of Tablet VII's first column, still unrecovered in the SB edition, Enkidu lies weeping before Gilgamesh as he relates his dream of the divine council. Enkidu laments his fate: "O my brother, dear to me is my brother! They will [never] raise me up again for my brother. [Among] the dead I shall sit, the threshold of the dead [I shall cross,] never again [shall I set] my eyes on my dear brother" (George 1999:55). Enkidu grieves the loss of Gilgamesh's companionship as much as his own mortality. After cursing the trapper and Shamhat, Enkidu is reminded by Shamash of his introduction to the human experience of bread, beer, and clothes by the courtesan. Shamash continues, "and she gave you as a companion (*tappâ*) the handsome (*dumqu*) Gilgamesh," whom he describes as "your friend and brother" (*ibru* and *talīmu*) (VII 136–37). Enkidu accepts the rebuke of Shamash, "his angry heart grew calm" (*agga libbašu inūḫ*; VII 147), and he is apparently placated for his short life by the reparative knowledge of his meaningful relationship with Gilgamesh.

Harris (1990:228–29) considers the possibly homosexual relationship between Enkidu and Gilgamesh when she observes: "Apart from his closeness to his mother, Gilgamesh's only other intimate relationship demonstrated by kissing, embracing, and the holding of hands is with Enkidu." Although the OB text (OBY i 19) notes their kissing, the SB epic does not describe the heroes kissing each other until Tablet XII 85: "They embraced and kissed each other" (*innedrū-ma ultaššaqū*).[73] The SB epic is apparently reticent to describe much physical contact between the heroes while they are both alive; even so, Gilgamesh and Enkidu do embrace or hold hands various times in the extant SB text.[74] More telling are Enkidu's words in Tablet XII, where Enkidu's ghost laments the decay of "my body that you touched so your heart rejoiced" (*zumrī ša talputū-ma libbaka iḫdû*; XII 93, 95). There are further clues to the heroes' intimacy. Before journeying to the forest of Humbaba, Gilgamesh and Enkidu formalize their relationship and cement their emotional bonds through one of the few conventional means available: Ninsun adopts the orphan Enkidu as her own son, making him Gilgamesh's brother (III 130 restored).[75] Like the covenant between David and Jonathan, this formal relationship could be a literary means to camouflage romantic love (Comstock 1992:21–23). After legitimating their relationship in the eyes of their society, Gilgamesh and Enkidu set off for the distant cedar forest of Humbaba on a type of heroic honeymoon. The couple flees the crowded city for the privacy of the wilderness where, like Achilles and Patroclos, they sleep together in the same tent. Their bonds are strengthened through heroic deeds and death-defying adventures as they devote themselves to each other's company. After their return and a triumphal parade through the streets of Uruk, Gilgamesh makes merry in his palace and then "the young men lie asleep in a bed at night" (*utullū-ma eṭlūtū ina mayāl mūši ṣallū*; VI 184), apparently sharing one bed. Since the text previously implies that neither Enkidu (II 49–52) nor Gilgamesh (I 222) requires sleep, their lying together is suggestive of intimacy as much as restfulness. A double entendre is also found in Shamash's statement to Enkidu that Gilgamesh "will lay you down on a magnificent bed" (*ina mayāl taknî ušnālkā-ma*; VII 139), a phrase with both wedding and funereal associations.

Many of these scenes and phrases are suggestive of romantic involvement, yet the epic is never unambiguous in its depiction of the heroes' erotic attachment. In explaining the difficulty of distinguishing between literary representations of homoerotic and other types of same-sex affection, Mark Lilly (1993:66) states, "Conventions of expression sometimes make brotherly affection, physical tenderness, and sexual desire all sound the same." The use of common poetic expressions to represent various forms of same-sex love provides grist for the mill of queer theory and its hermeneutics of suspicion as it deconstructs the dichotomy between platonic and erotic love. The Gilgamesh epic's reticence to define the physical quality of the heroes' love leaves the matter unresolved and equivocal. In fact, the epic most clearly conveys Gilgamesh's passionate desire for Enkidu in prophetic dreams prior to their meeting and in elegies after Enkidu's death. The descriptions of their physical relationship when both are alive are sexually suggestive without ever being sexually explicit. This careful presentation of their erotic attraction allows for a clear articulation of erotic desire without risking the image of the physical expression of homosexual passion. The text's ambiguity concerning Enkidu and Gilgamesh's relationship is in fact similar to the literary strategies of modern gay writers to sublimate homoeroticism through literary codes and conventions (see Comstock 1992:22). Significantly, two of the most common conventions to represent homoerotic desire in nineteenth- and twentieth-century male homosexual literature are the language of soldier-comrades and elegies for the dead (see Comstock

1992:21–22), two themes effectively utilized in the epic of Gilgamesh as well.

Scholars have long appreciated the heroic context and agonistic quality of the story of Gilgamesh and Enkidu as a precursor to the Western literary tradition that explores the intense emotional bonds of soldier-comrades (see Halperin 1990:75–87). The profound love, devotion, and loyalty between comrades-at-arms are seemingly difficult to convey without recourse to the erotic language of passion and desire. Love poetry from soldiers of the First World War is illustrative of these themes, as explained by Lilly (1993:64–82) in his consideration of gay men's literature. Lilly (1993:67–69) demonstrates the direct expression of love between men, the intense emotional gratification of comrades' affection, and the subsequent devaluing of women's love in this sentimental poetry, written by both heterosexual and homosexual men. These points are equally descriptive of Gilgamesh and Enkidu's mutual devotion as they shun heterosexual involvement to pursue their exclusive friendship.[76] Lilly (1993:65) notes the importance of the modern soldier as a symbol of a community's virility and power and states that "it would be difficult to overestimate the resistance amongst heterosexuals to the idea that men *upon whom otherwise they would wish to bestow their deepest admiration*, might have enjoyed other men carnally" (his emphasis). This same resistance is found among many interpreters of the Gilgamesh epic, who choose to neglect or ignore the implications of the poem's manifestly homoerotic images. Indeed, from ancient to modern times, heroism and homoeroticism are not inconsistent motifs in the androcentric poetry of warfare and adventure.[77]

The elegiac expression of homoerotic desire is also prevalent in the epic's latter half as Gilgamesh laments his fallen comrade. The unexpected death of Enkidu as divine punishment shattters Gilgamesh's equanimity. Apart from the explicitly sexual content of his prophetic dreams, Gilgamesh most clearly articulates his passion for Enkidu in his moving elegies and anguished mourning. Gilgamesh conveys the intimacy of their friendship and the depth of his love when he cries out in grief, "My friend, whom I loved so dearly, who experienced all dangers with me!" (*ibrī ša arammu danniš ittīya ittallaku kalu marṣāti*) (e.g., X 233). Gilgamesh eulogizes Enkidu with wild animal metaphors: "My friend, a wild mule on the run, a wild ass from the mountains, a panther of the steppe!" (*ibrī kūdanu ṭardu akkannu ša šadî nimru ša ṣēri*) (e.g., VIII 49). These epithets capture the untamed aggression and virility of the warrior Enkidu. In fact, *akkannu*, "wild ass," and *akkannu ṭardu*, "wild ass on the run," along with Gilgamesh's epithet *rīmu*, "wild bull," are used as quintessentially masculine images in Akkadian potency incantations (e.g., Biggs 1967:12). The gazelle's feminine gracefulness and the wild ass's virility combine in Enkidu's heroic build when Gilgamesh exclaims, "Your mother was a gazelle (*ṣabītu*) and a wild ass (*akkannu*) the father who sired you!" (VIII 3–4). The evocative quality of these animal metaphors is heightened by their juxtaposition with the cold-blooded images of Humbaba's insults that depict Enkidu as the "spawn of a fish who knew no father" (*mār nūni ša lā idû abāšu*) and a "tortoise, a turtle who suckled no mother's milk" (*raqqu u šeleppû ša lā īniqu šizib ummīšu*) (V 83–84).

Gilgamesh pays tribute to Enkidu with additional metaphors that denote their close companionship (VIII 45–48):

ḫaṣṣin aḫīya tukultu idīya	The ax at my side, in which my arm trusted,
namṣar šibbīya arītu ša pānīya	the sword in my belt, the shield before me,
lubār isinnātīya nēbeḫ lalêya	my festive garment, my sash of delight:
namtāru lemnu itbâm-ma īkimanni yâši	an evil fate rose up and robbed me (of them)!

The intimacy of the clothing metaphors—"my festive garment, my sash of delight"—suggests a tender relationship between the men, emphasized by *lalû*, "delight," which appears elsewhere in the epic with explicitly sexual connotations (e.g., I 178). More significantly, the ax at his side (*ḫaṣṣin aḫīya*) refers to Gilgamesh's dream of manifestly erotic involvement with an ax (*ḫaṣṣinnu*) that symbolizes Enkidu (I 257–72).[78]

Finally, at Enkidu's death, Gilgamesh commissions a luxuriant statue (*ṣalmu*, *minâtu*, *zumru*) of his friend's body, crafted in gold and adorned with lapis lazuli and precious gems (VIII 67–73). The unfortunately fragmentary description of Enkidu's image hints at a sensuous concentration upon Enkidu's masculine form in anatomical detail before the text breaks off completely (see George 1999:65). Indeed, Enkidu's body effectively symbolizes the theme of desire throughout the epic's twelve tablets. Enkidu's physical substance is introduced to the epic as an elemental piece of clay (*ṭiṭṭu*; I 85), worked in Aruru's hands and then cast into the wilderness as a primordial being (*lullû*; I 86). Enkidu is merely a shaggy animal running with the herds until he becomes human through the ministrations of Shamhat, whose expert touch transforms the rough creature into an attractive human, a man civilized by human customs and proper behavior. The heroic form of Enkidu is then celebrated by the citizens of Uruk as he becomes the boon companion and mirror image of the handsome Gilgamesh. With his death, however, Enkidu's body becomes even more powerfully evocative as a symbol of masculine allure brought to its inevitable ruin. Poetry through the ages has celebrated the athleticism of the warrior's beautiful body, which even in death is an object of dignity and admiration. Lilly (1993:78–80) considers WW I poetry that commemorates the masculine beauty of young soldiers' corpses unspoiled by old age, even as Vernant (1991:50–74) presents the ancient Greek image of the warrior's "beautiful death" (*kalos thanatos*) in Homeric epic. Death on the field of battle or in heroic adventure grants honor and glory to the warrior, as Gilgamesh foolishly boasts: "If I should fall, then I will establish my fame: 'Gilgamesh joined battle with ferocious Huwawa!'" (OBY iv 13–15; cf. George 1999:110). Enkidu, however, is deprived of a hero's death and posthumous glory by a decree of the assembled gods. He dies on his back, brought down by disease in an inglorious demise. Nevertheless, the heroic body of Enkidu retains its masculine beauty even as Gilgamesh attempts to rouse the corpse from its deathly slumber (VIII 54–57). It is only in acknowledging Enkidu's stilled heartbeat that Gilgamesh accepts his companion's death.

For seven days in a macabre wake, Gilgamesh weeps over Enkidu's corpse and refuses to surrender him for burial.[79] Gilgamesh clings to the body of his beloved friend until decomposition mars its allure, a point driven home by the gruesome depiction of a maggot dropping from the cadaver's nose (X 237–38). Vernant (1991:72) describes the humiliation of an unburied corpse left to decay in the open: "The body abandoned to decomposition is the complete reversal, or inversion, of a beautiful death. At one extreme is the youthful and manly beauty of the warrior whose body inspires amazement, envy, and admiration...; at the other is that which surpasses ugliness, the monstrousness of a being worse than nothing, of a form that has sunk into the unspeakable." Enkidu's body has thus passed from a desirable masculine form into a lifeless corpse, and now is further reduced to carrion. Ironically, Enkidu's ideal form is rendered immortal in gold, precious gems, and lapis lazuli even as his fleshly body descends into putrefaction. The stark juxtaposition of Enkidu's elegant statue with his rotting corpse hints at the impermanence of passionate desire for mortal beings. Gilgamesh, who was so quick to embrace a glorious death in his desire to battle Humbaba, shatters any illusions of a hero's "beautiful death" by impeding Enkidu's burial and thus revealing the harsh reality of death and decay. Gilgamesh will later lament that Enkidu's body "has turned into clay" (*ītemi ṭiṭṭiš*; e.g., X 72), thereby completing the cycle of his achievement and forfeiture of an alluring masculine form. By Tablet XII, discussed below, Enkidu is but a disembodied ghost, incapable of either inciting or responding to erotic desire.

Gilgamesh's morbid fixation upon the despoiling of Enkidu's beauty is expressed by his obsessive recounting of the maggot dropping from his friend's nose (X 65, 138, 238). The tragic acknowledgement of the beloved's eventual decomposition is similarly captured in the WW I poem by Herbert Read, "My Company (iii)" (in Taylor 1989:98; see Lilly 1993:78–79):

> A man of mine
> lies on the wire
> It is death to fetch his soulless corpse.
>
> A man of mine
> lies on the wire;
> And he will rot
> And first his lips
> The worms will eat.
> It is not thus that I would have him kissed,
> But with the warm passionate lips
> Of his comrade here.

The haunting image of the beloved's consumption by vermin serves as a brutal contrast to the warmth and charm of a living body in this soldier's poem of "unapologetically sensual" love for a comrade (Lilly 1993:78). Gilgamesh's horror at the degradation of Enkidu's physical form similarly alludes to the homoerotic bond between the two heroes as the attractive body that in life Gilgamesh loved to touch (XII 93) becomes repulsive and repellent. Like a rival lover, the maggot now possesses the beloved's body, effectively warding off all other suitors. Indeed, Gilgamesh's revulsion at Enkidu's moldering corpse signals the end of desire's thematic role in the SB epic.

In conclusion, David Comstock's (1992:23) analysis of the story of David and Jonathan applies equally well to the companionship of Gilgamesh and Enkidu: "The conventional and socially acceptable language and form of covenant, friendship, politics, elegy, and soldiering may have been used to tell a love story which needed both to remain within what was socially acceptable as well as to break with convention, that is, to tell a story that would appeal to and be heard differently by two different audiences." Comstock (1992:29, n. 53) suggests authorial intent to explain such coding, whose success may be measured by "the clarity with which gay persons to-day tend to read the David-Jonathan relationship as romantic and non-gay persons as political or friendly." Even without authorial intent to portray a homoerotic relationship in a coded manner, however, the Gilgamesh epic's ambiguity in describing intense sentiments of friendship and fraternal love generates conflicting readings of their relationship. These literary conventions to express love and devotion, whether platonic or sexually realized, contribute significantly to the poetic construction of desire in this ancient text. Halperin (1990:75) warns against the "insidious temptation to sexualize the erotics of male friendship," but even he (1990:81) must admit that Gilgamesh's affection for Enkidu is "described in terms appropriate for...objects of sexual desire" and is "explicitly modeled on sexual attraction."[80] This explicit modeling results in a poetics of desire that encompasses and promotes homoeroticism. In contrast to the erotic affairs of Shamhat and Ishtar, the powerful attraction between Gilgamesh and Enkidu results in intense emotional bonds, inseparable companionship, and mutual respect.

The heroes' subsequent neglect of sexual relations with women conveys the superiority of their same-sex love to heterosexual unions. By constructively channeling their energies, Gilgamesh and Enkidu's association allows them to realize their heroic potential in an alliance portrayed as mutually satisfying and completely fulfilling until its tragic interruption by death.

The Death of Desire

Gilgamesh experiences the loss of Enkidu's presence like an amputee who suffers the phantom pains of a severed limb. His violent reaction to their separation signals the depths of his passion and suggests that Gilgamesh loves Enkidu in a profound and extraordinary way. As Henry Staten (1995:xii) explains, to love a mortal being without restraint opens one up to unbearable grief and a despair that threatens the very foundations of rationality. In contrast to the transcendence of mortal forms and the sublimation of erotic desire into abstract ideals that are characteristic of Platonic philosophy, Gilgamesh loves unreservedly and thus risks himself absolutely in his attachment to the mortal Enkidu. Having achieved a complete union in their heroic friendship, Gilgamesh must now face an equally complete separation from his beloved companion. Herman Vanstiphout (1990:52) identifies the "renewed and much deeper loneliness" of the bereaved king that drives the epic plot after Enkidu's death. Gilgamesh will not risk cathexis or express desire for another person throughout the rest of the SB epic. His eros is transformed into *pothos*, defined by Vernant (1991:101) as a desire for what is absent, an unfulfilled longing that subsequently produces suffering, mourning, or regret. Tormented by his inner demons, Gilgamesh flees the city of Uruk to search for solace in the wilderness. He loses himself in the abyss of despair as he wanders the wasteland beyond the limits of human endurance. The narrator identifies the source of Gilgamesh's grief when he explains that Gilgamesh "weeps bitterly for his friend Enkidu" (IX 1–2) as he roams the steppe. Rather than discover an existential meaning to his life through ascetic contemplation, however, Gilgamesh is driven relentlessly onward by his wrenching heartbreak into isolation, despair, and madness.[81]

The specter of Enkidu's death haunts Gilgamesh with the prospect of his own mortality. Gilgamesh recognizes the ominous foreshadowing in the death of his mirror-image: "Enkidu, my friend whom I loved, has turned to clay! Shall I not be as he and so lie down, never to rise again for all eternity?" (X 73–75). The narrator identifies Enkidu as the source of his bitter weeping (IX 1–2), but Gilgamesh's words mourn his own impending demise: "I shall die and then shall I not be as Enkidu? Sorrow has invaded my heart! I am afraid of death and so I wander the steppe" (IX 3–5). The mixture of sorrow, anger, and fear in Gilgamesh's laments corresponds well to the numerous sources of his torment as he rages against human mortality. His anxiety at being "like Enkidu" expresses his dread of becoming "clay" (i.e., a decomposed corpse), as well as a repugnance at the sleeplike inactivity of the deceased.[82] Another worthy object of Gilgamesh's fear is the grim abode of the dead, described in the epic by Enkidu's harrowing Netherworld dream (VII 165–226) and the vision of Death's realm in Tablet XII. In combining the images of sleeplike inactivity, bodily decomposition, and the grim conditions of the Netherworld, the epic provides a comprehensive basis for Gilgamesh's desperate fear of death that precludes the possibility of further erotic cathexis.

Having lost the object of his desire with Enkidu's death, Gilgamesh now sacrifices his own allure in his extravagant grief. He rips off his finery (*damqūtu*) and tears out his curled hair (VIII 62–63) in traditional acts of mourning (see Anderson 1991:74–82; Abusch 1993a; 19934b). Moreover, his overwhelming grief and dread of the grave drive him to further self-mortification in his wearying journeys across the world. Gilgamesh becomes feral, killing lions and donning their skins to replace his worn-out clothes.[83] In a stylized dialogue, Siduri, Utnapishtim, and others remark upon his haggard and travel-worn appearance, his face burnt by frost and sun, and his wasted visage (*qatû zīmūka*; e.g., X 42). Utnapishtim's evaluation of Gilgamesh's desolate appearance also uses the verb *qatû* to emphasize the corruption of his allure: "Matted hair has enveloped his body; the pelts have ruined the beauty of his flesh" (*iktasû malû pagaršu maškū uqtattû dumuq šīrīšu*; XI 246–47).[84] As though in sympathy with Enkidu's bodily decay, Gilgamesh despoils his own attractive form through sleeplessness, hardship, and self-denial (X 254–55). Utnapishtim chides Gilgamesh for defiling a body that contains divine flesh (X 268–69) as he urges him to renounce his asceticism. In a scene that cleverly inverts elements of Gilgamesh's encounter with Ishtar, the bar-maid Siduri is repelled by Gilgamesh's ravaged features. While the beauty of Gilgamesh's body attracts the immortal gaze of Ishtar and kindles her desire for him in Tablet VI, Siduri's gaze upon his haggard form arouses within her only fear and revulsion. Ishtar comes down to seduce the king with coy words, while Siduri bars her door and flees to her roof in order to avoid his fearful presence (X 15–16; see George 1999:218–20). Looking through the eyes of Siduri and Utnapishtim, then, the epic text replaces the erotic gaze of Tablets I–VI with the vision of Gilgamesh's repulsive appearance.

Although it has been greatly truncated in the SB edition, Siduri's graceful speech to the distraught Gilgamesh in the OB epic urges him to abandon his futile quest and find contentment with life's simple joys.[85] Siduri's rhetoric is especially relevant to the poetics of desire as she says (OBM iii 12–13):

ṣubbi ṣeḫram ṣābitu qātīka	Gaze upon the little one who grasps your hand.[86]
marḫītum liḫtaddâm ina sūnīka	Let a wife ever delight in your lap.[87]

In an attempt to dissuade him from his pursuit of immortality, Siduri here counsels Gilgamesh to avert his gaze from erotic objects in order to focus upon family members. She evokes the tender image of a toddler clinging to his father's hand as a symbol of familial warmth. In encouraging him to take a wife as Enkidu's replacement, Siduri literally instructs Gilgamesh to become the object of a woman's erotic desire rather than the agent of his own passions: the Gtn-stem precative *liḫtaddâm* gives the active sexual role to the woman rather than the man. This is a rare and striking example of a woman's voice advocating feminine sexual agency in ancient Akkadian epic (cf. Leick 1994:222; *CAD* 15:387). Siduri's advice to let an anonymous wife delight in his lap rings hollow to the disconsolate Gilgamesh, however, and he disregards her counsel in order to continue his search for Utnapishtim (cp. Abusch

1993a:9–11). In its surprising excision of Siduri's speech, the SB edition seemingly reflects Gilgamesh's own rejection of erotic attachment as a meaningful goal of human endeavor. Desire itself has been edited out of the SB epic's final tablets.

Gilgamesh is the only person to traverse the wastelands, tunnel through the mountains' darkness, and sail the waters of death to arrive on the shores of Utnapishtim's immortal paradise. Yet, once there, he is powerless to claim any reward. Rather than a heroic victory over human limitations, his all-consuming and self-destructive journey is a vain struggle against death. Gilgamesh must eventually admit his quest's utter failure when he is unable to ward off even sleep. No comfort is offered in response to his desperate plea: "O Utnapishtim, what should I do and where should I go? A thief has seized my flesh! In my bedroom resides Death; wherever I turn, there too will Death be!" (XI 238–41). Even more pathetic is his desolation after losing his last hope, the Plant of Rejuvenation, to the serpent's stealth: "For whom, Urshanabi, were my arms wearied? For whom was my heart's blood poured out? I did not establish any benefit for myself, but for the 'lion of the ground' I established a benefit!" (XI 303–6). Gilgamesh's experience ironically affirms his youthful blustering on the futility of human endeavors: "As for a man, his days are numbered; whatever he may achieve is but wind" (*amēlutti manû ūmūša mimmû ēteppušu šārū-ma*; II 203–4, restored according to OBY iv 7–8). The hero's only recourse is to return to Uruk, empty-handed and bereft of hope.

John Maier (1984:32) expresses a common perspective when he interprets Gilgamesh's decision to take the Plant of Rejuvenation back to Uruk's elders as a metonymous symbol of his voluntary and contented resumption of royal duties. In fact, the text offers little support for this optimistic interpretation that sees altruism rather than egocentrism in the hero's decision to "put the Plant to the test" (*šamma lultuk*; XI 290) on others before ingesting it himself. Has Gilgamesh attained some penetrating insight that quells his illimitable mourning and reveals the secret of a satisfying life? The text does not mention any such transformation during his return from the land of Utnapishtim, nor does it suggest that Gilgamesh suddenly discovers his true vocation in wisely ruling Uruk. Indeed, a more tragic reading of the epic concludes that Gilgamesh returns home, broken, defeated, and resigned to his mortal fate. Ray (1996:316), for example, considers Gilgamesh's concluding words to Urshanabi, quoting the epic's introduction, as "utterly conventional phrases to cover up his true feelings of defeat and despair" (cf. Foster 1987:42). Gilgamesh merely conforms to societal expectations once he realizes the futility of his striving for immortality.

The epic text perhaps most cleverly indicates Gilgamesh's unhappy submission to cultural norms by referring to Ishtar's temple in his brief remarks on Uruk's magnificence in Tablet XI. In the tablet's final seven lines, Gilgamesh instructs Urshanabi to gaze upon the walls, bricks, and expanse of ancient Uruk, including the shrine of Ishtar (XI 319; cf. I 14, 20). The reference to Ishtar's temple carries great significance because it effectively symbolizes her patronage of the city. By invoking its grandeur Gilgamesh implicitly recognizes her authority over Uruk and submits to her power. In accordance with the king's principal duty to maintain proper worship of the gods (George 1999:xlii), the text's opening column praises Gilgamesh for reinstating ancient cultic practices (I 41–42). The reader can infer that Ishtar's proper worship includes the celebration of heterosexual passion in the Sumerian sacred marriage rite so vehemently rejected by Gilgamesh in Tablet VI. Gilgamesh's apparent submission to Ishtar's power and implied participation in her cult provides a shocking contrast to his earlier derision of the erotic goddess, who is in at least a small way culpable in Enkidu's death. From this tragic perspective, it is surely duty, not desire, that impels Gilgamesh by journey's end.

In tension with the text's reference to Ishtar in its closing lines is the curiously consistent presence of Urshanabi in the epic's final columns. A queer hermeneutics raises the suspicion that Urshanabi is meant to replace Enkidu as Gilgamesh's lover as well as travel companion.[88] The observant reader will recognize numerous parallels with Enkidu in the text's presentation of Urshanabi as an appropriate comrade for the semi-divine king. Both Enkidu and Urshanabi originally live far from human society and are introduced to Gilgamesh through the mediation of liminal women (Shamhat and Siduri). Urshanabi navigates the Waters of Death that surround Utnapishtim's realm of life, much as Enkidu guides the urban king along the dangerous wilderness path to Humbaba's mountain.

Although the SB text of their initial meeting is fragmentary, the OB account notes Urshanabi's lack of fear as he struggles in physical combat with Gilgamesh (compare X 102–3 with OBM iv 2–5; cf. George 1999:79). They travel to Utnapishtim and then to Uruk at the same super-human speed—a six-week journey in three days (X 169; XI 293–94, 311–12)—as Gilgamesh and Enkidu travel together on their heroic adventures (e.g., IV 1–4).[89] As a ferryman on the edge of the world, Urshanabi like Enkidu is a potent symbol of transitions and the crossing of boundaries. Finally, Urshanabi accompanies Gilgamesh in his return home, and it is through his gaze upon Uruk's walls that Gilgamesh may learn to appreciate his own city.

Yet, for all of the subtle clues to a possible alliance between the boatman and Gilgamesh, the narrator does not invite the reader to envision Urshanabi as a worthy object of erotic desire. As though in sympathy with Gilgamesh's rejection of desire after Enkidu's death, the language of attraction and allure is absent from the SB epic's final tablets. The text's utter disregard for Urshanabi's physical appearance and potential allure—similar to the narrator's purposeful neglect of Ishtar's appeal in Tablet VI—precludes an easy identification of him as Gilgamesh's new companion. The clever ambiguity of the narrator's presentation allows readers to interpret Urshanabi and his relationship with Gilgamesh in at least two ways: he is an erotic replacement for Enkidu or a minor character who coincidentally accompanies the hero to Uruk (cf. Foster 1987:42, n. 44). From a queer perspective, those readers suspicious of a homoerotic relationship need not be manipulated with sensual descriptions or overt references to appreciate the possibility of a new heroic lover. And those readers bound by a heterosexist bias need not be troubled by the implications of further homoerotic attachment. As Comstock (1992) argues, different audiences may thus appropriate the same narrative in quite distinctive ways based upon subtle textual clues.

In the end, Gilgamesh returns from his failed quest as a sadder but wiser man. Far from attaining a youthful immortality by his wearisome journeys, he has succeeded only in hastening his own bodily demise (X 302–5). Fortunately, Gilgamesh is able to restore at least some of his beauty through bathing and grooming (*ṭâbu zumuršu*; XI 250, 259) so that he may return to Uruk clothed in magically clean garments that befit his royal dignity (XI 252, 255). Enkidu's body, on the other hand, has been reduced to the clay whence it came (X 72). No restoration is possible for his physical deterioration as his spirit descends to the great world below. In what some interpreters take to be one last chance for love, however, Tablet XII portrays the heroes' brief reunion when Shamash retrieves the spirit of Enkidu for an interview with the bereaved Gilgamesh.[90] The text pointedly describes Enkidu as a wraith or spirit as he rises from a hole in the earth: "the ghost (*utukku*) of Enkidu came forth from the Netherworld like a phantom (*zaqīqu*)" (XII 84). The mythical portrayal of the disembodied spirit nevertheless allows for an ephemeral embrace with his living comrade.[91]

In a difficult bicolon, the text (XII 85–86) describes the tearful reunion of Gilgamesh and Enkidu:

innedrū-ma uttanaššaqū	They embraced and kissed each other,[92]
imtallikū uštannaḫū	They deliberated and sighed mournfully together.[93]

Some commentators have suggested that this scene promises the eternal reunion of the two friends in the Netherworld. Leick (1994:267–69), for example, holds that Gilgamesh's conversation with Enkidu's ghost demonstrates a "communion of spirits" that is the fulfillment of their love. There is nothing in the text, however, to suggest that this encounter is a foretaste of future communion or that Gilgamesh is consoled by the hope of reconciliation with his lost companion.[94] As Abusch (1986:186) argues, Gilgamesh is less concerned with Enkidu than with learning the order and administration of the Netherworld. Although Tablet XII does suggest that some people from this life could be recognized in the Netherworld, the epic offers no hope of a restored relationship between Enkidu and Gilgamesh after their deaths. Indeed, Gilgamesh's advice to Enkidu neither to kiss nor to slap his wives or sons (XII 23–26) implies that the expression of strong emotions and interpersonal attachments are foreign to the existence of the disembodied spirits. Contrary to other cultures' concepts of Paradise or Elysian fields, the ancient Mesopotamian realm of the dead is a dark and dreary place for even the most blessed of mortals. The complexities of the Mesopotamian Netherworld are beyond the scope of this chapter (see Cooper 1991; Scurlock 1995; Abusch 1998); here it must suffice only to point out that the Gilgamesh epic offers no consolation for the loss of a beloved friend or hope of love's fulfillment beyond the grave.

Furthermore, any hope of erotic desire based on the heroes' embrace and kiss (XII 85) is immediately dashed by Enkidu's lament: "My body, which you touched so that your heart rejoiced, the worm devours like an old garment!" (*zumrī ša talputū-ma libbaka iḫdû kīma lubāri labīri kalmatu ikkal*; XII 93–94). As earlier in the epic, the once-beautiful masculine form is reduced to its repulsive antithesis as a moldering corpse. Thus, in the same comment that resurrects the memory of erotic delight, Enkidu utterly eliminates the possibility of further erotic investment; the worm-infested corpse effectively quells all sexual desire. In fact, Enkidu's complaint precisely identifies the lack of an attractive physical body as an insurmountable obstacle to the lovers' postmortem reunion. Over the course of the epic, the narrator's erotic gaze has emphasized beautiful bodies that elicit desire rather than platonic notions of friendship and the transcendence of the physical. In his earlier dream-vision of the Netherworld (VII 165ff), Enkidu similarly laments the wraith-like existence of the dead, "clad like birds in coats of feathers," who eat clay in the dark and dusty world below (VII 189–90). Such disembodied beings can neither experience the physical passions and bodily yearnings of erotic response nor incite desire in others with their seductive allure (*kuzbu*).

In the *Epic of Gilgamesh*, then, desire has no place in Death's realm. Deprived of their heroes' youthful bodies, Gilgamesh and Enkidu cannot sustain their erotic relationship into the Great Beyond. Even the warrior's virile body, beautiful in death as well as in life, quickly suffers decay as its spirit sinks into the Netherworld. Indeed, the deterioration of the enticing body and its capacity for desire is inevitable, whether through exhaustion, old age, or premature death. Gilgamesh thus learns that allure is momentary, just as desire is unpredictable, because mortal bodies cannot endure.

Among its many lessons on the frailties of human existence, therefore, the *Epic of Gilgamesh* teaches the impermanence of allure and the fragility of desire.

CONCLUSION

Over the course of its twelve tablets, the *Epic of Gilgamesh* offers the reader a panorama of sexual experiences and erotic possibilities. The epic's discourse of desire encompasses an impressive array of alluring bodies, passionate yearning, and unrequited love before eventually concluding with the tragically ephemeral nature of desire. The epic's discourse of sexuality opens with the heterosexual indulgence of Enkidu and Gilgamesh as they exploit women's erotic availability with no regard for potential procreation. The text appears to assume a normative heterosexuality when Gilgamesh dispatches the enticing Shamhat to civilize the wild man through human sexuality. Enkidu's animalistic drive to mount the receptive woman also portrays heterosexual intercourse as natural, instinctual, and hence, normative. Yet, the text eventually resolves the erotic triangle of Shamhat, Enkidu, and Gilgamesh by neatly disposing of the female intermediary, thus leaving the two heroes to devote themselves exclusively to an intense, homosocial companionship. In their androcentric obsessions, both Gilgamesh and Enkidu shun women and scornfully reject Ishtar, the feminine embodiment of heterosexual passions.

Desire is indeed a fickle thing in the *Epic of Gilgamesh*. As in Enkidu's attraction to Shamhat, Ishtar's numerous passions, and the heroes' reciprocal love and attachment, erotic desire is always related to the apprehension of beauty or allure. Hence, in contrast to the hunting analogies of pursuit and conquest that are typical of much Greek mythology, the Gilgamesh epic constructs a discourse of sexuality that privileges seductive allure as a force that incites desire within the receptive beholder. Erotic desire is a response to allure rather than a physical appetite or bodily need. The epic similarly emphasizes the unpredictability of desire as it leads the reader through a labyrinth of erotic possibilities, of desire reciprocated and passions denied, before revealing the fragility of desire with the gruesome image of Enkidu's moldering corpse and

Gilgamesh's renunciation of erotic investment in the epic's last tablets.

Although many interpreters conclude that the *Epic of Gilgamesh* ultimately endorses marriage and procreation (e.g., Foster 1987), the SB text never actually links erotic desire with reproduction. It is true that a structuralist analysis of the epic may conclude that procreative sex symbolizes life and immortality through children, while unproductive eroticism represents sterility and death. In this symbolic context, same-sex love—like Ishtar's bestiality, Enkidu's sex with a prostitute, and Gilgamesh's taking of other men's brides—is identified with sterile eroticism because it does not produce legitimate sons and heirs. Tablet XII rehearses the patriarchal theme by stressing the necessity of numerous sons to perform funerary rites and maintain the ancestral mortuary cult. Desire is subordinated to the social responsibility of procreation in this patriarchal ideology that implicitly identifies the maternal womb as the proper locus of sexual activity. The point that men should become fathers to other men is communicated by Siduri's OB speech and Tablet XII of the SB epic, even though the protagonist himself neither agrees to nor follows through on this advice in any version of the epic narrative.

A rhetorical analysis of the text's poetics of desire, however, demonstrates how the poetic narrative challenges and subverts this structural message through its glorification of masculine homosocial companionship. The heroes' erotic relationship over the course of the epic is portrayed as foreordained, passionate, formalized, and satisfying; their friendship is described in terms of tender affection, fidelity, and self-sacrificing devotion. Their exclusive intimacy is strengthened through the sharing of adventures in a heroic world that excludes women. This hypermasculine ideal undergirds the text's misogyny as the narrative conveys the superiority of male homosocial experience to heterosexual relations.

The epic's androcentrism and misogyny are further reflected in its treatment of female subjectivity. The passing of the prostitute from man to man—the classic, patriarchal "traffic in women"—objectifies women as little more than bodies for male exploitation. Women can elicit and manipulate masculine desire, to be sure, as Shamhat baits the hunter's trap with her enticing figure, yet she essentially remains an erotic object rather than a subject of her own desires. The epic inscribes its masculine discourse of feminine sexuality upon the body of Shamhat in its receptivity to male advances but then counters this receptivity with the threat of Ishtar's aggressive and polymorphous desires. The clitoral locus of Ishtar's desire parallels a masculine, phallic sexuality in its focus on pleasure and sensual gratification instead of fertility and procreation. Yet even Ishtar with all her powers cannot force a reluctant Gilgamesh to desire her. She gazes upon him with libidinous intent but is unable to incite his passion because the narrator strategically neglects to establish her own feminine allure. The text thus depicts Ishtar's feminine subjectivity as an impediment to erotic investment and a threat to male sexuality. The representation of both Shamhat's availability and Ishtar's aggressive sexual agency is, of course, a male construction of feminine sexuality rather than an accurate portrayal of women's desire. The narrative employs feminine sexuality not as a subject worthy of inquiry in itself but merely as a literary trope to illumine the central discourse of masculine desire (see Halperin 1990:113–51).

The epic moves beyond the representation of merely homosocial relations between Gilgamesh and Enkidu in its utilization of sexual innuendoes, erotic metaphors, and sexually-charged dreams. The epic text introduces sexual allure (*kuzbu*) in the enticing description of Shamhat (I 124) and Uruk's prostitutes (I 214) but then turns its gaze to the appeal (*kuzbu*) of Gilgamesh's masculine body (I 220; cf. I 49–51). Like the fruit in the Garden of the Gods that is "lovely to look at" (*ana dagāli ṭābat*; IX 176)[95] and "delightful to behold" (*ana amāri ṣayāḫ*; IX 178), the bodies of Gilgamesh and his partner Enkidu are portrayed as objects worthy of erotic desire. The narrator gathers his readers to admire their masculine beauty much as "the people of Uruk gathered to gaze upon" the triumphant heroes as they paraded through the city streets (*paḫrā nišū ša Uruk idaggalāšunu*; VI 173). As part of its construction of desire, the text introduces the male reader into a patently homoerotic perspective by urging him to share its own fascination with heroes and their masculine bodies. The narrator thus attempts to seduce the reader into an appreciation of masculine allure, to arouse eros through the manipulation of the reader's masculine gaze. In portraying the heroes' relationship with homoerotic language and an emphasis on male embodiment, the SB Gilgamesh epic invites a sexual reading of their love. Standard codes for gay relationships in modern English literature—the language of comrades-in-arms and elegies—are employed to convey the heroes' intimate companionship. While the text does not necessitate a realized sexual component to the heroes' love, it clearly gestures towards this meaning through innuendo and implication.

The Gilgamesh epic further transcends traditional erotic categories and sexual identities by demonstrating the importance of erotic object-choice. Gilgamesh's clever reply to Ishtar's proposition emphasizes the transgression of normative sexual boundaries through her choice of a variety of erotic objects (divine, human, animal, bird). The diversity of Ishtar's boundless passions actually offers an expanded model of erotics and suggests the possibility of additional forms of unconventional love. While Ishtar maintains a strictly heterosexual experience, Gilgamesh and Enkidu contribute the theme of homoeroticism to the epic's repertoire of erotic investment. Thus, both sexual subjects and erotic objects are significant variables in the *Epic of Gilgamesh*'s discourse of sexuality and poetics of desire. Rather than replace the obligatory heterosexuality represented by Shamhat and Ishtar with a dichotomous, homosexual identity, however, the epic uses a continuum of homosocial affection to describe the heroic relationship. That is, the Akkadian text does not establish a sexual or social category of homosexual in binary opposition to an implied heterosexual ideology. Instead, like queer theory itself, the epic obscures the modern distinctions between hetero- and homo-sexuality, just as it destabilizes the dichotomy between erotic and platonic forms of same-sex male love. The Gilgamesh epic presents a continuum of homosocial relations that encompasses a wide spectrum of masculine activities, from athletic contest to intimate companionship, as it promotes a broader expanse of erotic possibility.

In conclusion, my intent in this chapter was to examine the SB Gilgamesh epic's literary construction of desire within its larger discourse of sexuality. The epic's clever manipulation of homoerotic imagery, metaphors, and innuendo represents an expansive erotic vision in subtle and sophisticated literary style. Queer theory exploits this complex and polyphonous discourse by providing a new lens through which to examine the poetics of desire in a text-centered analysis. By suspending a normatively heterosexist perspective, we are allowed to perceive a deeper struggle within the ancient text concerning desire, eroticism, and sexuality. We more fully appreciate the poetic text's inherent ambiguity and the contested quality of sexual categories when we do not impose a modern construct of sexuality upon the narrative. This chapter thus demonstrates how ideological criticism can refocus our own postmodern gaze upon ancient Near Eastern literature. In its fertile variations on the theme of erotic desire, the *Epic of Gilgamesh* negotiates between competing ideologies of sexuality even as it negotiates between competing visions of the satisfying life.

NOTES

[1]Although traditional interpretations attempt to summarize the Gilgamesh epic's message in neat formulas of "do your duty and enjoy your life to the full," recent analyses influenced by postmodern tendencies in literary criticism recognize the text's fundamental ambiguity and indeterminacy (e.g., Leick 1994:254; Michalowski 1996:188). Ray (1996) has most persuasively articulated the need for more nuanced approaches to appreciate more fully the Gilgamesh epic's incorporation of multiple perspectives and competing voices. This interplay of conflicting voices, none of which is ultimately authoritative, is perhaps best described by Bakhtin's use of the term polyphony (see Morson and Emerson 1990:231–68; cf. Vice 1997:78–83).

[2]Halperin (1990:40) identifies the cultural poetics of desire as "the processes whereby sexual desires are constructed, mass-produced, and distributed among members" of a society.

[3]Lambert (1987a:40, 43) dates Sin-leqe-unninni's composition to between 1300 and 1200 BCE. He calls it the "canonical edition" because it is the only version to survive into the first millennium. For a listing of the

numerous tablets used to reconstruct the epic, see Parpola (1997:xiii–xxvi). For a masterful survey of the epic's development through the centuries, see Tigay (1982).

[4]All references to the SB text follow Parpola (1997) unless otherwise noted. My vocalizations of Akkadian generally follow Huehnergard (1997), except in direct quotes from secondary sources. OBP refers to the Old Babylonian text of Tablet II in the University Museum of the University of Pennsylvania (see Huehnergard 1997:475–84) and OBY refers to the Old Babylonian tablet at Yale (see Thompson 1930:25–29, with restorations). OBM is the Old Babylonian fragment (VAT 4105) published by Meissner (1902). Basic bibliography prior to 1980 can be found in Tigay (1982). Maier (1997) excerpts more recent work in his compilation.

[5]According to many scholars, the integrated plot of the SB epic was probably extant by the end of the OB period, c.1600. See Tigay 1982:39–54; Lambert 1987a:43; Vanstiphout 1990:46, n. 6.

[6]Among numerous examples, see Bailey 1976; Doty 1993:73–85; Greenberg 1988:110–13; Hardman 1993:1–8; Jacobsen 1930; 1990:245; Kilmer 1982; Miller and Wheeler 1981:95; and Van Nortwick 1992:17. Compare Halperin 1990:75–87.

[7]See Foucault 1978; Halperin 1990:1–53. See Richlin (1993:523–30) for a convenient overview of the disagreements between the constructionist and essentialist arguments on homosexuality within classical studies (cf. Nissinen 1998:143, n. 36).

[8]Compare Henderson's (1988:1251) remarks on the social construction of sexual expression: "A Manchu mother, for instance, would routinely suck her small son's penis in public but would never kiss his cheek. For, among the Manchus, fellatio is a form of sexual behavior except in the context of mother and small son, whereas kissing of any kind is always sexual. We are perplexed because, in our culture, fellatio is always sexual, whereas cheek-kissing among kin never is."

[9]See Jagose (1996) for a convenient overview of queer theory. Jagose (1996:3) emphasizes queer theory's resistance to definition and its subversive volatility when she states that there is "no critical consensus on the definitional limits of queer—indeterminacy being one of its widely promoted charms...."

[10]See Thornton (1996:13–15) and Staten (1995:8) on the Greek concept of eros.

[11]See Lambert (1987b) on the figurative language of love in ancient Mesopotamian literature.

[12]The best of recent studies is Nissinen (1998:19–36) with its knowledge of recent gender studies, judicious treatment of cuneiform sources, and excellent bibliography. The careful study by Parkinson (1995), with attention to both literary forms and historical context, provides an example of the sensitive analysis one might expect from scholars of the ancient Near East. I retain the anachronistic word "homosexual" here for simplicity's sake in accordance with the studies under consideration.

[13]See Nissinen 1998:19–36, with references. For the sexual omens, see Guinan (1998).

[14]Lambert (1992:146) too quickly assumes a correspondence between literary representations and actual social practices when he states that lesbianism must have been quite rare in Mesopotamia since it is not included in astrological incantations that mention the erotic desire of a man for a woman, a woman for a man, and a man for a man, but not a woman for a woman. The patriarchal and androcentric nature of the literary tradition is more likely responsible for the lack of references to women's private lives in general.

[15]See Jagose 1996:51, with references. On the other hand, Foster (1995:2468) suggests that the Gilgamesh epic may actually parody male heroism by depicting the crucial intervention of women throughout the epic.

[16]Winter (1996:11–14) analyzes four Akkadian terms, each applied to Gilgamesh, that describe seductive allure: *banû*, "well-formed"; *damqu*, "auspicious, handsome"; *baštu*, "life force, vigor, vitality"; and *kuzbu*, "seductive allure." The term *lalû*, "delights," is also used in the epic to describe Gilgamesh's appeal (I 50) and Shamhat's erotic charms (I 178; VII 104, 114). The poet also applies the words *damqu* and *dumqu* to depict the physical beauty of Gilgamesh (I 190; VI 6; VII 136; XI 247). On *baštu* as "virility," see Winter (1996:13); other occurrences in the Gilgamesh epic (XI 252, 261) connote "dignity" (cf. *CAD* 2:142–44).

[17]*CAD* (8:614–15) defines *kuzbu* as "attractiveness, sex appeal, luxuriance, voluptuousness ... virility or sexual organs," as well as "abundance" (cf. Winter 1996:13–14; Leick 1994:181). *Kuzbu* is employed six times in Tablet I—but not once in the epic's other eleven tablets—to describe Gilgamesh (I 220), Shamhat (I 126, 147, 164, 172), and Uruk's courtesans (I 214).

[18]Winter (1996:19–23) argues that the iconographic representation of masculine *kuzbu* would be apprehended differently by women, who could relate libidinally to the image, and by men, whose normative heterosexuality would compel them to identify with the king's masculinity in political

and ideological terms. She (1996:21) plausibly suggests that the eroticization of the royal body would represent "for women, their subordination to desire and by men; for men, their fusion with authority at the same time as they are subject to it." I, however, would like to suggest a queering of these categories in the present analysis.

[19]For recent discussions of gender in ancient Near Eastern sources, see Asher-Greve (1997; 1998), Harris (2000), and Wyke (1998).

[20]Contra van Nortwick 1992:8; see *CAD* 17/1:71. On Enkidu as a wild man, see the bibliography and cogent remarks of Mobley (1997:220–23).

[21]OBP ii 5 observes that while making love with Shamhat, Enkidu "forgot where he was born."

[22]On prostitution in Mesopotamia, see Lambert (1992); Bottéro (1992b:185–98); and Leick (1994:147–69).

[23]See *CAD* 17/1:288–89. *CAD* (17/1:311) chooses not to translate the word *šamḫatu* but gives the general description "a prostitute, a woman connected with the temple." Bottéro (1992a:72) wittily translates her name into French as *Lajoyeuse*.

[24]Harris (1990:222, n. 14) similarly sees no distinction between a "temple" and a "commercial" prostitute in the Gilgamesh epic. On this hotly debated topic, see Lambert (1992), Cooper (1993), and Beard and Henderson (1998), with bibliographies.

[25]I derive the verb from *šaḫātu* instead of *šaḫāṭu*, contra Parpola (1997:140). See *CAD* 17/1:84–95.

[26]In her analysis of the modern mage of the femme fatale, Mary Ann Doane (1991:2) describes the seductive woman whose allure appears "to blur the opposition between passivity and activity." Her body has an agency of itself, as though the woman's power of attraction is not subject to her own control.

[27]Compare also the parallel reference to a "young woman who has not had pleasure in her husband's embrace," *ardatu ša ina sūn mutīša kuzba lā ilputu* (*CAD* 15:387). Leick (1994:181, 292) suggests that the phrase here refers to orgasm.

[28]*CAD*11/1:305; Foster 1987:24. George (1999:6) and others translate "she took his scent," which, while philologically plausible, is a rarer meaning of the term and not in keeping with the general tendency of this passage.

[29]*CAD* (6:2) gives two roots: *ḫabābu* A, "to murmur (said of water)" and "to hum, low, chirp" and *ḫabābu* B, "to caress(?)." *AHw* (1:301) derives all attestations of *ḫabābu* from one root and suggests "whisper" to describe Gilgamesh's actions over the meteorite. Note the similar metaphor

for lovemaking like "twittering birds" (using the verb *ṣabāru*) (Lambert 1987b:28; cf. Livingstone 1989:31). Kovaks's (1989:9, n. 10) comment that the verb "normally refers to quick repeated sounds" suggests the grunting of strenuous intercourse rather than languid moaning. Other possibilities include, "His passions will surge over you." Dalley's (1989:55) suggestion, "his love-making he lavished upon her," is poetic but imprecise. Dalley (1989:126) notes the redundance of *eli ṣērīša*, "over her back," and suggests an image of him mounting her from behind, as animals mate; but one would expect the verb *rakābu* for such an image.

[30]The verb *reḫû* is also used in OBP iv 25, missing in SB, to describe Gilgamesh's copulation with the brides on their wedding days. The verb *reḫû* can also mean "to impregnate, sire" (as Parpola 1997:138 notes; e.g., *CAD* 1/1:288), but the lack of any other reference to pregnancy and childbirth convinces me of the epic's emphasis on eroticism in contrast to procreation; see below. The verb *reḫû* is also used in the epic numerous times to describe sleep (*šittu*) that spills over people.

[31]Although the god Sumuqan does inseminate (*reḫû*) the herds in Akkadian texts (see Cooper 1996), we have no evidence for similar activity on Enkidu's part.

[32]One tablet has *ultaḫḫit*, another reads *ultaḫḫi*, and the third has only [...-*ḫ*]*a* (*CAD* 17/1:92). Parpola (1997:73, 140) reads *ultaḫḫiṭ* in I 182 and, similar to *CAD*, provides three different G-stem roots for *šaḫāṭu*: "to leap, jump"; "to strip, tear off, detach"; and "to fear," which *CAD* reads with /t/ rather than /ṭ/. Parpola (1997:140) derives the verb in I 182 from "jump," apparently meaning "Enkidu jumped up, his body purified." The verb *šaḫāṭu*, "to jump," rarely occurs in the D and only means "to attack" in *CAD* references; *šaḫāṭu*, "to fear" means "to frighten" in D; *šaḫāṭu* (u) "to take off" means "to remove" in D. The Gilgamesh epic has been punning on this root in its descriptions of Shamhat stripping off (e.g., I 147) her clothes and not fearing (I 173) Enkidu's approach.

[33]*CAD* (17/3: 207–8) gives three roots: "to have illicit sexual intercourse"; "to remove, abolish"; and "to ruin, destroy." Enkidu uses this root in his curse of Shamhat: "May mud ruin your fine garment" (VII 107) (cp. *CAD* 17/3:208; Parpola 1997:142). Some translators understand *ullulu* in this context to mean "weak, flaccid" without explanation (e.g., Hecker 1994:678; Tournay and Shaffer 1994:56).

[34]This text is from Lambert's (1992:129–31) edition of an Middle Babylonian tablet from Ur (UET VI 394) that includes both the curse and the subsequent blessing. Contra Leick (1994:166), the verb *tušemṭînni* is an

Š-stem verb from *maṭû*, meaning "to weaken, diminish, humiliate, treat badly" (cf. *CAD* 10/1:434–35). Lambert (1992:130) translates, "you have humiliated me, the innocent." An attractive variant of VII 129 is: "Yes me, the innocent, you expelled from my wilderness!" (*yâši ella teddînni ina ṣērīya*) (Parpola 1997:96, 133). See also Tournay and Shaffer (1994:168, n. 65) for a reconstructed text, including the variants.

35See Whiting 1985:180–81; Cooper 1996. Cf. Wilcke 1985; Foster 1993:123, 144.

36See Whiting 1985:181–82. Note the euphemistic use of *birkān*, "knees," for "genitals" in *CAD* s.v. *birku*.

37A nominative phrase, *mudû libbašu* could be the subject of the verb, as in *CAD* 10/2:166 (1977), "his (Enkidu's) wise heart searches for a companion," but I am treating it as a nominative absolute as *CAD* 7:6 (1960), "he longed for a congenial companion," and Tournay and Shaffer (1994:57). George (1999:8) interprets the phrase as "he knew by instinct, he should seek a friend."

38Bell (1994:1, 11) argues that Western discourse by prostitutes begins with the two courtesans in Plato's philosophical conversations, Diotima and Aspasia—whom she calls the "philosopher/whore"—but she neglects the earlier literary narratives about prostitutes in the Bible and the ancient Near East. Bell (1994:20–22) explains that she is purposefully reading against the grain; she (1994:193, n. 1) also acknowledges that Halperin (1990:124) and other classicists do not identify Diotima as a prostitute.

39Enkidu continues to make love with Shamhat after protecting the shepherds in OBP iv 1–2: "He lay with her and took his pleasure," *ittīlam ittiša ippuš ulṣam*.

40 Foster (1987:32, n. 35) notes that the collation of tablets suggests a short conversation between Shamhat and the two heroes after their initial wrestling match in the OB version.

41Note the last of Enkidu's blessings on Shamhat for this opposition: "For you may the mother of seven (sons), the first wife, be abandoned," *aššumīka linnezib ummi sebet ḫīrtum*; VII 161.

42Compare the rhetoric of Siduri's advice to Gilgamesh in the OB edition, "let a wife ever delight in your lap" (*marḫītum liḫtaddâm ina sūnīka*; OBM iii 13) (see Abusch 1993a). This speech is excised from the SB epic.

43Bell (1994:24) is clearly mistaken in her assertion that "the sexual, the reproductive, and the spiritual were simultaneously embodied in the sacred prostitute in the ancient world." Leick (1994:263) is equally mistaken when she accuses Foster of "a serious anachronism" in introducing an

"Aristotelian" and "Christian dichotomy" between reproductive and non-reproductive sex.

[44]For a detailed analysis of the entire episode, see especially Abusch 1986. Note also the comments of Vanstiphout (1990:46, 49, 52) on Tablet VI's function as a center and pivot within the epic.

[45]Leick (1994:123) suggests that references to the clitoris in ancient feminine poetry have been neglected by male scholars. Other genres of Akkadian poetry also attribute an active sexuality to goddesses such as Ishtar and Nanaya; see Leick 1994:180–92 with references.

[46]Even when portrayed as a prostitute sitting outside of the tavern, Ishtar remains an active partner, "loving" (*rāʾimtum*) rather than being loved (see *CAD* 6:101). For her insatiable sexuality, see Foster (1993:590).

[47]Leick (1994:125–26) states that the erotic lyrics depict the woman bathing her body, dressing her hair, and preparing the bedroom in order to evoke passion within her husband. Here of course, it is the bathing king who attracts the goddess's attention.

[48]Gilgamesh refers to a *ḫāmiru* and *ḫarmu* (VI 42, 44), apparently acknowledging the validity of her marriage proposal. Note Abusch's (1986:161–73) insightful and thorough literary analysis of Gilgamesh's recitation of Ishtar's past lovers.

[49]See Foster (1987:35) on line 69. I read *šūṣâm-ma* following Parpola (1997:92) but a variant is *lištēṣâm-ma* (also from the root [*w*]*aṣû*), "may your hand be sent forth."

[50]Guinan's (1998:42) remarks are commenting upon the following two omens: "4. If a man repeatedly stares at his woman's vagina, his health will be good; he will lay his hands on whatever is not his. 5. If a man is with a woman (and) while facing him she repeatedly stares at his penis, whatever he finds will not be secure in his house."

[51]Cf. Winkler (1990:202–6) on Greek myths of goddesses who abduct mortal men for their sexual pleasures and the males' subsequent loss of manhood.

[52]See Gurney 1960:114–15, 118–19; Leick 1994:249–53 and bibliography. A second viewing of her body is actually required to break Nergal's resolve, but the threat of confinement to the Netherworld is a serious obstacle to eliciting male desire. Ereshkigal's success on the second attempt demonstrates her allure.

[53]On Gilgamesh's role in the Netherworld, see the references in Abusch (1986:150, n. 13); see also George (1999:195–208) for the most recent translation of the Sumerian tale, "The Death of Bilgames."

[54]Abusch's (1986) extended argument is too complex to consider in detail, but this episode is only part of the necessary transformation of Gilgamesh prior to his eventual acceptance of his judicial rule in the Netherworld (see Abusch 1986:183–84).

[55]The only other references to the *agû* in the epic are to the kings in the Netherworld (VII 193–94) and Ninsun donning hers as queen mother (III 40).

[56]Gilgamesh has previously declared that he would celebrate the New Year festival (*akītu*) after his return from the Cedar Mountains (II 228–30), so it is possible that his return is coincident with such a festival at the beginning of Tablet VI. The sacred marriage rite was perhaps enacted at the New Year festival, so one might assume that this is the intended context even though the text provides no further hints.

[57]After this period all of the evidence suggests only the symbolic copulation of two deities by placing their statues in bed together. Furthermore, none of the later sources refer to Inana-Ishtar's involvement. See Cooper (1993:94), with references to earlier literature.

[58]On the relation between this scene and the sacred marriage ritual, see also Abusch (1986:173, n. 68; 178, n. 71, with references).

[59]See Vanstiphout (1990:46, 49, 52) on Tablet VI's pivotal role in the epic.

[60]Guinan (1998:44–47) analyzes the four examples of male homosexual relations in the omen series. The most important omen, for my purposes, is 16: "If a man has sex *per anum* with his social peer [*meḫru*], that man will become foremost among his brothers and colleagues." Guinan (1998:45) explains: "The omen turns on the switch of positions from 'behind' to 'in front' and on the paronomastic relationship between the words *qinnatu* ('anus') and *kinātu* ('colleagues'). Thus, one can put oneself ahead of one's peers in the community by penetrating one of them from behind." It is important to note that Guinan's analysis of the sexual omens focuses on competitive social status while the Gilgamesh epic's discourse of sexuality is more concerned with desire and erotic object-choice.

[61]See Jackson (1982) on the dichotomy between the king and the warrior in later Western epics.

[62]See Abusch (1986:161–73) for a detailed literary analysis.

[63]The only evidence of lesbianism in ancient Mesopotamia, according to Lambert (1992:153), is an omen that reads, "If one dog mounts another, women will copulate" (*šumma kalbu kalba irkab sinnišātu igarrušā*). One wonders how common this sight would have been.

[64]On the centrality of male friendship in this ancient epic, see especially Furlani (1977), von Weiher (1980), Halperin (1990:75–87), Doty (1993:73–85), and Leick (1994:267–68). Doty (1993:82) describes the heroes' friendship as the most ideal of male bonds, while Harris (1990:228) suggests that "on a subliminal level if not overtly, the composers of the epic were critical of so intense a relationship between men."

[65]On the *droit de cuissage* or *ius primae noctis*, see Lambert (1987a:42), Leick (1994:257), and George (1999:xlvii). Note also the possible pun between the Gt-stem participles *muttakpu*, "rampaging" and *muttaqbu*, "deflowering, raping," in Gilgamesh's epithet *rīmu muttakpu*, "a rampaging bull" (I 28).

[66]Gilgamesh's obscure description as a "happy-unhappy man" (*ḫādi-ū*ʾ*a*; I 217) may connote his failure to achieve contentment even through his frenetic striving for happiness (cf. Leick 1994:263). Scholarly opinion is divided on the phrase's meaning. Compare Parpola (1997:126), "sadist"; Dalley (1989:57), "man of joy and woe"; *CAD* (6:24), "person with quickly changing moods"; Kovaks (1989:10), "man of extreme feelings(?)" or "man of changing moods"; and George (1999:9), "a man happy and carefree."

[67]In interpreting Gilgamesh's dreams, for example, Ninsun says "I will make him your equal" (*anāku ultamaḫḫaršu ittīka*; I 249, 269), probably referring to her adoption of Enkidu into Gilgamesh's cultic votaries (III 123–25).

[68]On this difficult issue, see Dalley (1989:126); Lambert (1992); Maul (1992); Henshaw (1993:197–201, 284–89); and Nissinen (1998:28–36).

[69]Cooper (1977:43) and George (1999:10) understand the phrase this way, but others (Dalley 1989:57; *CAD* 9:114) take *šerri la*ʾ*î* as hendiadys for a plural subject and conclude that the men are like children. The nuance in question is whether the men kiss Enkidu's feet out of joy, as one kisses the tiny feet of an infant, or whether they are like children in contrast to his size and might. Foster (1987:26–27) translates "like infantile urchins" to convey the poet's "contempt for the gawking crowd." With its characteristically shorter lines, OBP i 11 and 21 read only "the men kiss his feet" (*eṭlūtu unaššaqū šēpīšu*) with no reference to a baby. In other contexts, kissing feet commonly denotes submission before royalty or the acknowledgement of superiority.

[70]Vernant (1990:472, n. 14) quotes the *Symposium* (192aff): "'These are the best of boys and youths, being the manliest by nature... . They are resolute, brave, and virile—qualities they also seek out and value in their

lovers—which is shown by the fact that, once they have grown up, they are the only ones to show themselves real men in political life.'"

[71]Alternatively, line 11 could be read *iṣṣabtū-ma kīma lîm,* "they grappled like bulls." OBP vi 16–17 repeats the phrase with a different poetic division: "They gasped each other, like wrestlers/bulls they bent down."

[72]Jacobsen (1990:237) holds that Enkidu defeats Gilgamesh in the wrestling match, which explains why Gilgamesh does not go through with the marriage. The majority of interpreters, however, conclude that Gilgamesh wins the match but is sufficiently impressed by Enkidu that he loses interest in the bride.

[73]Following Parpola (1997:116). See *CAD* (4:30) and (1/2:422) for different readings.

[74]Some OB texts provide evidence of the heroes holding hands in the unfortunately fragmentary Tablet II of SB (cf. III 19). In one such broken context, "They grasped each other as one... they clasped hands like...." (*iṣṣabtū-ma mitḫāriš... innedrū-ma qātīšunu kī...*; II 152–53). The two heroes "clasped hands and went forth" (*iṣṣabtūnim-ma illakūni*, VI 171) in their triumphal return to Uruk after killing the Bull.

[75]On Enkidu's adoption by Ninsun, see Foster (1987:27, 33), Lambert (1992:140), Tournay and Shaffer (1994:105), and especially George (1999:27, 212–20). This passage's textual difficulties are now resolved by George's (1999:212–20) collation of tablets from the British Museum. George (1999:27) reads part of Ninsun's speech: "...henceforth your brood [*atmûka*] will belong with the votaries of Gilgamesh, the priestesses, the hierodules and the women of the temple." George's (1999:xxxix) conclusion that Enkidu is associated with foundlings raised by the temple women is more compelling than Foster's (1987:27) comment that Enkidu "thus joins the ranks of prostitutes and temple women." Note also Doty's (1993:81) provocative suggestion that Enkidu's adoption into the ranks of the oblates makes him "Ishtar's castrated priest or male temple prostitute." More likely is the explanation that adoption is one of the few means available to socially recognize a homosocial relationship within formal kinship structures (see Halperin 1990:75).

[76]Compare David's famous lament for Jonathan: "Your love to me was wonderful, surpassing the love of women" (2Sam 1:26).

[77]In his sociological analysis of homosexuality throughout history, Greenberg (1988:110–13) argues that aristocratic warrior societies such as ancient Mesopotamia are actually conducive to homosexual relationships among its young men in military service.

[78]"My son, the ax you saw is a man. You will love him and embrace him like a wife" (*mārī ḫaṣṣinnu ša tāmuru amīlu tarâmšū-ma kī aššate taḫabbub elīšu*; I 267–68).

[79]See Abusch (1993b:9–10) for the proper custom of immediate burial, followed by a period of mourning. Enkidu's lack of burial may be in fulfillment of Humbaba's dying curse (V 256, with George 1999:44).

[80]Halperin (1990:81) mistakenly argues that the "point of these analogies to kin and objects of sexual desire seems to be that Enkidu's friendship affords Gilgamesh a proleptic taste of the pleasures of human sociality, including marriage and paternity, with which he will be invited to console himself by the ale-wife after Enkidu's death." Siduri's speech, however, is edited out of the SB epic. On the contrary, Gilgamesh's relationship with Enkidu competes with, rather than points toward, responsibility to family and society. Although Halperin (1990:75–87) repeatedly notes the work of Hammond and Jablow (1987) on the anti-social aspects of male bonding, he virtually ignores their conclusion concerning the essentially immature quality of the friends' relationship and the damage to society through its mitigation of familial bonds.

[81]Contra Held (1983:139) and others who argue for Gilgamesh's continued ethical development in his wanderings, as well as Leick (1994:269), who holds that in his grief Gilgamesh has "internalized Enkidu to such an extent that his friend's physical presence is obsolete."

[82]Note Gilgamesh's complaint to Shamash in the OB text, "Will not sleep be plentiful in the Netherworld? I will lie there all through the years!" (OBM i 11–12; see *CAD* 15:74; Tournay and Shaffer 1994:198, n. 7; cf. George 1999:71).

[83]In his savagery and wearing of lion skins, Gilgamesh is portrayed as the antithesis of the civilized royal figure. See Watanabe (1998) on the specifically royal connotations of the lion hunt in Assyrian sources.

[84]*CAD* (17/3:115 and 13:183) translates this passage with "hidden" rather than "ruined," but the D-stem of *qatû* means "to bring to an end, destroy."

[85]On Siduri's role in the OB epic, see Harris (1990:224–25) and Abusch (1993a; 1993b).

[86]The D-stem verb *ṣubbû* means "to inspect, survey, look at from afar" (i.e., to peer intently). Here it connotes an earnest, intent, or loving gaze. *CAD* (16:226) suggests "look (with pride)" for this poetic context.

[87]On the rare word *marḫītum*, see Abusch (1993a:8–9), including his suggestion (n. 38) that the word originally meant "prostitute, harlot" in-

stead of "wife." The SB epic also applies the term to Utnapishtim's wife (XI 210, 213, 217, 267).

[88]Miller and Wheeler (1981:102) predict that Urshanabi will replace Enkidu as Gilgamesh's "consort," according to the pattern they claim to establish. The name Urshanabi may mean "servant of two-thirds," as a play on Gilgamesh's identity as two-thirds divine (Foster 1987:42, n. 44). Urshanabi may thus merely be a servant to Gilgamesh and not a suitable candidate to replace Enkidu as his intimate companion. On the other hand, Enkidu is called Gilgamesh's servant in the Sumerian traditions and again in Tablet XII (lines 7, 54) of the SB epic.

[89]Urshanabi and Gilgamesh "crew" the boat (*irkabū*; XI 265–66) on their trip, parallel to Enkidu acting as the helmsman (*rākib*; V 252; see George 1999:47) when he and Gilgamesh return from the Cedar Mountains.

[90]Although Tablet XII is not easily integrated into the eleven-tablet SB narrative, its inclusion by the SB compiler as part of the twelve-tablet cycle cannot be ignored in an analysis of the theme of desire. Enkidu's self-sacrificing love for Gilgamesh is demonstrated by his volunteering to retrieve Gilgamesh's *pukku* from the Netherworld. Why Gilgamesh would allow him to take such an inordinate risk on his behalf is unclear, unless one takes recourse to the historical explanation that Enkidu is merely Gilgamesh's servant in the original Sumerian tale. Note that even in the Akkadian version, Enkidu is called Gilgamesh's servant (*ardu*; XII 54) and Enkidu identifies Gilgamesh as "my master" (*bēlī*; XII 7). When Enkidu's spirit arises from the Netherworld, however, they each address the other as "my friend" (*ibrī*; XII 87 and 89). Parpola (1997:116) and others read Nergal but George (1999:194) identifies Shamash as the god who allows Enkidu's ghost to ascend to Gilgamesh.

[91]Compare Achilles's dream of Patroclos's ghost (*Iliad*, XXIII) and Odysseus's vain attempts to embrace his mother in Hades (*Odyssey*, XI).

[92]Alternatively read *innedrū-ma ul uššarū,* "they embrace and do not release," following Thompson (1930:69), *CAD* (4 [1958]:30), and Tournay and Shaffer (1994:263). In order to agree with the Sumerian original, Hecker (1994:742) and *CAD* (1/2 [1968]:422) emend the text and read *uttanaššaqū*, "they kiss each other" (Dtn-stem durative). Parpola similarly suggests *ultaššaqū*, apparently an Št-stem durative. See also George (1999:187, 194).

[93]Thompson (1930:69) reads line 86: *im-tal-il-ku uš-ta-an-na-[ḫ]u.* Scholars routinely emend the third sign (from *il* to *li*) to read *imtallikū* (e.g., Parpola 1997:116, 131). *CAD* (4:30), however, suggests the alterna-

tive *imtallilu*, "they danced for joy," as though from the irregular verb *mēlulu*; but see *CAD* (10/2:16–17) and Huehnergard (1997:461) on the unlikelihood of this form. *CAD* (10/1:157) suggests *uštannâ*, apparently from *šanû* in hendiadys, as well as *uštannaḫū* (4:30) for the final verb. Parpola (1997:121) defines the Št-stem of *anāḫu*, "to emit sighs" (cf. *CAD* 1/2:105).

[94]George (1999:196) states that the Sumerian text of "The Death of Bilgames" describes his reunion with beloved family members and friends, including Enkidu. However, the text (translated in George 1999:195–208) states only that Bilgames will go to the place where they lie (i.e., the Netherworld), yet he should not despair because, unlike them, he will sit among the ruling Anunna gods. Moreover, even if Sumerian texts were to describe the happy reunion of loved ones in the afterlife, the Akkadian *Epic of Gilgamesh* does not communicate such eschatological hope. See Abusch (1986:179–87) on Gilgamesh's Netherworld role among the Annuna gods.

[95]Following *CAD* (16:66) instead of Parpola (1997:102).

CHAPTER 2

On the Couch with Horus and Seth: A Freudian Analysis (Or, The Case of Pharaoh's Mommy)

INTRODUCTION

In 1979, Robert A. Oden, Jr. presented a structuralist interpretation of "The Contendings of Horus and Seth," an Egyptian myth recorded in a hieratic text from the 20th Dynasty (c. 1160 BCE).[1] Oden surveys earlier scholarly literature on "The Contendings" and addresses the methodological weaknesses of previous inter-pretations, most of which are purely euhemeristic, prior to his own structuralist analysis of the myth. A short response by an Egyptologist characterizes Oden's article as "an aesthetically satisfying but overly simplistic interpretation of the story," yet offers no alternative interpretation of the complicated myth (Wendte 1979:371). Indeed, in the two decades since Oden's article, Egypt-ologists have neglected to produce convincing analyses of this myth's bizarre content and complex symbolism to challenge Oden's structuralist interpretation.[2] This chapter is thus a belated response to Oden's pioneering application of contemporary methods of myth analysis to an intriguing ancient Egyptian text of divine conflict and desire.

The plot of "The Contendings" revolves around a primordial court trial between the youthful Horus and the virile Seth to determine who will replace the deceased Osiris as King of Egypt. Isis supports the right of her son Horus to inherit the throne from his father. The patriarchal sun god Pre prefers Seth, who is "great of strength" and a mighty warrior. At stake is the royal ideology of succession through inheritance rather than charismatic power or physical prowess. Apart from "The Contendings," the conflict between Horus and Seth constitutes a central theme of Egyptian religious literature and art from the third-millennium *Pyramid Texts* through Hellenistic sources. Each god is wounded in the fray, with Horus losing an eye and Seth losing his testicles. Ancient Egyptian texts variously identify Seth as the uncle or older brother Horus, an inconsistency based upon divergent mythological traditions and a variety of gods named Horus in the Egyptian pantheon.[3] "The Contendings" always describes Horus as the son of Isis and Osiris, while Seth is the son of Nut. The traditional confusion about Horus and Seth's relationship, however, is allowed to complicate the issue of primogeniture in "The Contendings" as it once refers to Seth as Horus's elder brother (4, 8).

Oden's application of structuralist theory to "The Contendings" emphasizes the multiple layers of symbolic communication and the particular importance of kinship relations as one symbolic code.[4] He (1979:366) demonstrates some of the ways in which the underlying structure of the text works itself out and concludes that this "series of relationships...is the meaning of the myth." While Oden's analysis is insightful, I cannot agree that the text's structure constitutes the "meaning" of the myth. This is in fact the methodological limitation of structuralism for many critics who are not willing to conclude that the meaning of a text has been exhausted once its structuralist codes have been deciphered. Although structuralism may reveal the text's structure, it is unable to disclose the text's semantics. Oden (1979:369), however, argues that "a semantic interpretation" of the myth is "incorrect and misguided" in light of the structuralist explanation. Oden's (1979:363) criterion for evaluating interpretations of "The Contendings" is their power to explain the most elements of the myth. He thus poses the methodological question: "Can the structuralist method account for more of this myth's manifold elements and episodes than could the methods heretofore applied to this text?" Oden's analysis succeeds in explaining aspects of the text that previous interpreters had ignored; yet, the emphasis on structural relations obscures many elements of the myth's bizarre symbolism. Since Oden's (1979:363) motivation in applying structuralism is "the search for a more adequate method for interpreting myths," I propose we consider the utility of other methods in interpreting "The Contendings of Horus and Seth."

Although previous interpretations have revealed much about "The Contendings," they have not adequately explained or interpreted some of the most striking features of the myth: the fantastic episodes of maternal decapitation, homosexual rape, consumption of semen, excision of eyes, loss of hands, exhibitionism, and masturbation. Philological and historical approaches, while necessary, are not capable of adequately treating the symbolic and psychological content of these episodes. Although many of the myth's details have cultic or cultural allusions that are lost on the lay reader, the more bizarre aspects of the text are often equally nonsensical to the Egyptologist. These fantastic episodes require a more appropriate method that emphasizes symbolic interpretation from a semantic perspective. As Alan Dundes (1980:55) points out, "It is never easy to make sense of nonsense, but that does not mean that nonsense is meaningless." Therefore, I suggest the application of Freudian psychoanalysis to interpret more fully this ancient narrative.[5] I take my cue from the eminent Egyptologist Erik Hornung (1986), who proclaims the "discovery of the unconscious" by ancient Egyptians. Although Hornung's sympathies are with a Jungian approach, the subject matter of "The Contendings" suggests that a Freudian lens might bring the manifest and latent content of the text into sharper focus. While Oden (1979:363) holds that structuralism "heightens the significance of each and every fact," I argue that a Freudian interpretation can explain a greater number of elements of this particular myth. Indeed, I take as my own measuring stick a variation of the question posed by Oden: Can a psychoanalytic approach account for more of the myth's manifest elements than previous interpretations?

Oedipus in Ancient Egypt

The present interpretation does not defend the methodological rigor or correctness of Freudian analysis but merely applies its theories to "The Contendings of Horus and Seth."[6] To be sure, the manifest content of a myth about a young boy's successful attempt to replace his father with the support of his mother easily calls to mind the categories of classical Freudian theory. "The Contendings" is especially amenable to Freudian interpretation because the myth's manifest content deals with the usually latent issues of oedipal struggles and sexual anxieties. The explicitly sexual and familial concerns of the myth therefore allow for a psychoanalytic interpretation of the myth's contents without necessarily adopting all of the functionalist assumptions of Freudian theory.[7] This literary approach focuses on the actual text of "The Contendings" but my analysis also draws upon various mythic traditions from ancient Egypt in order to supplement and contextualize the myth's content, much like an analyst would require the analysand to provide personal information in interpreting a particular dream. Though many writers overly stress the parallel between an individual's dream and a culture's myth, there is heuristic value in the analogy. The use of complementary and even contradictory mythic traditions is thus not meant to reconstruct a hypothetical version of "The Contendings," but only to point out some of the possible symbolic associations and cultural context of the myth's manifest content. For example, although "The Contendings" never mentions Seth's guilt in the drowning murder of Osiris, one should not assume that the New Kingdom audiences were unaware of this venerable tradition. To the contrary, we must utilize all of the available cultural information to interpret elements of this strange Egyptian text.

For the purpose of this analysis I presuppose the Freudian categories of displacement, infantile sexuality, and the Oedipus Complex. My treatment thus adheres more closely to classical Freudian theory than to neo-Freudian ego-psychology or later developments in psychoanalytic thought.[8] In his defense of psychoanalytic approaches to ancient myth, Richard Caldwell (1990:350–56) identifies symbolism, projection, and decomposition as the three main forms of displacement of repressed ideas in myths and dreams. Projection is the tendency to attribute to another person one's own internal impulses or feelings that are often too painful or unacceptable for conscious awareness. Such projection may even invert the original impulse, such as when a boy's oedipal rivalry with his father is replaced in a myth by the father's murderous intentions toward the son (see Dundes 1996). The mechanism of decomposition explains how one figure may appear in dreams or narratives as multiple characters. This element of Freudian analysis is explicit in ancient Egyptian myth in the relationship of various deities as hypostatic manifestations of one another.[9] Unlike mythological systems in which the gods have well-established personalities and relatively consistent attributes, ancient Egyptian deities are often fluid in their identities, roles, and relationships. Deities are routinely equated in one context, only to be distinguished in another. "The Contendings" illustrates this mechanism by its depiction of the sun god in his three manifestations of Pre, Atum, and Khepri but also as one composite deity as the Lord of Heliopolis. Since the text reflects the decomposition of the sun god into three distinct characters, it is plausible to suggest that the psychological roles of the mother and father have likewise been divided in the myth as part of the unconscious process. I will argue that Isis, Hathor, and Neith represent aspects of Horus's mother figure, while Osiris, Pre, and Seth represent the decomposed father figure in "The Contendings."[10]

Since one of the most relevant areas of psychoanalytic theory for the interpretation of myth is childhood psychosexual development, the text's portrayal of Horus as an infant is particularly significant. Caldwell (1990:361) explains that an oedipal situation is reflected "wherever we find a triangular relationship between a hero, the forbidden object of his desire, and a prohibiting figure who denies the hero access to his own possession. Usually these mythical figures are not literally son, mother, father...." In "The Contendings," the goddesses (mother figures) support Horus in his struggles against older males (father figures) who block his access to the throne. Otto Rank (1990:66–67) notes that a boy's anger with his actual father may be displaced on to some other male in order to alleviate feelings of guilt. This displacement, or decomposition of the father figure, allows the father to remain a positive image on the manifest level while the son vents his anger at the replacement figure, who often plays the role of a tyrannical persecutor. The replacement father figure may attack both the boy and the original paternal figure, thus allowing the son to avenge his persecuted father by battling the displaced father figure. These projective mechanisms help explain Horus's positive relationship with Osiris and conflicts with the aggressive Seth in "The Contendings."

According to classical Freudian theory, the fear of paternal retribution for the son's oedipal desires leads to castration anxiety. As the boy becomes aware of his inferiorities in comparison with his father, he compensates by fantasizing about himself as the sexually powerful and conquering male instead of the physically immature and helpless child. More recent psychoanalytic thought, however, holds that castration is more typically executed by mother figures than father figures in world mythology.[11] Caldwell associates this fear of the castrating mother with male sexual performance anxiety, caused by the boy's realization that he would be physically unable to satisfy his mother sexually if he were to replace his father. Such infantile feelings of sexual inadequacy may haunt the male throughout his life. Thus, as Caldwell (1990:366) summarizes, the mythic hero's need to overcome a male figure to gain his prize usually represents the classical oedipal rivalry between father and son in psychoanalytic theory; a female antagonist often reflects a boy's "feelings of impotence, inadequacy, and limitation" and sexual performance anxiety brought on by awareness of maternal sexuality. These anxieties and conflicts are reflected in "The Contendings." Pre's insult to Horus—"You are feeble in body, and this office is too big for you, you youngster whose breath smells bad!" (3, 8)—emphasizes Horus's physical immaturity on the text's manifest level, since Egyptologists routinely identify the charge of bad breath as a reference to the odor of milk on a baby's breath. Plutarch's (*DIO* 19) description of the infant Horus as "weak in his lower limbs" is even more transparently symbolic of impotence or genital immaturity.[12] Seth's phallic confidence, by contrast, is symbolized by his threat to kill all the gods with his "4,500 pound scepter" (5, 2). The outcome of "The Contendings," however, is the repeated and eventually unanimous declaration of Horus's virility and competence to satisfy the demands of his father's office. I will argue that "The Contendings" resolves these conflicts and anxieties for Horus in a specifically pharaonic manner.

A CONTENTIOUS COURT: TWO EPISODES

The legal dispute between Horus and Seth can be settled only by the decision of the gathered Ennead, which seems too fickle a group to be trusted in rendering such a momentous verdict. The gods engage in petty arguments and disagree on the relative merits of royal succession through might or inheritance. While the reader knows that Horus will eventually triumph over Seth, the course of the narrative meanders through various scenes and episodes before reaching this rather anti-climactic conclusion. Prior to the three contests between the litigants are two comedic episodes that deserve particular attention in a psychoanalytic treatment of the myth. The strange exhibitionism of Hathor and the devious machinations of Isis are not necessary to the narrative's plot yet their inclusion in the text signals their integral role in the myth's symbolic system. In addition to depicting the contentious nature of divine politics, the interventions of Hathor and Isis convey important clues to sexual themes and symbolism in "The Contendings of Horus and Seth."

The Insult and the Enigma (3, 9–4, 3)

One of the first confrontations in "The Contendings" occurs when the god Baba insults Pre by charging that his "shrine is empty," presumably referring to a lack of worshipers (3, 10). Baba, also called Babai or Bebon, is a minor deity who often appears in baboon form. In the Papyrus Jumilhac (16, 7 ff) Thoth retaliates against a false allegation by Baba by stealing his phallus, after which Pre (here called Re) ridicules him.[13] Baba's phallus, however, is certainly functional in other magical and mythical texts where he acts as a deity of sexuality. Furthermore, Spell 93 of the *Book of the Dead* reads, "O you phallus of Re, this which is injured by uproar, whose inertness came into being through Babai" (Faulkner 1990:88). Faulkner's interpretation suggests that Baba is the cause of Re's impotence, which would be in accordance with other traditions that describe Re as an otiose god who has removed himself from the active rule of earth to his place in the sky on the back of the Celestial Cow. Why Baba is blamed for Re's loss of virility is unclear, but this motif helps to explain his role in "The Contendings" because it establishes the antagonism between Baba and Re in certain contexts. Thus, we have one god, whose phallus was stolen at least once, insulting another god, whose phallus the first had made impotent. If this line of interpretation is correct, then Pre's depression in "The Contendings" may be based more upon a reminder of his loss of sexual virility than the inconsequential insult.

Pre is brought out of his sulk by the goddess Hathor, who "uncovered her vulva before his face" (4, 2). Frequently symbolized by the wild cow of the Delta, Hathor is a goddess who represents fertility and abundance, as well as the excesses of inebriation and jubilation. Although we lack any explicit texts of her erotic adventures, such as the well-known Mesopotamian love lyrics of Inana and Dumuzi, Egyptologists routinely refer to her as a goddess of love. The "Story of the Herdsman" in Papyrus Berlin 3024 may depict her as a wild, nude female who accosts a shepherd tending his herds in the Delta (see Goedicke 1970; Drenkhahn 1977). Hathor has the epithet "mistress of the vulva" (*nb.t ḥtp.t*) and wooden phalloi were discovered in her sanctuary at Deir el-Bahri (Bleeker 1973:40–41). Thus, the exhibition of her vulva to Pre is not out of character. Nevertheless, scholars have not adequately explained the significance of the action in this particular context. I suggest that the psychoanalytic approach offers a coherent reading of this scene in "The Contendings."

According to later Christian writers, Greek mythology includes a similar episode in which the goddess Demeter grieves for the abduction of her daughter Persephone by the god Hades but is made to laugh by the licentious jokes and skirt-raising gesture of a woman or goddess named Iambe or Baubo.[14] The earliest Greek tradition related to the Baubo motif is in the Homeric Hymn to Demeter, where the servant girl Iambe successfully diverts Demeter's attention from her grief through words alone. Perhaps the first Freudian "talking cure," Iambe's monologue consists of jests and obscene jokes. In his description of figurines associated with Baubo, Maurice Olender (1990:104) refers to the "female body where the mouth above is juxtaposed with the mouth below" as a means of connecting the talkative Iambe and the exhibitionist Baubo. Hathor, in contrast to Iambe, lifts Pre's spirits not by persuading him with the sounds of words from her mouth, but with the glance from her "other mouth." (We will return to the importance of looking and seeing in Freudian analysis below.) Her silent argument is quite effective in persuading Pre to resume his duties with the Ennead, just as Baubo's pose restores Demeter to an active role.

Since laughter is the necessary catalyst in each of these cases, the genital display could be understood as a joke, with no deeper conscious meaning. Winifred Milius Lubell (1994:39–40, 173–78) emphasizes that laughter lightens the seriousness of life; Hathor possibly intends merely to shock Pre out of his current state of mind with one of the few means at her disposal. It is exactly this type of action, however, which often carries a deep, unconscious meaning. Even if laughter is simply a surprised reaction to unexpected nudity, much like the humor of "streaking" in the 1970s, such exhibitionism still requires an explanation of the symbolic values which make it humorously shocking. The unconscious or primary process is the most obvious source of this intuitive understanding.

The potent image of the goddess lifting her skirts has captured the imagination of contemporary writers, yet the lengthy discussion of this motif has not arrived at any consensus regarding why this act of exposure causes a lifting of spirits and return to normal activities. In contrast to the humorous effect of the genital display in the Greek and Egyptian scenes, the scholarly discussion of related acts in world literature often refer to the symbolic power of the feminine generative organs. George Devereux's (1983) book-length study examines various psychoanalytic aspects of feminine exhibitionism and focuses on the sexual content of the image. In an exploration of the image throughout the world, Lubell (1994:55) advocates for the sacred power of Baubo's skirt-raising gesture as a "metaphor for the transformative power of female sacred sexual energy" for renewal and regeneration. Lubell (1994:55) connects the "bawdy joke" of Baubo to the solidarity of females as the source of creation, renewal, and regeneration against patriarchal oppression in rape and abduction. She suggests that the gesture communicates to Demeter the central function of their wombs in procreation; women are transformers of reality and must not surrender to the masculine forces of death and destruction. Whether or not Lubell's phenomenological interpretation applies to other sources, it surely does not apply to the male Pre's reaction to Hathor's exposure.[15]

Many commentators have emphasized the repellent quality of the action and note examples of the warding off of demons who exhibit terror at the sight of the female pudenda (see Olender 1990:104, n.119; Devereux 1983:176). Philip E. Slater (1968:320), for example, notes the display of the female genitalia as a "common apotropaic device" based upon its powerful fertility symbolism. The special characteristics of the vulvas of virgins, mothers, and prostitutes have all come under consideration in the critical literature in attempts to isolate the essence of the gesture. A classic example of the terror-inspiring quality of the female genitalia is found in the ancient Greek tradition of the hero Bellerophon, slayer of monsters and rider of Pegasus. Caldwell (1990:364–65) aptly describes the image of the spear-wielding warrior astride the flying stallion as a "doubly determined symbol of phallic superiority," yet this mighty hero is routed by the mere sight of the Xanthian women's pudenda (see also Slater 1968:333–36). To be sure, the spectacle of all the city's women, lined up on the walls and bent over to expose their genitals *en masse*, would be a shock to any unsuspecting traveler, but Bellerophon's reaction in falling off his mount in mid-air seems extreme and fraught with Freudian overtones of performance anxieties.

To return to "The Contendings," Freudian scholars might suggest various interpretations of this scene as a projection of psychological processes. The terse narration of this event leaves the reader ignorant of both Hathor's intent and Pre's unconscious reaction expressed by laughter, but these "facts" are less significant than how the scene reflects unconscious concerns. Freud's theories lead one to hypothesize that Pre, intimidated by the female pudenda, masks his anxiety with laughter. This scene may portray the fear of aggressive feminine sexuality, symbolized by female genitalia, in which case Hathor's display would constitute an aggressive sexual overture. The "Herdsman's Story" depicts a nude goddess whose seductive advances prove terrifying to the herdsman. If that goddess is Hathor, as many Egyptologists assume, then the fearsome nature of her sexual passion could be a motif shared by this episode in "The Contendings." Pre's recumbent position also alludes to Osiris's corpse, lying on its back, which Isis aggressively mounts in order to conceive an heir. Thus, Pre could remain on his back, face Hathor's seductive advances, and risk not satisfying the demanding goddess of love; or he could arise and flee the scene in surrender to his performance anxiety. In this scenario, Pre chooses a dignified exit under the pretense of amusement in order to cover his actual embarrassment. This interpretation is further bolstered by Hathor's identity as Pre's mother or daughter in various Egyptian traditions (Bleeker

1973:65). Thus, his fear of her sexuality would in fact be either an aversion to her incestuous suggestion or a denial of his own incestuous attraction which we may presume he felt but could not consciously acknowledge.

Another interpretation based upon Pre's unconscious fear of the female pudenda relates to Freud's analysis of castration anxiety. Freud explains that a boy's exposure to the maternal genitalia leads to his belief that the female lack of a penis is the result of castration. The fear of his own castration is thus brought on by this sight. Hence, one could argue that Pre's anxiety at Hathor's display is caused by unconscious castration anxiety. On the other hand, one could also suggest that his laughter reveals his proud recognition that he does have a penis while the goddess does not. In direct contrast to Lubell's interpretation of the Baubo and Demeter story as an affirmation of their shared genitalia, then, a psychoanalytic interpretation could stress the humorous quality of this encounter based upon the difference between the male and female genitalia. That is, Baba's insult, "your shrine is empty," becomes meaningless when Pre realizes that his genitalia are not "empty" as Hathor's are.

Conversely, Pre's expression of delight in seeing Hathor's pudenda could be an authentic response to either a humorous jest or erotic enticement.[16] While Pre may indeed be compensating for an unconscious anxiety concerning feminine sexuality, I interpret Pre's laughter as an authentic expression of his good humor caused by Hathor's pose. Thus, he enjoys the titillation of the woman's advances and his bodily rising from the ground symbolizes his sexual arousal and phallic erection.[17] This interpretation is especially appealing if one recalls that Pre is downcast from the insult of Baba, who may be the cause of Pre's impotence, according to the *Book of the Dead*. We may then interpret Pre's response to Hathor's display of her vulva as sexual arousal. Freudian theory commonly associates the display of female genitalia with the severed head of the Gorgon Medusa, who could turn men into stone with a mere glance (see Clair 1989). Contrary to Freud's explanation that petrification symbolizes erection as a defense against the fear of castration, Slater (1968:321–22) convincingly argues that "immobility is much more suggestive of impotence." In fact, the literal display of female genitalia to Pre results not in his immobility, but in his movement.

That is, Hathor's exposure of her vulva causes the prone and immobile father to arise and reassert his role as leader of the Ennead. The sensitive male ego that was immobilized by Baba's insult is healed by Hathor's erotic display; the sexual impotence caused by Baba is countered with phallic tumescence caused by Hathor. Just as Isis revives the dead Osiris's phallus, here Hathor restores life to Pre's inert form. Pre's joyous laughter is therefore in reaction to his stirred libido and the rejuvenation of his sexual powers. While this interpretation reads much into the few lines of "The Contendings," the data from other contexts support this unconscious, latent meaning.

In summary, a number of anxiety-producing fears (performance anxiety, denial of incestuous urges, fear of aggressive maternal sexuality, castration anxiety) might motivate the overwhelmed male to make a hasty retreat. Taken within the context of the Iambe and Baubo traditions, the purpose of Hathor's illicit act could be simply to elicit laughter from Pre. Yet, even if critics prefer this reading, they must still explain the symbolism of female genitalia. While the fear of father-daughter incest or aggressive female sexuality in general may play a role in this scene, I interpret Hathor's display of her vulva as erotic titillation to restore Pre's sexual vitality. The depression brought on by Baba, the cause of Pre's impotence, is brought to an end by the intervention of the erotic goddess. This interpretation is consistent with Hathor's role in a later episode, discussed below, and this consistency is what motivates my interpretive decision. Of course, with Freud we can have our cake and eat it too: Pre can be both sexually aroused yet also wary of the incestuous advances of his daughter with the Electra Complex.

Island Intrigue (4, 4–8, 1)

While Hathor's exploits effectively motivate Pre to reconvene the Ennead, no immediate resolution to the conflict is forthcoming. The gods still disagree concerning both the principle of succession and Seth's identity as either elder brother or maternal uncle of Horus. The lack of decision leads to the vocal intervention of Isis and Seth's subsequent demand that she be excluded from the proceedings. Pre aligns himself with Seth and calls the council to reconvene on the

Island-in-the-Middle. He warns the ferryman Nemty to keep Isis from crossing over to the new location. Ironically, Seth's attempt to flee from Isis's presence only results in his most intimate contact with her in the myth. Rather than avoiding her, he ends up trying to seduce her; while attempting to elude her influence, he is caught in her web of intrigue. That the wise Isis can trick the doltish Seth into admitting the superiority of Horus's claim to the throne is unsurprising. While Seth was able to dupe Osiris into the wooden case which became his coffin, he is no match for the magical enchantments and cunning of Isis.

Isis's transformation into a beautiful young maiden entices Seth into assuming the aggressive role as the male pursuer, but when Isis reveals her true identity Seth realizes that she is the manipulative mother rather than the innocent virgin. Afterwards, Seth foolishly complains to Pre about "that evil woman" who has tricked him again (7, 3). While he was confident about seducing a mere girl, he admits his inadequacy when faced with the mature Isis. In fact, other episodes in Egyptian myth portray the sexual antagonism between Isis and Seth. The lecherous god deeply desires Isis, but his lust is unfulfilled as she consistently eludes his grasp. Just as in this case, she turns his losses into her own victories and "unmans" the hapless god through her scorn.

The Papyrus Jumilhac (II, 26–III, 5) recounts the most explicit episode of Seth's humiliating sexual performance:

> When Seth saw Isis in this place, he transformed himself into a bull in order to run after her, but she disguised herself by assuming the appearance of a dog with a knife at the end of its tail. Next she began to run before him, and Seth was not able to overtake her. Then he scattered his seed on the ground and the goddess said, "It is an abomination to have scattered (your seed), O Bull." His seed sprouted on the Gebel into plants....[18]

Seth's inability to catch Isis may symbolize an unconscious anxiety about male sexual performance. Much like the *vagina dentata*, the image of Isis as a bitch with a knife on her tail obviously depicts the threat of castration to the one who would sexually approach the goddess. This implied threat, as well as her taunting of Seth for his premature ejaculation, conveys a male performance anxiety. As noted above, Freud identified male performance anxiety in the Oedipus Complex when the boy realizes that he, whose body and penis are so much smaller than his father's, would be incapable of satisfying the sexual desires of the mother. Seth's failed encounters with Isis aptly illustrate a male anxiety about the inability to satisfy the aggressive mother, as well as a fear of castration from the erotic female.

Although Isis is certainly feminine and erotic in these scenes, it is important to note the phallic qualities of this mother goddess with the horned headdress. In his 1945 article, "Aphrodite, or the Woman with a Penis," Géza Róheim explicates the concept of the phallic mother who threatens men with castration.[19] Indeed, the mortal danger of the erotic female is not an uncommon theme in world mythologies. Furthermore, the phallic nature of Isis is emphasized in the Papyrus Jumilhac's depiction of Isis turning herself into a snake (an obvious enough phallic symbol) whose stinging venom slays the allies of Seth with its powerful poison (Hollis 1990:174–75). "Poison" and "semen" are translations of the same Egyptian word (*mtwt*). Thus, rather than describe the allies of Seth injecting their poison into Horus, this myth portrays Isis playing the masculine role comparable to insemination. Isis not only threatens castration with a knife, she also usurps the traditionally male role of injecting her poison/semen into her prey's male bodies.

"The Contendings" is more subtle in its presentation of Isis as a castrating or phallic mother, but the motif is evident. The Island scene first establishes the sexual lure of the nubile maiden among the sycamores, trees sacred to the erotic goddess Hathor. Then Isis transforms herself into a kite or falcon and flies up to perch on an acacia tree in order to taunt Seth with his own stupidity (6, 14–7, 1). The height of her perch not only represents Seth's inability to obtain her but also may symbolize the inadequacy of his erection; his phallus is insufficient for her. Since the upward motion of flight symbolizes erection and birds are often phallic symbols in Freudian thought, Isis's metamorphosis into a kite may also symbolize her role as the erect phallic mother (see Slater 1968:324). In addition to the usual Freudian interpretation of bird symbolism, Isis's manifestation as a kite is a subtle snub to the erotic intentions of Seth as well as a jab at his own guilt in the death of Osiris, Isis's true lover. Recall that it is as a kite that Isis alights upon the corpse of the slain Osiris. After she has flown down to his prostrate corpse, she reinvigorates his penis in order to impregnate herself. Thus, her manifestation as a kite with Osiris conveys both her erotic availability and her aggressive sexuality. In fact, the Papyrus Louvre 3079 describes Isis as having "played the part of a man" in conceiving Horus, since she initiates and dominates the sexual encounter with the flaccid body of Osiris (Manniche 1987:59). Isis provides the necessary energy by breathing life into the corpse—or at least into the phallus—and assumes the dominant sexual position. Thus, her bird imagery combines feminine eroticism and phallic erection in a way that results in sexual intercourse and procreation in the Osiris myth. Conversely, in "The Contendings" her phallic bird form wards off the unwanted sexual advances of Seth after she has successfully aroused him in a different manifestation.

Seth's return and complaint to Pre, in which he tells the story on himself, illustrates Isis's effective humiliation of her brother. Seth takes out his aggression against the ferryman, Nemty, by having his toes cut off (7, 13). This castration symbolism underlines Seth's own symbolic emasculation at the hands of the clever Isis. In this vein, Seth deprives Nemty of phallic symbols (toes) because Seth's own phallus is useless in pursuing Isis. In fact, Isis's gift of a golden ring to Nemty may symbolize her sexual availability to him, since finger rings are common vulva symbols in psychoanalytic interpretation (Dundes 1989:114–15). This sexual symbol is introduced only after Isis's appearance as an elderly mother who offers nourishing food, so Nemty's punishment may be in response to his repressed oedipal desire. In contrast, Isis initially appears to Seth as an erotic maiden in order to get what she wants as a maternal nurturer. The clever manipulation of feminine sexual symbolism in this episode communicates both the unattainable quality of Isis's sexuality to Seth, as well as her own superiority to him as a phallic mother. Seth is here defeated by Isis just as he will be defeated by Horus in their phallic contests.

In conclusion, the two episodes with Hathor and Isis present conflicting images of the goddess as erotic female, nurturing mother, and phallic mother. Hathor is effective in her healing role explicitly because she has female genitalia; Isis is effective in eventually unmanning Seth because she is a phallic mother. The juxtaposition of these two scenes at the myth's beginning emphasizes the importance of feminine symbolism and male anxieties in "The Contendings." These episodes establish a symbolic context for Horus's oedipal competition with Seth and his own interactions with the erotic and maternal goddesses.

THE THREE CONTESTS

Seth proposes three contests to demonstrate his physical superiority over the child Horus, but the bizarre content of the contests is hardly relevant in determining royal competency. A psychoanalytic interpretation of the contests' manifest elements can expose the Freudian categories of the psychological processes and unlock their latent meanings.

Under the Water (8, 9–10, 11)

The first contest, to maintain a submerged hippopotamus form for three months, gives Seth an obvious advantage since the hippopotamus is one of his theriomorphic manifestations. The watery setting of the challenge is in direct contrast to Horus's own falcon manifestation and sky associations. Water is also the medium of Seth's murder of Osiris, so one can also see an implicit threat to Osiris's son in the choice of this venue. Later iconographic traditions, however, routinely depict Horus harpooning hippos as a symbol of royal ideology. Seth's odd challenge therefore alludes to the symbolism of the pharaonic hippopotamus hunt, a motif present in the third contest as well.

The ancient Egyptians knew the male hippo to be a violently aggressive and territorial beast. Egyptian sources also use the male hippo as a Sethian symbol of evil.[20] More significant to a Freudian analysis, Plutarch (*DIO* 32) states that ancient Egyptians identify the hippo with "shamelessness; for it is said to violate its mother after killing its father" (Griffiths 1970:169). John Gwyn Griffiths (1970:423) remarks that neither parricide nor mother-incest are ascribed to Seth or the hippopotamus in ancient Egyptian sources apart from this late reference, but he neglects the psychological import of Plutarch's quote in identifying Seth's motives. Seth is in fact guilty of killing Osiris and lusting after Isis. While Seth is their sibling in some traditions, Isis and Osiris also represent parental images in these myths when Seth is called the brother of their son Horus. Thus, Seth's murder of Osiris and lust for Isis constitute a symbolic realization of the oedipal complex. Similarly, Horus's agreement to become a hippopotamus may also represent unconscious oedipal wishes.

The first contest is interrupted by Isis, who fears that Seth will kill her young son. She constructs a harpoon and accidentally stabs Horus before impaling Seth on her phallic weapon. Although Isis does not explicitly threaten to castrate anyone in this scene, she plays the role of the phallic mother by interfering in the masculine contest. Isis symbolically emasculates Horus by publicly doubting his prowess and his ability to contend with the virile Seth. In his fierce anger over her interference, Horus comes out of the water and decapitates his mother: "He cut off the head of his mother Isis, took it in his arms, and ascended the mountain. Then Isis changed herself into a statue of flint which had no head" (9, 9). Contra Plutarch, who refuses even to discuss what he describes as one of the "most outrageous episodes" of a myth with "barbarous views about the gods," this scandalous event requires careful analysis.[21] Psychoanalytic theory helps explain the scene's meaning for the modern reader.

A boy's relationship to his mother is a stereotypically Freudian preoccupation, but the relationship of Horus and Isis is in fact central to "The Contendings." Dundes (1980:258) explains, "In Mediterranean family structure, one of the crucial problems for boys remains breaking the strong bond existing between them and their mothers so as to join the world of mature men." Within this context, I interpret Horus's decapitation of Isis as his means of symbolically castrating the phallic mother. Horus establishes his masculine independence from the overprotective Isis by arising in symbolic erection from the water and depriving her of her head, a common phallic symbol. The text further communicates Horus's phallic superiority by noting that the blade with which he decapitates Isis is sixteen times heavier than the harpoon with which she pricks his body (8, 12 and 9, 9). Horus's violent overthrow of the phallic mother, however, does not result in the guilt-producing image of a bloody woman or headless corpse since Isis merely transforms herself into a headless statue (see Slater 1968:303–6). The result is a generic female body with neither head nor phallus. As noted above, the rigidity of stone is often symbolic of impotence rather than erection, so the headless stone statue is a particularly appropriate symbol for the castrated phallic mother.[22] The loss of her head also deprives Isis of her voice, the weapon with which she tricked Seth in their Island encounter. She is now silent, as well as impotent. Yet, rather than return to his manly contendings with Seth after asserting his independence from maternal control, Horus takes Isis's severed head and retreats into the desert highlands.[23]

Horus's attachment to his mother's head reflects the complexity of the mother-son relationship in this myth. Horus resents his mother's phallic intrusion into his affairs yet clings to her head as he wanders off by himself. Citing strong Freudian precedent and the maxim of "displacement from below to above," one can easily interpret the woman's severed head as symbolic of female genitalia. Hence, Horus's retention of Isis's head may represent his sexual desire for his mother; Horus retains Isis's mouth when he actually wants possession of her vulva.[24] Likewise, his ascent of the mountain symbolizes his phallic erection and sexual excitement. In other words, Horus cuts off Isis's head because it is a phallus but then takes it with him because it is a vulva. Such are the vagaries of Freudian symbolism! While this sexual interpretation of Isis's severed head may seem forced to some readers, Griffiths (1960:48–50) cites Egyptian sources in which Horus actually does sexually violate his mother. Griffiths states that this scene of incestuous rape actually replaces the decapitation episode in these texts, supporting my interpretation of the latent meaning of this scene in "The Contendings."

Although Isis does not complain about her treatment, Pre is angered by Horus's aggression and demands his punishment. The next scene depicts Horus reclining under a tree in a desert oasis. "Then Seth found him, seized him, and threw him on his back upon the mountain. He removed his two eyes from their places and buried them upon the mountain" (10, 4). Horus's oedipal drive is satisfied by his acquisition of Isis's "head" for himself but he now faces retaliation for usurping the paternal rights to the mother. Thus, Pre's condemnation and Seth's physical punishment reflect the fear of the paternal rival for the mother's genitalia. Blinding is a common Freudian symbol of castration and the classical punishment for Oedipus's sin of incest. Therefore, Horus's loss of his eyes may reflect castration anxiety produced by oedipal guilt. While seeing Hathor's pudenda is healing for the mature Pre, the sight of the maternal genitalia remains threatening to the young son. The transformation of Horus's eyes into lotuses further emphasizes the sexual nature of this episode since flowers are common vaginal symbols in Freudian analysis. The symbolic rebirth of the sun god from the lotus in the form of the Horus-child further substantiates the genital symbolism of the flower in this context.[25] As the phallic mother is emasculated with the loss of her head, so Horus is threatened with feminization by his symbolic castration and the transformation of his eyes into vulva symbols.

The erotic goddess Hathor, who appears in the myth for the first time since her exhibitionism to Pre, restores Horus's excised organs. Hathor approaches the wounded god as he lies weeping in the desert and replaces his eyes by pouring gazelle milk into his empty sockets.[26] Although Isis is more frequently depicted as breast-feeding the infant Horus, Hathor also nurses Horus in Egyptian myth when Isis is attending to the burial of Osiris. Indeed, Hathor is one manifestation of Horus's mother, as mentioned above. Thus, it would not be unexpected for this goddess, routinely depicted as a wild cow, to use her own milk to heal Horus. I submit, however, that it is the erotic manifestation of the mother, rather than the phallic or lactating maternal form, that is required to heal Horus in this instance. In other words, it takes the erotic mother to heal the sexual wound of symbolic castration. We will return to the symbolism of maternal milk in another context. After restoring his loss, Hathor instructs Horus to open his eyelids so she can inspect his new eyes, an act that signifies the erotic mother's approval of her son's sexuality. That is, after the symbolic castration at Seth's hands for his viewing of the maternal genitalia, the mother restores Horus's virility and explicitly approves of his new phallic symbols. The symbolic equivalence of vision with sexual libido thematically unites this healing act with Hathor's revitalization of Pre in their previous encounter. Hence, Hathor's role in each of these strange episodes, in my interpretation, is to restore the sexual vitality of the impotent male.

In summary, Horus symbolically castrates the phallic mother and is himself symbolically castrated by Seth in this first episode. His mother then comes to him in the form of the erotic Hathor and restores his sight. As we will see again in the next episode, the realization of castration anxiety over oedipal guilt is alleviated by maternal support and eventual victory over the displaced father figure.

In the Bed (11, 2–13, 1)

The second contest is explicitly sexual in character. After hosting Horus for a meal, Seth invites the boy to sleep in his bed. During the night, "Seth caused his phallus to become stiff and inserted it between Horus's thighs. Then Horus placed his hands between his thighs and caught Seth's semen" (11, 3–4). While earlier texts relate Seth's homosexual desire for Horus, the intent of his attempted rape in "The Contendings" is to disqualify Horus from the throne.[27] Seth attempts to feminize the younger Horus but is unsuccessful in penetrating Horus's body. Horus runs to Isis to show her what Seth has done to him. This return to Isis demonstrates Horus's continued dependence on his mother in his struggles with Seth. While he cannot tolerate the phallic mother's dominance, Horus still depends on Isis's maternal support.

The text describes what happens next: "He opened his hand and let her see the semen of Seth. She cried out aloud, seized her knife, cut off his hand and threw it into the water. Then she made a new hand for him" (11, 5–7). Since the hand is a common phallic symbol, this is a clear example of symbolic castration by the mother. Horus emasculates the phallic mother in a previous episode, but there is residual anxiety about Isis's powers.[28] Isis immediately alleviates this anxiety, however, by creating a new hand for him, similar to Hathor's restoration of his eyes. The manifest sexual character of this episode continues in the immediately following lines, which read: "And she took a dab of sweet ointment and put it on the phallus of Horus. She made it become stiff and inserted it into a pot, and he caused his semen to flow down into it" (11, 7–8). A Freudian could conclude that this scene represents the projection of the boy's oedipal desires onto the mother: "It is not I who desire her, but she who desires me." This projection alleviates any guilt over repressed incestuous desires. Isis's symbolic castration of Horus's semen-covered "hand" is rectified by providing a new one; its phallic symbolism and proper heterosexual use is demonstrated by her sexual overture in masturbating him. Far from being the castrating phallic mother, Isis now incites his sexual arousal and induces his orgasm with no demands for her own pleasure.

The "aromatic ointment" that Isis applies to Horus's phallus to aid in his ejaculation may symbolize female sexual secretions, just as the jar into which she inserts Horus's phallus is a standard symbol of female genitalia in psychoanalytic thought. Thus, we have a rather explicit reference to mother-son sexual intercourse only partially veiled by the mechanism of sublimation. More graphic than Isis's head in the arms of Horus, this scene clearly communicates the erotic quality of the mother-son relationship. Moreover, this episode forestalls any risk of the mother's aggressive sexuality overwhelming the young boy. Róheim (1972:185–87, 197) describes the infantile belief that the phallic mother can enjoy sex only because she has a penis and that the possibility of female orgasm, symbolized by ointments, evokes the image of the sexually demanding woman. Horus, however, has already deprived Isis of her symbolic phallus in a previous episode and has thus removed her ability to enjoy an orgasm, according to Róheim's argument. The substitution of the jar for the vagina on the text's manifest level further precludes Isis from experiencing any sexual pleasure. Horus's successful orgasm at the hands of his mother as well as the text's negation of female sexual pleasure in this episode should obviate any potential male performance anxiety. Isis's initiation of the heterosexual encounter also relieves Horus of any oedipal guilt for his own incestuous desires.

The next morning Isis goes to Seth's garden and surreptitiously places Horus's semen on Seth's lettuce, a plant whose milky sap symbolized fertility in ancient Egypt (Griffiths 1960:45–46). When Seth eats the lettuce, he unknowingly becomes pregnant with Horus's seed.[29] "The Contendings" exploits the potent symbolism of semen, whose ominous power the Egyptians recognized by using the same word for "semen" and "poison" (*mtwt*), as noted above. Caldwell (1989:87) describes the symbolism of semen as "the combination of fire and water, a liquid that contains the spark of life." Recall the scene in the Papyrus Jumilhac where Isis, in the form of a knife-tailed bitch, jeers at Seth for spilling his seed upon the ground. By contrast, Isis carefully collects Horus's apparently valuable semen in "The Contendings." Like the Freudian discussion of toilet training in which the ambiguity of the otherwise dirty feces is communicated to the child by the parents' pleasure at the child's "gift," here one sees Isis's delight in Horus's production of the very substance that had horrified her when on his hand. Thus, it seems that semen—like dirt—is only dirty when out of its proper place. Significantly, Seth's semen keeps ending up in all the wrong places in Egyptian myth. His attempted rape of Horus results in the wasting of his semen in the marsh; his pursuit of Isis ends with his seed spilled upon the ground to produce only plants; and his attack on the Seed-goddess in the Chester Beatty Papyrus actually gives him a debilitating headache when the semen flies to his own forehead (see van Dijk 1986). Thus, Seth's ejaculation produces no heirs or supporters, while Horus's fertile seed impregnates Seth with the golden moon disk.

"The Contendings" is not the only myth from ancient Egypt that depicts Isis as a manipulator of semen, as she also "steals" the seed of the dead Osiris in order to conceive Horus. After draining her husband's energy to create the child in her womb, Isis produces her own bodily fluid (milk) to nurture the son who will replace his father. In fact, a symbolic relationship between semen and maternal milk is not uncommon in world mythology.[30] The ubiquitous image of Isis nursing the infant Horus embodies her maternal nature and the intimate bond between mother and child in Egyptian myth. Yet "The Contendings" makes no direct reference to this paradigmatic relationship, except in the form of Pre's insult that Horus's breath stinks (presumably from mother's milk). Instead, the present scene inverts the traditional mother-child relationship: the mother draws semen from her son's phallus instead of the son drawing milk from his mother's breast. I submit that this inversion reflects Horus's own repudiation of his infant status in order to attain adulthood. That is, the myth intentionally portrays Horus as a sexually mature male who produces semen rather than ingesting maternal milk. Hathor's earlier use of milk—but not her own milk!—in healing Horus's eyes may therefore reflect a symbolic rejection of the lactating mother in preference for the erotic mother. That the maternal Isis masturbates Horus emphasizes her promotion of Horus's male sexuality without invoking the threat of feminine sexual gratification associated with Hathor. Horus's ambivalent relationship to his mother requires this decomposition into the erotic and the castrated maternal manifestations of the mother for a resolution to his oedipal conflict.

When the two litigants return to court, Seth assumes that he will prevail through his declaration that he has "played the man" with Horus (12, 3). His trick backfires when the call for his semen elicits a response from the marsh while the call for Horus's semen elicits a reply from within Seth's body. The semen exits Seth through his forehead as a golden disk. Seth not only fails to "do the deed of a man" to Horus, he is forced to play the feminine role in giving birth to Horus's offspring. Thus, Horus's masculinity is vindicated in the Ennead as he strives for recognition of his right to his father's throne.

On the Boat (13, 3–11)

The mode of competition moves from semen to seamen with Seth's proposal of a boat race (13, 3–4). While the significance of "stone ships" is lost on modern readers, Seth's ancient association with ships gives him a clear advantage in this contest (see Griffiths 1960:48). Floating is standard erection symbolism in Freudian analysis. Boats, however, are feminine symbols because of their capacity to carry people, as well as the crescent shape of female genitalia. Horus's successful sailing therefore symbolizes his masculine sexual ability, while the sinking of Seth's stone ship conveys impotence and performance anxiety. Horus's phallic superiority is further represented by his harpooning of Seth in his hippo manifestation, as well as the erectile symbolism of raising a sail. Indeed, Horus is adept at the mechanisms of hoisting a sail and then traveling downstream to Neith, the divine mother, to whom he repeats his many victories over Seth. One might easily interpret this as another oedipal wish to show off his sexual prowess to his approving mother.

Meanwhile, the Ennead sends a letter to Osiris to ask his opinion in the matter of succession. Osiris forcefully supports Horus and the Ennead eventually agrees. After another unspecified contest won by Horus, Seth is bound in fetters by Isis as yet another example of her emasculating power over him. Seth finally concedes Horus's right to the throne and Horus is installed as King of Egypt. The gods rejoice in celebration of Horus's enthronement as Isis proclaims that "Horus has arisen as ruler" (16, 6). Once again, the contrast between Horus's arising and Seth's immobility is clear. Seth, however, is neither killed nor driven out of the gods' assembly, as in later versions of the conflict. Pre resolves this issue by adopting Seth as his own son and giving him a place in his heavenly ship. The fact that Osiris's letter is ultimately decisive underlines the importance of the father figure to this myth of Horus's maturation. The mother figures consistently support Horus's claim to the throne and in this episode the father figures (Pre, Seth, and Osiris) each conclude that Horus deserves to replace Osiris. Horus has won the support of all characters and repeatedly proven his victorious prowess. A place in the cosmos is found for the defeated Seth, who is impotent in his dealings with Isis but powerful in defeating threatening monsters for the sun god. Thus, Seth is no longer a serious rival for the affection of Horus's mother.

CONCLUSION

The application of classical Freudian theory to "The Contendings of Horus and Seth" highlights the resolution of Horus's oedipal conflicts and related anxieties. As an example of its culture's projection systems, this myth may reflect similar anxieties on the part of its author and audience who identify with Horus in his psychosexual development. Even listeners without these anxieties, however, could enjoy the wish fulfillment of common infantile fantasies.

"The Contendings" begins with the convenient oedipal scenario of a mother, a son, and a deceased father. Osiris is effectively castrated when Seth dismembers his corpse and scatters the fourteen pieces throughout Egypt. According to at least one Egyptian tradition, Isis recovers all but the male member of Osiris's body, so Osiris spends eternity without a phallus.[31] Far from being a rival to Horus, Osiris's death and emasculation doubly disqualify him from sexually possessing Isis. Dundes (1980:246) notes that "the castration of the father by the son would, like the virgin birth, be an ultimate expression of the son's repudiation...of his father" since it denies the father any sexual access to the mother. In fact, Isis's impregnation of herself from Osiris's corpse is similar to the symbolic function of a virgin birth in its rejection of the father. Moreover, Horus replaces Osiris as the provider of semen for Isis's use in "The Contendings," a fact that emphasizes Horus's virility on the myth's manifest level. And given the Egyptian concept of death, Osiris is still capable of staunchly supporting his son as his replacement on earth since he is unable to fulfill his royal duties. This scenario is indeed perfect for a boy's oedipal fantasy.

The decomposition of the father provides other male characters to obstruct the realization of Horus's oedipal desires. The father is displaced by an uncle who hates and persecutes the boy in competition for Isis's affections. This inversion allows Horus's oedipal aggression to be projected onto Seth while Osiris remains an object of love and support. Indeed, Horus can assuage any latent guilt by avenging his father and punishing Seth. The inadequate Seth is not a serious rival for Isis in any case, as his unsuccessful attempts at seduction result in humiliating rejections by Isis. Indeed, other traditions frequently describe Horus's actual castration of Seth, a sexually deviant god married to Nephthys, "the imitation woman who has no vagina."[32] The repetitious portrayal of Horus's superiority to Seth reflects over-compensation for Horus's anxieties caused by challenges to his virility. Horus's loss of eyes and hands reflects his own castration anxiety, but this anxiety is resolved when mother figures (Hathor and Isis) restore his phallic symbols. Isis's masturbation of Horus further suggests the mother's approval of his heterosexual capabilities. Horus's phallic superiority is thus progressively affirmed throughout "The Contendings."

Oedipal impulses, sexual anxieties, and decomposition can also help explain Horus's complex relationship with mother figures in "The Contendings." The decomposed mother image allows Horus to deal differently with different aspects of the mother. Isis's decapitation in the first contest establishes Horus's freedom from the phallic mother's control, while his dependence upon Hathor, Neith, and Isis in other scenes emphasizes his continued relationship with the erotic and maternal manifestations of the mother. The three contests depict Horus's progression from passive to active roles as part of his psychosexual development. The text further projects the boy's oedipal desires onto the mother, as Hathor and Isis follow him, promote his cause, and engage in at least symbolic sex with him. In theory, the proper resolution of the classic oedipal complex comes when the child accepts his inability to replace his father and possess his mother. As he identifies with his father, the boy transfers the object of his sexual desire from his mother to other women. Yet, Horus cannot resolve his oedipal complex in this way because his desire to replace his father is gloriously fulfilled.[33] This conclusion, however, is an appropriately pharaonic adaptation of the classical oedipal complex rather than an example of stalled psychosexual development. One must recall that Horus symbolizes the pharaoh, ancient Egypt's God-King, who is in fact both the son and spouse of the goddess. Unlike other boys, who must adopt the reality principle, the pharaoh Horus can enjoy maternal comfort as well as erotic association with his divine mother.

The emphasis on legitimate succession by descent in "The Contendings" relates to the divine status of the ancient Egyptian king, who is himself a manifestation of Horus and the son of the deceased Osiris, the previous pharaoh. The esoteric Kamutef concept, from the Egyptian term *kꜣ-mwt.f*, "Bull of his mother," helps explains the process by which each divine king is an incarnation of Horus.[34] Essentially, the god is reborn through impregnating his wife, who then becomes his mother. In this way, Hathor is called the mother and wife of every pharaoh, just as she is both the mother and wife of Horus in various traditions (see Hollis 1990:137–38). The "Bull of his mother" therefore has no need to transfer the object of his sexual desires from his mother to another woman. Although Isis is usually the comforting, nurturing, and supportive mother of Horus, she also plays an erotic role in Egyptian myth. The decomposition of the mother figure in "The Contendings" does not strictly separate the erotic Hathor from the maternal Isis, since Hathor is nurturing and Isis is erotic in some episodes. This ambiguous situation, in which the mother can be both maternal and erotic, may explain Horus's relationship with Isis throughout the myth. He overcomes the threatening phallic mother by symbolically castrating her, but then relies upon other mother images for comfort and support in the rest of the myth. I interpret this ambiguous relationship as the pharaonic resolution to the oedipal conflict in which Horus can have his mother as a protective, nurturing figure, as well as the object of his erotic impulses, without fear of being overwhelmed by her. Horus does not outgrow his attachment to Isis, as one would expect, and he therefore has no need for a new source of erotic pleasure. Thus, "The Contendings" may serve as the uniquely pharaonic wish fulfillment for the boy caught in the oedipal struggle who works out his self-doubts about his maturity and sexual capability to achieve an ideal situation. The myth's audience could also experience a vicarious satisfaction in the complete fulfillment of oedipal fantasies through this particularly pharaonic resolution.

To return to the original, methodological question, "Can a psychoanalytic approach account for more of the myth's manifest elements than previous interpretations?", I argue in the affirmative. A Freudian perspective on the "The Contendings" is especially proficient in explaining the most bizarre elements and fantastic episodes in a consistent fashion. Note, however, that I apply Freud's theories to a myth whose manifest content describes what Freud says should be latent. Application of the same categories to another myth might not be so productive or compelling. In asking which methodological approach make most sense of the greatest number of elements of this particular myth, the psychoanalytic method makes a strong case. But is this the best methodological question to pose? The criticisms of the Freudian approach to myth interpretation are well-known; detractors charge, among other things, that it is functionalist, universalist, unempirical, reductionist, and culturally relative. Furthermore, psychoanalytic approaches usually result in *causal* explanations for the origins of myths rather than interpretations of literary texts. This type of analysis becomes a circular argument to validate psychoanalytic theory. Recall the numerous options in interpreting Hathor's exhibitionism in my own analysis. While Freudian theory offers various possible motivations for Pre's reaction, how can the interpreter determine the correct one? I merely chose an interpretation consistent with my analysis of other scenes.

My point here is not to engage the methodological debate about Freud so much as to offer an analysis of "The Contendings" from a novel perspective, to provide a new lens through which to view this enigmatic myth. I certainly do not mean to suggest that ancient Egyptians would have consciously understood the myth in these terms. Nevertheless, Freudian theory is useful in examining psychological categories and symbolic associations, and in this case it helps to interpret some very strange episodes in a consistent framework. On the other hand, many important elements of the text are left unexplained by a psychoanalytic approach. Most of these elements concern culturally-specific content, such as the roles of Thoth and Neith or the royal ideology of the hippopotamus hunt. A psychoanalytic approach highlights elements of the myth that otherwise remain opaque, but the theory-driven character of the method and the subjective quality of its application lead me to conclude that the benefits of psychoanalytic approaches are of a limited nature. While Freudians may blanch at my timidity, I am content to agree with Wendy Doniger and suggest that Freud is appropriate when the myth is manifestly about castration, incest, and sexual anxieties but perhaps not when these elements are missing.[35] A methodologically conscientious pluralism recognizes that different myths call for different methods. Furthermore, different methods will emphasize and examine different aspects and symbols within the same narrative, resulting in disparate interpretations.

In conclusion, rather than advance my Freudian reading of "The Contendings" as a rival to Oden's structuralist interpretation, I advocate a pluralistic approach to myth interpretation and retain both analyses as complementary (if not always consistent) interpretations of one multivalent myth. Certainly, the oedipal tensions are there for the reader who wishes to perceive them, yet the myth has other things to say to those without a Freudian preoccupation. The political and ideological dimension of the text should be equally clear to the perceptive reader, and a structuralist analysis further demonstrates the importance of many details of the text's construction. Interpretations of myth should not be mutually exclusive since the multivalent nature of myth can produce many different readings. Let us continue Oden's (1979:363) "search for a more adequate method for interpreting myths" without sacrificing the benefits of one method for the insights of another. A combination of approaches will allow us most fully to appreciate an ancient myth like "The Contendings of Horus and Seth."

NOTES

[1]Quotations from "The Contendings" generally follow the translations of Gardiner (1931:8–26), Wendte (1973), and especially Lichtheim (1976:214–23) (cf. Junge 1995). The most thorough treatment and bibliography is by Broze (1996).

[2]Broze (1996:221–75) provides the only detailed analysis of the myth in response to Oden. The genre of "The Contendings" constitutes a point of controversy among its interpreters. Some call it a myth, others call it a fairy tale, satire, farce, or humorous diversion. Though I assume that the text represents an authentic myth, my analysis remains the same regardless of the narrative's genre. On the identification of myth and other genres in Egyptian literature, see also Sternberg (1985:14–20), Baines (1991; 1996), and Loprieno (1996b). Note also Brunner-Traut (1986; 1988).

[3]The Elder Horus is a sibling of Osiris, Isis and Seth, while the Younger Horus is the son of Isis and Osiris. Griffiths (1970:338, n.1) notes fifteen different forms of Horus in ancient Egyptian texts. On the conflict, see Griffiths (1960), especially 28–41 for the mutilations. Plutarch describes a statue of Horus holding the severed genitals of Seth in *De Iside et Osiride* 55 (hereafter *DIO*) (see Griffiths 1960:207, 333–34). For Seth, see Hornung (1975) and te Velde (1977). On the ambiguity of the male kinship term *sn*, see Robins (1979)

[4]Apparently unknown to Oden, Leach (1976) has also offered a structuralist analysis of the "mother's brother" motif in this myth. I thank Gay Robins for the citation.

[5]See also Robert Paul's (1996) consideration of Oedipus in ancient Egypt (esp. 1996:30–33). I found Paul's book only after the completion of my own analysis.

[6]For descriptions of psychoanalytic theory and its relevance for myth interpretation, see Caldwell (1989:18–70; 1990). Caldwell (1989:ix) assumes that "myths have three purposes in addition to whatever nonpsychological functions they may fulfill: these are (1) to allow the expression of unconscious, usually repressed, ideas in a conventional and socially sanctioned form; (2) to use the emotional content attached to these ideas to energize the nonemotional function of myth; and (3) to provide a societal response to psychological needs, whether universal or culture-specific, shared by individuals who make up the society." See also Eisner (1987) on psychoanalytic approaches to ancient texts. The folklorist Alan Dundes has long argued for a psychoanalytic approach to various cultural projection systems, including myths and folklore (see 1980:33–61; 1987; 1996).

[7]While much Freudian analysis focuses on either the origins of myth in childhood fantasy or the function of myth in its original social context, I have the more modest goal of a literary interpretation of the text's contents (see Willbern 1989).

[8]Wright (1998) provides a critical overview of Freudian and post-Freudian psychoanalytic approaches to literary and cultural criticism. On ego-psychology and myth, see the bibliography in Segal (1990:xxxiv, n. 16).

[9]See Hornung 1983. The complicated relationship between deities is also manifested in the identity of one as the ba or ka of another (see Hornung 1992:183–84).

[10]Egyptian mythology often identifies Isis and Hathor as aspects of the same goddess (Hollis 1990:174–75). Hathor is the actual mother of Horus in some ancient Egyptian sources. Her name (*ḥt.ḥr*) means "House of Horus," with "house" poetically referring to the womb.

[11]See Lederer 1968:218–19. On castration in Egyptian myths, see Hollis (1990:104–14).

[12]Griffiths 1970:147. Note also Rank's (1990:36) discussion of the hero's common physical defect at birth.

[13]Pre is a common New Kingdom writing of the name Re with the addition of the definite article.

[14]See Lubell 1994, Olender 1990, Clair 1989, and Devereux 1983. The earliest sources do not mention the skirt-raising gesture in their description of the lewd jokes told by the maidservant Iambe, but scholars routinely associate this mythic scene and ancient iconography with the divine name of Baubo.

[15]Contra Lubell (1994:178), who argues that Re has a bisexual nature and suggests that Hathor may be unveiling herself to the "mother aspect"

rather than the "father aspect" of Re.

[16]We can only speculate about humorous possibilities not mentioned, such as whether Hathor was shaved smooth, as some of the Baubo traditions suggest, or revealed a hermaphrodite identity.

[17]Contra Lubell (1994:178): "In my reading, this is no simple act of seduction. No erotic arousal is implicit in Hathor's stance. The lady of the southern sycamore is not attempting to titillate her father; she is arousing his humor, his laughter, in order to return Re to a saner view of the problem, to help him regain balance." Lubell's depiction seems markedly inconsistent with Hathor's usual mythological roles. Compare Devereux 1983:55–57.

[18]Hollis 1990:174. The Papyrus Jumilhac is discussed and translated by Hollis (1990:47–48, 68–70, 171–76), with notes and bibliographic references.

[19]See Róheim 1972. Róheim explains that at some point in the child's development the boy identifies with his mother to the extent that he believes that they must both either have or not have a penis. Rather than confront the possibility that the mother has been castrated, the child fantasizes that the mother also has a penis. Citations are to the reprint.

[20]See Säve-Söderbergh (1953:34–35). Note the aggressive and violent depictions of hippos attacking each other, biting crocodiles, etc., in the comprehensive study by Behrmann (1989: documents 78, 89a, 90b and c, 215c, and 221). Säve-Söderbergh (1953:45–55) also considers the more positive symbolic value of the female hippopotamus, such as Opet and Taweret. He (1953:46) states, "In ancient Egypt…the evil aspect of the animal applied to the male animal only, whereas the female hippopotamus was practically always a benign and good divinity, a form of mother goddess, who protected pregnant women, small children (including the Horus child), sleepers and the weak or sick."

[21]Plutarch *DIO* 20, in Griffiths (1970:147, 149). Various psychoanalytic interpretations of Isis's role in this scene are certainly possible. My focus on Horus's oedipal complex, however, emphasizes only the role of Isis in relation to her son's psychosexual development.

[22]In his discussion of Perseus and Medusa, Slater (1968:310) describes the decapitation of the mother as "maternal de-sexualization" in which the emotional goal is "to restore the mother to the son as a nurturing, nonsexual being who gives all and asks nothing." In contrast to Slater, I will argue that Horus's oedipal drive causes him to desire Isis as both a maternal and a sexual figure.

[23]An alternative Freudian analysis of these episodes could interpret Horus's violent anger as the result of his desire to return to the pre-birth symbiotic state, symbolized by his immersion in the water. Horus's anger at Isis would be for removing him from the bliss of the womb through the stimulation of pain (see Caldwell 1990:358). Horus may be caught between his regressive desire for the womb's symbiotic state and his developing desire for individual autonomy, Slater's (1968:88) "oral-nascissistic dilemma." The violence of his attack on Isis could similarly be explained as the preoedipal child's body-destruction fantasy in reaction to his frustrated desires (see Róheim 1992:23; 1972:189, 194–95).

[24]E.g., Slater 1968:319–20. Note also the essays in Eilberg-Schwartz and Doniger (1995).

[25]On lotus symbolism in Egypt, see Dittmar (1986: passim, 132–33), Griffiths (1970:290), Hornung (1992:41), and Spells 81a and 81b in Faulkner (1990:79).

[26]The symbolism of gazelle milk is unclear to me, although Broze (1996:248–251) argues that the gazelle is in fact a manifestation of Hathor in this context. The gazelle is identified with dangerous Sethian animals in the Horus cippi, magical incantations to ward off scorpion and crocodile attacks (see Ritner 1993:106, n. 518), but it is also associated with the nude goddess in various Egyptian and Canaanite sources, and nude young women generally in Egyptian art. Unfortunately, we cannot explore, much less resolve, the complexities of Egyptian gazelle symbolism in this chapter.

[27]On homosexuality in Egyptian literature, see Manniche (1987:22–27) and Parkinson (1995). Seth's sexuality is unconventional by most standards. His wife, Nephthys, is called the "imitation woman who has no vagina" in Pyramid Text 1273 (Faulkner 1969:201).

[28]A psychoanalytic reading could also identify latent anxiety over masturbation. Dundes (1980:53) remarks, "Hands are commonly used in initiating masturbatory fantasy and therefore might provide appropriate 'sinning' objects to be punished." Horus projects his guilt by saying that it is Seth's semen, not his own, on his hands.

[29]World mythology has numerous examples of oral impregnation; for examples see O'Flaherty (1980:48–53). Compare the oral impregnation of Bata's wife by a splinter of wood in Egyptian myth (see Hollis 1990:152).

[30]Compare O'Flaherty's discussion of the symbolic value of semen, milk, and blood in Hindu myths (1980:17–61).

[31] Plutarch *DIO* 18; see Griffiths 1970:145, 342–43; see also Hollis 1990:108–9.

[32]Pyramid Text 1273, in Faulkner 1969:201. In addition to Horus's traditional castration of Seth, the Papyrus Jumilhac (III, 18–19 and XX, 16–18) twice depicts Anubis emasculating Seth (see Hollis 1990:171, 174). Seth's strained relationships with females is further reflected in his violent and unnatural birth through Nut's side instead of her vagina (Plutarch *DIO* 12, in Griffiths 1970:135).

[33]Ironically, Seth is the more appropriate role model in his transition from the Pleasure to the Reality Principle. Neith's suggestion that he be given Re's daughters as wives (3, 4) demonstrates his opportunity to transfer the object of his erotic desire from Isis to other women. Seth makes the transition from his impossible oedipal desires at the beginning of the myth to accept the reality of his position at the end, where he receives a new father (16, 4), wives, and a respectable position among the gods.

[34]See Hollis 1990:153–55, with bibliography. Griffiths (1960:91) also points out the clearly sexual overtones of the title, "Bull of His Mother."

[35]Doniger writes, "Often the explicit content of a myth will give a broad hint as to how it might be interpreted: if it is about castration, try Freud; if it is about heresy, try theology. In the first analysis, it pays to be literal-minded…" (O'Flaherty 1980:5).

CHAPTER 3

Desire in Death's Realm: Sex, Power, and Violence in "Nergal and Ereshkigal"

For love is as strong as death;
Passion, as fierce as the grave.
Its flames are flames of fire,
  a roaring blaze.
(Song of Songs 8:6–7)

INTRODUCTION

"Nergal and Ereshkigal" is a small but brilliant gem of a myth that sparkles with intrigue and wit.[1] It is a fiery story of passion and conflict, seduction and betrayal, struggle and surrender. Its narrative spans the chasm between heaven and hell as it dramatizes the thin line between love and hate. Called a "love story" by some scholars, the myth of Nergal and Ereshkigal appears to be a simple but elegant tale of boy meets girl, boy loses girl, boy gets girl—or, more accurately, boy insults girl, girl tries to kill boy, boy and girl make passionate love, etc.[2] Yet, the plot is more elusive and the subject more profound than the travails of adolescent infatuation. The narrative deftly combines elements of romance and political intrigue with dark humor and a macabre setting to depict the passions and pathos of desire. Nergal and Ereshkigal's stormy affair begins as a contest of strategy and guile. Their courtship progresses as a fencing match with feints and posturing, thrusts and parries, sudden attack and strategic withdrawal. Seduction and erotic delight are introduced as mere tactics in the negotiations as the deities vie for dominion. In the end, however, the flames of passion prove to be fiercer than the threat of hell in this winsome myth of desire in Death's realm.

As a myth about politics and sovereignty, "Nergal and Ereshkigal" portrays the schemes and quarrels of the gods—their powers and privileges, honors and responsibilities. This clever myth of divine affairs and political agendas expresses an ironic sense of humor, a whimsy that belies its fearsome setting in the land of the dead.[3] Jean Bottéro (1992b:245) suggests that the entire myth is a play on words or trick of Ea, in that Ereshkigal summons Nergal to the Netherworld "for death" (*ana mūti*) but instead takes him "for a husband" (*ana muti*).[4] A dark comedy at best, the myth determines who will rule in hell. The Netherworld context symbolically conveys the dangers inherent to political and sexual negotiations. Like a Hollywood horror film, the myth threatens to open the gates of hell and set free its inhabitants in an ancient "Night of the Living Dead," when corpses arise from their graves to feast on living flesh. The reader is made to understand that sex and politics arouse fierce and consuming passions. It is no coincidence that Camille Paglia (1990:3) uses underworld imagery to describe the power of sex and its taboos when she says, "Eroticism is a realm stalked by ghosts. It is a place beyond the pale, both cursed and enchanted." The ancients recognized a similar truth as they told the passionate tale of divine courtship set within Ereshkigal's dark domain.

The myth of Nergal and Ereshkigal survives in two related but distinct versions (see Foster 1993:410–13). The earlier edition (c. 1500–1300 BCE) is represented by a short text of about 90 lines in a Middle Babylonian (MB) dialect discovered among the ruins of el-Amarna (EA 357).[5] The later recension is attested by a large (c. 440 lines), eighth-century Assyrian tablet from Sultantepe and fragments of a Late Babylonian tablet from Uruk.[6] Both editions begin with a banquet of the heavenly gods. Ereshkigal's emissary, Namtar, arrives to collect her portion from the feast, since she cannot leave her Netherworld domain to visit heaven. All of the gods except Nergal show their deference to Namtar and his queen by rising and kneeling. When Ereshkigal learns of her envoy's reception, she is incensed by Nergal's disrespect and demands that the insolent god present himself before her. Nergal eventually descends to the Netherworld to confront the angry queen. Although the two editions diverge in their treatment of Namtar's missions to heaven and Nergal's descent(s) to the Netherworld, both editions apparently conclude with the union of

Nergal and Ereshkigal as king and queen of the Netherworld. In contrast to the Amarna text's terse yet vivid style, the Sultantepe edition reflects a developed literary style with elaborate, formulaic language and a high degree of intertextuality with other Standard Babylonian (SB) mythological literature of the first millennium (see Voglezang 1992:271–77). This study follows the Sultantepe edition, using O. R. Gurney's (1960) citations of columns and lines, with additions from the Uruk tablet (Hunger 1976:17–19) to restore broken lines.[7] The Amarna text is cited mainly for contrasts and comparisons with the later edition. In an effort to avoid confusion between recensions, quotes from the Amarna tablet are always cited by EA, followed by the line number from Shlomo Izre'el's (1997) edition. Before turning to the Sultantepe edition of "Nergal and Ereshkigal," a summary of the Amarna myth's distinctive features is in order.

There is little intrigue and no eroticism in the Amarna text's simpler story of honor, respect, power, and violence. The imperious Ereshkigal is outraged by Nergal's insult and immediately charges Namtar to fetch the disrespectful god from heaven with an explicit intent: "Bring him to me that I may kill him!" (*ana muḫḫīya šūbilannīšū-ma ludūkšu*; EA, 27). The gods do not resist Ereshkigal's authoritative demands, but Namtar is unable to identify the disguised Nergal and returns to his queen having failed in his mission. Although the next lines are fragmentary, it appears that Ereshkigal takes no further action at this point (EA, 39–40). Ea, however, instructs Nergal to descend to the Netherworld, perhaps to deliver a chair to the offended queen. Nergal is truly afraid of Ereshkigal and her infernal realm in this edition: "Nergal was weeping before Ea his father, 'She will see me and not let me live!'" (*iba*[*kki Nergal*] *ana pāni Ea abīšu immaranni ul uballaṭanni*; EA, 43–45). Ea has a scheme, of course, and tells Nergal to have no fear (*lā pal*[*ḫāta*]; EA, 45) since he will be accompanied on his journey by fourteen divine helpers. When Nergal and his entourage arrive at the Netherworld gates, the gatekeeper sends for Namtar to identify the visitors. Namtar is elated (*ḫadi danniš*) when he recognizes Nergal, and he quickly runs (*ilsum*) to tell his mistress that the missing god is at the gate (EA, 57–58). Still intent on punishing the impertinent deity, Ereshkigal instructs Namtar to bring Nergal before her, "that I may kill him" (*ludūkšu*; EA, 60). Nergal, however, stations his troops at the gates and rushes in to Ereshkigal's courtyard, where "he overcomes his fear" (*ḫurbāša ina tarbaṣi ittakis*; EA, 74) and launches a swift assault.[8] With courage renewed, Nergal confronts the enthroned queen (EA, 77–79):

ina libbi bīti iṣṣabat Ereškigal	In the midst of the house he seized Ereshkigal
ina šartīša uqeddidaššī-ma ištu kussî	by the hair. He pulled her down from the throne
ana qaqqari qaqqassa ana nakāsi	to the ground in order to cut off her head.

Nergal's brutal violence and lethal intentions stand in stark contrast to the negotiations and diplomacy of the Sultantepe text, as we will see below. Grabbing Ereshkigal by her hair demonstrates Nergal's complete domination of the woman and the situation.[9] Rivkah Harris (2000:133–34) notes this passage's use of the verb *quddudu*, "to bend over, to make prostrate," to emphasize Ereshkigal's humiliation as she lies prostrate at Nergal's feet.[10] Rather than kneel in homage to the Netherworld queen, Nergal forces her to bow before his superior power.

Ereshkigal, who wanted Nergal killed for not showing proper deference to her authority, is unmasked as a defenseless woman who cannot resist the warrior god's violent aggression. In her terror, Ereshkigal makes a desperate plea to save herself in the tablet's final lines (EA, 80–88):

lā tadūkanni aḫūya amāta luqbâkku	"Do not kill me, my brother! Let me speak a word to you."
išmīšī-ma Nergal irmâ qātāšu ibakki uddaḫḫas	Nergal heard her and loosened his grip. She was weeping and distraught (as she said,)
atta lū mutī-ma anāku lū aššatka lušeṣbitka	"You be my husband and I will be your wife! Let me cause you to seize

šarrūta ina erṣeti rapašti luškun ṭuppa	kingship over the wide Netherworld. Let me place the tablet
ša nēmeqi ana qātīka atta lū bēlu	of wisdom in your hand. You be lord,
anāku lū bēltu Nergal išmē-ma annâ qabâša	I will be lady!" Nergal listened to what she said.
iṣbassī-ma unaššaqši dimtaša ikappar	He seized her and kissed her; he wiped away her tears (saying,)
minâm-ma terrišīnni ištu arḫānī ullûti	"What do you desire from me? For many months...."
adu kīnanna	Thus far.[11]

Ereshkigal's subjugation is complete as she voluntarily surrenders her authority to Nergal (*lušeṣbitka šarrūta*; *luškun...ana qātīka*; EA, 82–83). Nergal's brute strength, supported by Ea's wisdom, is more than sufficient to overcome the powers of the Netherworld and compel the submission of its queen.

The Sultantepe edition differs from the Amarna plot by incorporating two descents of Nergal to the underworld and the deities' greater use of deceit and manipulation as they vie for dominance. The violence of the Amarna text is replaced by deception and seduction, as Nergal spends six days in bed with the Netherworld queen on his first visit before sneaking out of her realm during the night. Yearning for the return of her lover, Ereshkigal threatens the gods with catastrophic retribution if they do not send him back to her. She dispatches Namtar to heaven, but he is unable to locate the disguised Nergal. Eventually, Nergal again descends to the dark realm, where he and Ereshkigal go passionately to bed for another week. The last lines of the Sultantepe tablet have not been recovered, but it is most likely that Anu's message confirms their new relationship as the king and queen of Death's realm. Violence gives way to deception, and aggression is transformed into passion by the Sultantepe recension of "Nergal and Ereshkigal."

The stormy romance of Nergal and Ereshkigal adeptly represents the discourse concerning gender and sexual ideology in ancient Mesopotamian literature.[12] The importance of seduction, deception, and violence in the myth suggests that a feminist theory of power will provide a useful hermeneutical perspective on the mutli-faceted tale of courtship, politics, and conflict. This chapter thus explores the interrelated themes of sex, power, and violence in "Nergal and Ereshkigal" using a feminist analysis of power (see Allen 1999).[13] We will consider the use of manipulation, persuasion, coercion, and domination as strategies and techniques employed by characters to compel or constrain other characters' actions. We will investigate how the myth legitimates structures of authority and power, as well as how it challenges and subverts them. In applying a specifically feminist method, we will be especially concerned with how the exercise of power effects the goddess Ereshkigal, and how she in turn utilizes her resources to contest and resist the powers of the male pantheon.

As Cheryl Exum (1995:65) explains, feminist criticism "seeks to expose the strategies by which men have justified their control over women," to understand "women's complicity in their own subordination," and to consider how women have "adapted to and resisted the constraints" of patriarchal authority and power (cf. Torsney 1989). Exum (1995:69–70) writes that feminist literary criticism analyzes how a text both represents and suppresses women, women's voices, and women's concerns. It seeks to uncover the gender assumptions operative within a text and to explore their ideological ramifications. As a hermeneutics of suspicion, feminist criticism should inquire, "Whose interests are being served?" and "What androcentric agenda does the text support?" Does the text affirm the patriarchal control of female power to avert social chaos or does it portray women as positive and responsible role models? Exum stresses feminism's openness to multiple readings of a text, including reading against the grain, as forms of resistance to androcentric, patriarchal control of texts and their interpretation.

In response to these and related concerns of feminist theory, Amy Allen constructs a theory of power to help feminist theorists "comprehend, critique, and contest the subordination of women" (1999:121). Allen (1999:122–23) describes feminism's need to understand how men dominate women; how women are empowered to act while being dominated and as a response to domination (resistance); and the collective power of feminist solidarity and coalition-building. She refers to these three modalities as power-over, power-to, and power-with (see Allen 1999:123–29). Power-over is essentially the relational ability to constrain another's choices, up to and including oppressive domination. Power-to is roughly synonymous to "empowerment," an individual's ability to achieve a desired goal, with resistance as a form of empowerment that works "to challenge and/or subvert domination" (Allen 1999:126). Power-with is collective strength that applies to feminist solidarity as a means of affecting change. Allen emphasizes that the three categories are not forms of power so much as they are analytically distinguishable features within usually complex power relations. Among its other goals, a feminist theory of power needs to recognize the power of resistance wielded by subordinate or disenfranchised actors in "the complicated interplay between domination and empowerment" (Allen 1999:3). Allen thus provides analytical perspectives that will enable feminists to analyze and explain "masculine domination, feminine empowerment and resistance, and feminist solidarity and coalition-building" (1999:123).

Giving Death its Due

As the Sumerian etymology of her name reveals, Ereshkigal is the Queen of the Great Earth, the grim underworld of Mesopotamian mythology.[14] Among its many titles and euphemisms, the most important Akkadian literary terms for her dark realm include the Netherworld (*erṣetu*, literally "earth"), the Land of No Return (*erṣet lā târi*), Arallû, and Irkalla (from Sumerian eri-gal, "Great City").[15] The Netherworld is assigned to Ereshkigal as a gift or dowry (sag-rig$_7$) when the primordial cosmos is divided among the ruling gods in the Sumerian myth, "Gilgamesh, Enkidu, and the Netherworld."[16] While the male gods each carry off a share of the cosmos to rule, their unmarried sister receives a dowry that would transfer to the control of her husband upon marriage. Historically, Ereshkigal is paired with a variety of consorts at different times and places, including Gugalanna and Ninazu.[17] The myth of "Nergal and Ereshkigal," however, explains how Nergal becomes Lord of the Netherworld and Ereshkigal's (first) husband, a tradition reflected in

Old Babylonian (OB) religious texts that describe them as "Enlil and Ninlil of the Netherworld."[18]

Ereshkigal dwells in Ganzir, a palace at the entrance to the Netherworld, where she presides over the Anunnaki, "the gods of hell who delight in deathly stillness" (*Anunnaki rā'im šaḫrarti*).[19] Her primary role seems to be receiving the dead as they arrive and instructing them in the rules and practices of her infernal domain (Scurlock 1995:1887). As a goddess, Ereshkigal does not share in the repulsive or fearsome characteristics of other underworld denizens.[20] Rather than an angry devil who delights in the demise of others, Ereshkigal is a doleful figure in Mesopotamian myth, a benevolent goddess who rules over the realm of ghosts (*eṭemmu*) and demons (*gallû*). "The Underworld Vision of an Assyrian Prince" provides a rare glimpse of Ereshkigal making an appearance in a man's dreams, where she graciously says, "Let me hear your prayer that I may reveal what you desire" (*anākū-ma suppīka lušme ḫišiḫtaka lukallimka*; line 35) (Livingstone 1989:68–76; cf. Foster 1993:730–37). The man is then allowed a vision of the Netherworld in all of its terrifying splendor.

Similarly, at the beginning of "Nergal and Ereshkigal," the Netherworld queen is an authoritative and gracious ruler. The powerful god Namtar, whose name means "fate" and thus "death" (*CAD* s.v.), unquestioningly follows her orders, and the celestial gods accord her great honor and respect. Indeed, throughout the Sultantepe text, the gods kneel in obeisance only to Ereshkigal and her vizier (*sukkallu*), Namtar. When Anu's messenger, Kakka,[21] enters Ereshkigal's courtyard, he kneels and kisses the ground before her (*ikmisi iššiq qaqqaru maḫrīša*; i 28′). Queen Ereshkigal's reception of Kakka is gracious and cordial, as she inquires about the well-being of various celestial deities (i 39′–43′). Her polite questions contrast with Anu's abrupt message, which begins without greetings, salutations or blessings, and contribute to her portrayal as a gracious and noble queen. When Nergal arrives before the throne of Ereshkigal, he also kneels and kisses the ground before her (*ikmis iššiq qaqqara maḫrīša*; iii 49′) in a (belated) display of submission to her authority. More suprisingly, the assembled gods kneel before Namtar (*ilānī ina pānīšu ištēniš kansū*) as one who bears the authority of the Netherworld gods (*ukalla parṣī ilānī*) when he enters the heavenly courtyard (ii 4′–7′). In his study of messengers in the ancient Near East, Samuel Meier (1988:159) concludes that the subordinate character always pays homage to the superior or his/her representative in Mesopotamian etiquette. Since Ereshkigal certainly possesses a lower rank and status than Anu, Enlil, and Ea, it is rather the fearsome character of her realm that must motivate the gods to show such deference in this myth.[22] The supernal gods understand that death must be given its due.

Nergal, however, refuses to kneel in honor of death's emissary. Ea accuses Nergal of only pretending not to understand his signals to kneel before Namtar (*têrāta lā mudê-ma*; ii 10′). The myth does not explain Nergal's motivation for his reckless disregard for Ereshkigal's authority; it may be chauvinistic pride, disrespect for the realm of the dead, or unthinking hubris. Ereshkigal's initial response to Nergal's insolence is also unfortunately lost to breaks in the Sultantepe tablet (c. twenty-six lines at the end of the first and beginning of the second columns). In the Amarna text, the Netherworld queen commissions Namtar to retrieve Nergal so that she may kill him (EA, 27), but it is unlikely that Namtar is sent to fetch the impertinent god in the Sultantepe edition. Rather, Namtar returns to Ereshkigal's realm, where he nurses a grudge until Nergal shows up at the Netherworld gates (see iii 20′–22′). Indeed, Benjamin Foster (1993:410–11) suggests that Namtar returns home empty-handed in protest of Nergal's disrespect and that Ereshkigal, in mortification or outrage, refuses to sit on her throne and rule the Netherworld (as in v 7′). Her abdication throws the celestial gods into consternation and Nergal is required to descend to the Netherworld to appease the offended queen (cf. Gurney 1960:111). Foster's suggestion is plausible, since Anu's message to Ereshkigal seems to be for her to resume her royal duties (iii 51′–52′, following Uruk iv 6–7):

ina kussî annî tišab-ma	Sit upon this throne and
dīnī dīnī ša ilānī rabûti	Render judgment for the great gods,
ilānī rabûti āšibi qereb Irkalla	the great gods who dwell in the midst of Irkalla.

Interpreters, however, disagree on the significance of this passage.[23] Gwendolyn Leick (1994:251–52), among others, holds that Anu's instructions are addressed to Nergal, who repeats them to Ereshkigal to convey his willingness to rule the Netherworld in her place. If so, then Anu and Ea have given Nergal contradictory instructions about sitting in the chair (ii 40′) as part of a ruse of some kind. It seems more likely, however, that Anu's instructions are for Ereshkigal to resume her royal duties after Nergal has placated her with proper obeisance to her authority (iii 49′).

In fact, scholars have put forward various explanations for Nergal's motives in traveling to Ereshkigal's realm. A summons to the Land of No Return by its imperious ruler is a one-way journey for all but a select few. Inana-Ishtar's presumptuous decision to enter the dark realm without invitation leads directly to her death. The fact that gods can die in ancient Near Eastern myth needs no elaboration (see Cassin 1987:226–35; cf. Abusch 1998). In the Sultantepe tablet, Nergal's fragmentary remarks (ii 17′–20′) and Ea's reply (ii 21′–24′) indicate that Nergal makes the journey of his own volition (or the gods' urging) rather than in response to Ereshkigal's imperious summons. The relevant text (ii 12′–20′) is fragmentary, but Nergal shows no fear concerning the journey as he does in the Amarna text (EA, 43–45) where he is summoned to come and die.

Erica Reiner (1985:56) argues that Nergal arrives in the Netherworld "incognito and under false pretenses" as Anu's messenger. She (1985:57) states that only messengers have the diplomatic immunity to move freely between the realms of heaven and the Netherworld, while the gods cannot transgress these boundaries without penalty.[24] Ereshkigal refers to Nergal as "Anu's messenger" (*mār šipri ša Ani*; e.g., iv 44′; Uruk v 1) because he relays Anu's words to her, but Reiner's argument that Nergal is in disguise is harder to substantiate. Ereshkigal identifies Erra as her absconded lover in her complaint to the gods (iv 53′–56′). Although there is a long and ancient tradition of their common identity, Reiner (1985:58–59) suggests that Nergal is distinct from Erra in this myth.[25] In her interpretation, Nergal impersonates another god to keep from revealing his true name to the Netherworld queen. When Nergal arrives at the Netherworld and the gatekeeper calls for someone to identify the unknown visitor (iii 9′–13′), Namtar recognizes him as the god who refused to pay him homage in heaven (iii 24′–27′; cf. Uruk iii 1–3) and reports this fact to his queen. Reiner neglects to note that the narrator affirms that "Namtar looked at Erra" through the bars of the gate (*ippalaššu Erra*; iii 20′) and later "brought in the god Erra" (Uruk iii 21′), thus identifying Nergal with Erra. Although Nergal will resort to various stratagems and tricks in his contest with Ereshkigal, there is little evidence that he pretends to be other than he is: a brash and arrogant warrior god, unafraid of even Death's realm. Likewise, it is difficult to believe that Ereshkigal is unaware of her visitor's identity before she seduces him.

Finally, Nergal may enter the Netherworld with the intention of usurping the throne, seducing Ereshkigal, or otherwise pacifying the angry Netherworld queen. His motives remain unclear to modern interpreters. Whatever his intention, however, Nergal risks all by traveling to the abode of Ereshkigal, where death awaits in the form of an alluring woman.

CRUCIBLE OF DESIRE

The biblical book of Proverbs warns against the "forbidden" or "alien woman" (*šiššâ zārâ, nokrîyâ*) who lures the simple young man into her house with promises of illicit sex (Prov 7:5). She coaxes the youth to her perfumed bed with seductive speech, saying, "Come, let us drink our fill of love until the morning, let us delight ourselves with lovemaking" (*lkh nrwh ddym ğd-hbqr ntğlsh bšhbym*; Prov 7:18). The young man is admonished to resist her charms and reject her invitation (Prov 7:26),

> For many are those she has brought down to death,
> And numerous are her victims.
> Her house is the path to the grave,
> Leading down to Death's inner chambers.

The young man's defense against the forbidden woman, whose houseguest is already counted among the Netherworld shades (Prov 9:18), is the teachings of Lady Wisdom, who invites him into her house for instruction in righteousness. Like Proverbs, the myth of "Nergal and Ereshkigal" employs the threat of the dangerous woman who seeks to seduce and lead to death. Indeed, what woman could be more forbidden, what land more alien, than Ereshkigal and her Netherworld domain? But just as Wisdom's instruction will guard the youth against the deceitful hospitality of the alien woman, Nergal is protected from Ereshkigal's lethal charms by the wise counsel of Ea, the cunning god of wisdom in Mesopotamian mythology.

The trickery of Ea plays a crucial role in "Nergal and Ereshkigal," as it does in many other Mesopotamian myths.[26] Ea is responsible for transforming Nergal into an unrecognizable form (iv 31′–32′) so that he may elude capture by Namtar, as Ereshkigal shrewdly realizes (v 39′–41′). Ea also counsels Nergal on the construction of a particular chair that seems to have a crucial, if enigmatic, function in at least one of Nergal's descents.[27] In the Amarna version, Ea seems to play his usual role as "the god of last resort" (Kramer and Maier 1989:129) when Nergal comes weeping to him about his (enforced) descent to Ereshkigal's realm (EA, 43–47). Ea provisions Nergal with fourteen divine helpers and probably suggests the plan to attack the undefended queen (EA, 46–47). In the Sultantepe edition of the myth, Ea chides Nergal for not bowing in honor of Namtar (ii 8′–11′) but then counsels him for success in his mission to the Netherworld. Although the details of Ea's scheme are lost to a fragmentary text, the myth recounts Ea's intentionality as "he said to himself, 'I will bring it about…'" (*zikra ittami ana libbīšu [lušt]ēpiš*, ii 21′–22′). Bottéro (1992b:245) surmises that Ea only pretends to help Nergal remain among the supernal gods while he purposefully manipulates events to insure that Nergal will become the new Netherworld ruler. According to Bottéro, Ea perpetrates this ruse in order to "colonize" the Great Below for the celestial gods by installing their own representative on the throne. While Ea may indeed manipulate events for his own purposes, gender is a more significant factor than family in this myth of divine politics.

Especially relevant for the analysis of "Nergal and Ereshkigal" is Ea's clever machinations in the myth, "Adapa and the South Wind." Adapa is called to heaven to account for breaking the south wind through magical power learned from Ea. The wily god instructs Adapa on how to ingratiate himself with Anu's counselors and thus avoid a severe punishment. When Adapa finally arrives in Anu's court, he is offered the food of the gods to make him immortal (lines 77–80):[28]

akal balāṭi ilqûniššum-ma ul īkul	They brought him the bread of life but he did not eat.
mê balāṭi ilqûniššum-ma ul ilti	They brought him the water of life but he did not drink.
lubāra ilqûniššum-ma ittalbaš	They brought him a garment and he put it on.
šamna ilqûniššum-ma ittapšiš	They brought him oil and he anointed himself.

Anu laughs when he recognizes the hand of Ea behind Adapa's inconsistent behavior and unwitting rejection of immortality:[29]

Anu ana epšēt Ea šaqîš iṣīḫ-ma	Anu laughed heartily at what Ea had done,
ina ilānī ša ani erṣetim mala bašû mannu kiam ippuš	"Of all the gods of heaven and earth, who else could accomplish something like this?
qibīssu ša kīma qibīt Anu mannu uwattar	Who else could make his own command outweigh the command of Anu?"

In a particularly ingenious bit of subterfuge, Ea had previously misled Adapa concerning Anu's hospitable intentions, saying (lines 36–41):

akala ša mūti ukallūnikkum-ma lā takkal	They will offer you the bread of death, so do not eat.
mê mūti ukallūnikkum-ma lā tašatti	They will offer you the water of death, so do not drink.
lubāra ukallūnikkum-ma litbaš	They will offer you a robe; put it on.
šamna ukallūnikkum-ma piššaš	They will offer you oil; anoint yourself.
ṭēma ša aškunūka lā temekki	Do not neglect the instruction I have given you,

amāta ša aqbâkku lū ṣabtāta	You should accept the advice I have shared with you.

Thus, through manipulating both Adapa and, indirectly, the ruling gods of heaven, Ea achieves his purpose of keeping the mortal Adapa in his service on earth.

Similarly, in "Nergal and Ereshkigal" Ea instructs Nergal to avoid the food and drink of the Netherworld (ii 36′–48′):[30]

u šâšu issī-ma išakkanaššu ṭēma	(Ea) spoke to him and gave him instructions,
mār ḫarrāni terrišu tallak	"Traveler, if you desire to go,
mimmû têrēti … ina libbi …	[Take] to heart all of the directions [I give you.]
ultu ullânum-ma kussâ našûnikka	When you are there and they bring you a chair,
ē-tamīr-ma ē-tušib ina muḫḫi	You must not proceed to sit upon it.
nuḫatimmu alkī našīka ē-tamīr-ma aklīšu ē-tākul	When the baker serves you bread, you must not proceed to eat his bread.
ṭābiḫu šīra našīka ē-tamīr-ma šīršu ē-tākul	When the butcher serves you meat, you must not proceed to eat his meat.
sirāšû šikarī našīka ē-tamīr-ma šikarī ē-tašti	When the brewer serves you beer, you must not proceed to drink the beer.
mesītu šēpē našīka ē-tamīr-ma šēpēka ē-tamsi	When someone brings water for your feet, you must not proceed to wash your feet.
šī ana narmaki īrum-ma	When she herself enters the bath,
lubūši … illabiš	And she is clothed in a … garment,
… zumurša uštabarrâkka	… and she reveals her body to you,
atta ša zikar u sinniš ē-tašši libbīka	You must not become aroused as a man for a woman.

Ea's advice seems genuine in this case, as he apparently intends to protect Nergal from Ereshkigal's attempts to kill or imprison him. Indeed, Ea has tricked Ereshkigal before. He cheats her out of her rightful spoils of battle when he commissions his creatures to resurrect the corpse of Inana-Ishtar in both the Akkadian and Sumerian versions of Ereshkigal's conflict with her younger sister. In "Inana's Descent to the Netherworld," Enki (Ea) specifically instructs his two agents to accept no water or food from the underworld queen (lines 246–48; Sladek 1974:172). Thus, Ea's support of Nergal against the inimical powers of Ereshkigal is consistent with his actions in other myths and shows the intertextuality of the mythological corpus.

Ereshkigal's Wiles

Nergal delivers his message to the Netherworld queen (iii 50′–53′) and, as Ea predicted, is immediately offered a chair, bread, meat, beer, and a footbath, all of which he declines (iii 54′–59′). The sumptuous food offered to Nergal is inconsistent with the meager fare usually associated with Netherworld cuisine. In fact, the narrative has already informed the reader that Irkalla is a severe and destitute realm, "whose inhabitants are deprived of light; where dust is their sustenance and clay is their bread" (*āšibūšu zummû nūra ašar epru bubūssina akalšina ṭiṭṭi*; iii 2–3, restored from parallels). We will return to this matter below. The text moves quickly on, however, as in the very next line (iii 60′) Ereshkigal enters her bath and exhibits her nude body to Nergal. He apparently heeds Ea's counsel, restrains his ardor, and resists her feminine allure before the text breaks off completely (iii 63′). In light of Ea's explicit directions to avoid all forms of Netherworld hospitality, it is most plausible to assume that acceptance of Ereshkigal's gifts would somehow imprison Nergal within the realm of death. This magical prescription is nowhere stated in the myth of "Nergal and Ereshkigal," but the example of Adapa, who would have been immortal had he partaken of the gods' food while in heaven, suggests this understanding (Reiner 1985:52). In addition, there is the attractive parallel from Greek mythology of Persephone's seasonal residence in Hades's realm as a consequence of eating pomegranate seeds. So, while it remains possible that Ea's instructions have some other devious purpose, it is most likely that Ereshkigal does offer Nergal the equivalent of the food and drink of death. Ereshkigal's fraudulent hospitality thus invokes the image of the deceitful woman who attempts to poison a male guest in her home.

Beginning her survey with Eve offering Adam a bite of the forbidden fruit, Margaret Hallissy (1987) investigates the motif of the poison lady or "venomous woman" in Western literary tradition. Hallissy identifies as venomous the woman who secretly poisons men under the facade of hospitality. As readers of murder mysteries know, after all, poison is a woman's weapon of choice. Poison is hard to detect and harder to prove; it surreptitiously avoids the violence of direct confrontation. A woman's conjugal or social duty to prepare and serve food and drink provides her the opportunity to exert her power over an unwary male (1987:9). Cooking is already a mysterious and transformative process, analogous to alchemy, witchcraft, and the brewing of magical potions. The literary theme of the venomous woman, according to Hallissy (1987:xiv), manifests a male fear of women's mysterious and secret powers, as symbolized by their hidden reproductive organs. Carole Fontaine (1988) similarly addresses the common association of deceptive women with food, sex, and death in the Hebrew Bible and ancient Near Eastern myth. While she acknowledges the feminist critique of this androcentric motif's negative portrayal of women, Fontaine (1988:85) argues that the motif accurately reflects how any marginalized and disempowered person may resort to deception and manipulation in order to achieve desired goals. Fontaine (1988:97) holds that the ideological message of Jael, Judith, and Proverb's alien woman is that the hostess who offers food, drink, shelter, and sex may also be serving death. Although she does not mention this myth, we see the same theme at work in Ereshkigal's deceptive hospitality toward Nergal as a means to gain power over him.

Hallissy (1987:3) further associates the motif of the venomous woman with male mobility and female seclusion in the home. Like a black-widow spider patiently spinning a web to ensnare her prey, the woman waits for the man to enter her domestic space in search of refuge and relief. Hallissy (1987:3–4) explains the power dynamic implicit in this motif:

> What happens in the house is an indication of the balance of power between male and female. In the patriarchal order, he is supposed to be able to take from her what he needs and leave again, his powers restored. She meets his various needs: food, warmth, shelter, rest, sex. If she is not content to follow this role, her intent can be to keep him there, in her place. Seduction is one way to keep him there; poison is another. To keep the man inside is the triumph of the female; to go away again, having taken what he needs from the female but remaining free of her domination, is the triumph of the male.

Hallissy's remarks have a striking correlation with the power struggle between Nergal and Ereshkigal. As Fontaine (1988:96–97) points out, the meal or banquet scene gives the advantage to the host, who may lull the guest into a false sense of security before springing the trap. Nergal is not disarmed by Ereshkigal's subterfuge, however, because he has been forewarned by Ea's crafty insight. When Nergal rejects the poisonous food that she offers, Ereshkigal immediately turns to seduction as a means to overpower and dominate her visitor.

The goddess of death tempts Nergal with the sight of her nude body as she prepares to bathe. The text breaks off as Nergal, still following Ea's advice, resists Ereshkigal's allure (iii 63′). When the tablet is again legible (iv 5′), Ereshkigal is taking yet another bath. What transpires and how the plot progresses in the missing fourteen lines in unknown. Regardless, the Netherworld queen engages in a purposeful and manipulative provocation of Nergal by once again parading her nude form before his masculine gaze. The virile Nergal is unable to restrain his ardor any longer (iv 8′) and the two deities go off to bed for a week.

Like the modern image of the femme fatale (see Doane 1991:2), Ereshkigal's body is an enticement to death that she wields as a weapon, eventually overcoming the virile god's resolve to resist her charms. Ereshkigal's manipulation of Nergal's gaze alludes to other Akkadian myths, especially the Gilgamesh epic and "Ishtar's Descent to the Netherworld."[31] As mentioned in a previous chapter, the motifs of bathing and female nudity—whether Inana, Ninlil, Ninhursag and her daughters, Shamhat, Hathor, or Bathsheba—are powerful enticements to male arousal in ancient Near Eastern literature (see Hutter 1985:85–87). Ereshkigal's seduction of Nergal shares numerous elements with Shamhat's seduction of Enkidu, including the woman's silent exposure of her body, the male initiation of the actual lovemaking, a six-day sexual marathon, and the male's eventual residence in the Netherworld as a significant plot element. While Shamhat educates the innocent Enkidu in order to make him human, Ereshkigal manipulates Nergal as part of their power struggle. Each woman seduces the male in order to control him. The motif of Ereshkigal's nudity also alludes to the nakedness of Inana during her descent to challenge her sister's rule of the dead. The erotic goddess is stripped of her clothes before her audience with Ereshkigal as a sign of her powerlessness (see Katz 1995:221–25). In contrast, Ereshkigal's voluntary and provocative nudity represents her power over Nergal. Finally, as a successful seduction of a resistant male, this scene also provides an ironic contrast to Ishtar's failed seduction of Gilgamesh. Ereshkigal simply removes her clothes and incites Nergal to passion, even though he knows that it may mean his incarceration in the Netherworld; Ishtar's use of slippery language in her attempt to bed Gilgamesh fails partly because he recognizes the lethal truth behind her deceptive words. Female nudity incite males to passion, but female speech does not arouse men in these narratives. Literary allusions such as these combine to depict Ereshkigal as a desirable and powerful woman who plies her feminine charms more successfully than Ishtar, the goddess of eroticism.

Although Nergal's lack of restraint at the sight of a nude female is a typical male sexual response in Mesopotamian mythological literature, the text does not simply portray his arousal and initiation of sex. Instead, the text emphasizes the mutual passion of the two deities: "The two of them embraced one another and went passionately off to bed" (*innadrū-ma aḫāmeš kilallān ana mayyāli šitmuriš īterbū-ma*; iv 9′–10′; cf. vi 35–36). Far from the rape of the frigid queen of the dead, this is a fevered affair between two amorous deities (Harris 2000:135; cf. Hutter 1985:87–92). Ereshkigal's eagerness suggests a release of pent-up sexual energies in an explosion of erotic expenditure. Indeed, the dreary entrance to hell becomes a palace of pleasures for Nergal and Ereshkigal as they luxuriate in their passion for six days and nights. The significance of this impetuous scene is accentuated by the fact that it is the only instance of sexual activity within the Netherworld in all of ancient

Mesopotamian myth. Other texts may hint at the possibility—such as Enlil repeatedly seducing Ninlil as they travel toward the Netherworld (see Cooper 1980), or the more rustic example of Baal having sex with a cow on the pleasant shores of Death's realm in the Ugaritic corpus (see Smith 1997:148)—but none actually depicts sexual intercourse within the Land of No Return. As I argue in a previous chapter, the twelfth tablet of the SB Gilgamesh epic contends that passion is not possible for the insubstantial shades within the Netherworld. And, according to "Inana's Descent," underworld demons "never enjoy the pleasure of sexual intercourse."[32] Yet, poor Ereshkigal is neither shade nor demon; she is a living goddess, relegated to the infernal regions of the earth as caretaker of the dead, herself subject to the desires and frustrations of all women.

The harsh juxtaposition of fleshly sensuality—feasting, drinking, bathing, and sexual abandon—and the austere abode of the dead reaches its climax in this scene of Nergal's seduction. Scholars have perhaps over-emphasized the alleged taboo against sex in the underworld and the dichotomy between fertility and sterility in their interpretations of cuneiform literature (e.g., Sladek 1974:91), but there is indeed a natural opposition between healthy sexuality and the dismal realm of death and decay. Georges Bataille (1991:95–101), however, argues that prohibition, taboo, revulsion, and disgust all heighten the intensity of erotic pleasure and that "the knowledge of death deepens the abyss of eroticism" (1991:84) (cf. Dollimore 1998:249–57). Bataille (1986:20) envisions an intrinsic relationship between desire and death: "If the union of two lovers comes about through love, it involves the idea of death, murder, or suicide. This aura of death is what denotes passion." Whether or not Bataille's erotic philosophy is applicable to other contexts, it is most appropriate for the libidinal energy of "Nergal and Ereshkigal." Ereshkigal knowingly offers death to her lover, and Nergal risks virtual suicide by surrendering to his passions. Rather than being repulsed by the dreary realm of death, Nergal and Ereshkigal seem inspired to erotic extravagance.

Sex is introduced as part of the struggle for dominance between the competing deities. If eating Ereshkigal's food would have condemned Nergal to an eternity in the Netherworld as a dead god, do sexual relations with the Queen of the Dead consign him to the same fate? Ea's advice suggests that the enjoyment of Ereshkigal's body is part of the Netherworld hospitality to be avoided. If so, then Nergal has been defeated once he surrenders to Ereshkigal's allure. Alternatively, sexual provocation may be a desperate last resort for Ereshkigal after Nergal has foiled her plans to defeat him with the food of death. Perhaps Ea meant to warn Nergal against the entanglements of love simply because he knew Ereshkigal would compel him to remain in the Netherworld as her lover. Or, thirdly, Reiner (1985:53, 59, n. 6) suggests that Nergal may have been warned by Ea not to spend seven full days in the Netherworld, parallel to the rabbinical tradition that an angel who remains on earth for seven days cannot return to heaven. Perhaps Ereshkigal uses her allure to distract or stall Nergal, to keep him in her realm until his time runs out. The myth does not answer these questions or resolve these ambiguities as it emphasizes interpersonal dynamics more than legalities. Regardless, Ereshkigal overcomes Nergal with her sexuality; she conquers him through the traditionally feminine art of seduction in an effort to bend him to her will. As Susan Niditch (1989:52) points out, "Feminist scholars tell us that sex is politics; sex is a visceral means of asserting power." In this context, sex is a form of warfare.[33]

Ereshkigal sets the game when she attempts to conquer Nergal through deceptive hospitality and sex rather than outright combat. Like other venomous women, she is perceived as especially dangerous because her attack is surreptitious, in contrast to a warrior's direct confrontation. Having been coached by Ea, however, Nergal plays along by her rules and counters her attacks with his own strategic defenses. He gives in to her sexual overtures but then slips away from her realm—and out of her control—after exhausting the Netherworld queen with six days of erotic delight. Like Enkidu, who attempts to rejoin the running herds after his week with Shamhat in the Gilgamesh epic (I 178–85), Nergal abandons his lover to return to the company of his fellow gods in heaven. In contrast to Enkidu, however, Nergal is neither weakened nor transformed by sexual intercourse. In a reversal of the sexual stereotype, their erotic expenditure has exhausted Ereshkigal but failed to deplete his own masculine energies. The indefatigable Nergal makes good his escape while Ereshkigal enjoys her well-earned sleep.[34] Even if he must furtively sneak away before the dawn, Nergal triumphs in cutting loose the shackles of the Netherworld. To repeat Hallissy's (1987:3–4) explanation of the domestic politics, "To keep the man inside [the house] is the triumph of the female; to go away again, having taken what he needs from the female but remaining free of her domination, is the triumph of the male." Nergal thus receives a hero's welcome in heaven, where the gods celebrate his sexual prowess by hailing him as the "son of Ishtar" (iv 29′).

In addition to the trope of a lover absconding before the dawn, this scene in the Sultantepe text plays on the similarities of sleep and death. Ereshkigal has threatened Nergal with death, but he saves himself by lulling her to sleep with love. Sleep, like both love and death, pours over people, overpowering them and taking control of their senses (cf. Vermeule 1979:145–54). When chided by Shamash for wandering sleepless in his grief, Gilgamesh retorts that there will be plenty of time to sleep when he is dead: "Will not sleep be plentiful in the Netherworld? I will lie there all through the years!"[35] Nergal must escape his lover's embrace to avert a similar fate. The metaphor used by Gilgamesh in his mortal fear is literally true for him: "In my bedroom resides Death, and wherever I turn, there too will Death be!" (XI 240–41). Yet, Nergal can cheat death because he, unlike Gilgamesh (XI 207–12), is able to elude sleep for seven full days. In an unexpected twist on Ereshkigal's seduction, the warrior Nergal proves that he too can wield sex like a weapon to overcome his adversary. Through the shrewdness of Ea's advice and his own impeccable timing, Nergal survives his encounter with the desirable but venomous Ereshkigal and emerges from her lair before the morning light.

A GODDESS SCORNED

Unaware of Nergal's nocturnal flight from her domain, Ereshkigal apparently goes about a leisurely morning routine of bathing and ritual cleansing before taking her throne.[36] The imperious queen announces that her guest, who previously declined her hospitality, will now share her meal (iv 44′–45′; Uruk v 1):

mār šipri ša Ani abīni ša illikannâši	"The messenger of Anu, our father, who came to us,
aklīni līkul šikarni lišti	Let him eat our bread and drink our beer."

The polite invitation to table masks an ominous hazard. As in Ereshkigal's initial offer of hospitality, Nergal's acceptance of her food would acknowledge his imprisonment in her realm. Ereshkigal's statement thus implies that the visitor, having been seduced and detained for seven days, has already become a resident in her abode and a subject of her rule. As such, Nergal should no longer refuse her fare; indeed, he should be grateful to share in her royal provisions. Rather than gracious hospitality, therefore, Ereshkigal's invitation is a ploy to confirm Nergal's status as a permanent resident in Death's domain.

The duplicity of Ereshkigal's invitation is further indicated by her offer of bread and beer, when Netherworld residents usually consume only clay and muddy water. Ereshkigal may herself suffer similar privations as Mistress of the Dead, as she complains in "Ishtar's Descent": "For bread I eat clay; for beer I drink muddy water!" (*kīma aklī akkal ṭiṭṭa kīma šikari ašattâ mê dalḫūte*; 33) (see Borger 1963:88). The baker and brewer apparently tempt Nergal with real bread and beer in the first column of "Nergal and Ereshkigal," and a few other texts also depict the Netherworld gods enjoying a cuisine more suitable to their divinity. It is thus possible that Ereshkigal's words in "Ishtar's Descent" are rhetorical questions rather than declarative statements: "Shall I eat clay for bread?" (Reiner 1985:38). Nevertheless, Ereshkigal's complaint about her *akalu* and *šikaru* is consistent with other literary portrayals of the bleak condition of the dark Netherworld (including iii 3, quoted above). Similarly, in the Sumerian "Descent of Ur-Nammu" (lines 82–83), a deceased king is seated at the underworld banquet, where he discovers, "The food of the Netherworld is bitter; the water of the Netherworld is blood" (Kramer 1991:203; cf. 1967:118). Yet, even if Ereshkigal, as queen, enjoys bread and beer while the Netherworld inhabitants consume only clay and water, her defeat of Nergal would make him a subject of her realm, not its ruler. So, if Nergal were to accept the tempting bread and beer of Ereshkigal's palace, he would unwittingly consign himself to an unrelenting future of inconstant Netherworld fare.

Instead of confirming her dominance over Nergal with a celebratory meal, however, Ereshkigal discovers that the tables have been turned and she has been abandoned by her lover. Namtar breaks the news, "The messenger from Anu, our father, who came to us, made off before the light of dawn" (*mār šipri ša Ani abīni ša illikannâši lām urra inammiru šadâšu ītelû*) (iv 48′–49′; Uruk v 3).[37] No longer imperious and self-satisfied, Ereshkigal is exposed as a woman deceived and betrayed. Her anguished response expresses her desperation (iv 50′–56′; Uruk v 4–9):

Ereškigal uktabbit-ma iltasi malīt	Ereshkigal was stricken and let out a wail.
ultu muḫḫi kussî ana qaqqar intaqtu	She fell from her throne to the ground.
ultu qaqqar ušēšir ina īnēšu dimātu izannun	She got up from the ground as tears rained from her eyes.
eli dūr appīšu illakū dimāssu	Her tears flowed down her cheeks (as she cried),
Erra ḫāmeru lalêya	"Erra, my delightful lover!
ul ašbâ lalâšu ittalkanni	I was not sated with his delights when he left me!
Erra ḫāmeru lalêya	Erra, my delightful lover!
ul ašbâ lalâšu ittalkanni	I was not sated with his delights when he left me!"

Ereshkigal is truly heartbroken by her abandonment, for what began as a contest of wills has now turned into a romance for the lonely goddess. Having sought to enchant Nergal with her seductive allure, Ereshkigal instead finds herself constrained by her desire for the absconded god. Nergal's absence establishes his victory over the power of the Netherworld and the guile of its queen. In addition to relating her emotional distress, this scene is a portent of Ereshkigal's eventual dethronement by Nergal, as the queen falling to the ground foreshadows the god pulling her from her throne to the ground at the myth's conclusion.[38]

Ereshkigal's sorrowful wailing (*malītu*), swoon, and copious weeping express her grief in a manner that evokes traditional mourning rites for the dead. As ruler of the Netherworld she is no stranger to others' lamentations and woe, but Ereshkigal's anguished reaction attests to the depth of her own passions. In fact, Mesopotamian literature traditionally depicts Ereshkigal in a state of mourning.[39] Andrew George (1999:176) describes the "awful spectacle of Ereshkigal herself, who lies prostrate in perpetual mourning for her son Ninazu. The clothes torn from her body, she rakes her flesh with her nails and pulls out her hair." In "Ishtar's Descent" (lines 34–36), Ereshkigal describes her bleak realm and the sorrows of her office:[40]

lubki ana eṭlūti ša ēzibū ḫīrēti	Must I weep for the young men who leave behind wives?
lubki ana ardāti ša ultu sūn ḫāʾirīšina šallupāni	Must I weep for the young women who are torn from their husbands' laps?
ana šerri lakê lubki ša ina lā ūmēšu ṭardu	For the tender infant taken before its time, must I also weep?

Thus, even though Ereshkigal embodies the inimical power of the grave that separates humans from their loved ones, she is also a compassionate woman who weeps for the pitiful souls in her charge. In a leap of mythological imagination, the Queen of the Netherworld is also portrayed suffering her own bereavement. And, as if to compound her woes, the myth of "Nergal and Ereshkigal" adds to her troubles the betrayal of an absconded lover.

Indeed, Ereshkigal's lament for the absent Nergal is similar to a bride's grief over a deceased husband (cf. Alster 1983). Ereshkigal exhibits *pothos*, the unrequited yearning for a missing loved one (see Vermeule 1979:145, 154–55). Like Romeo and Juliet in modern English, the tragic motif of young lovers separated by untimely death is proverbial in Mesopotamian literature. In "Inana's Descent," rapacious underworld demons (gal_5-lá) "tear the wife away from the husband during intercourse, carry off children from their fathers' knees, and remove the bride from her marriage chamber."[41] An Akkadian incantation similarly accuses a demon: "You (demon) snatched the young man from the lap of the young woman; you snatched the young woman from the lap of the young man" (*eṭla ina sūn ardati tušēli ardata ina sūn eṭli tušēli*) (*CAD* 15:388). A dying woman's sadness at separation from her beloved husband is expressed in a poignant Assyrian elegy (Livingstone 1989:37–39; cf. Reiner 1985:85–93):

mūtu ina bēt mayyālīya iḫlula ḫillūtu	Death slunk stealthily into my bedroom,
issu bētīya ussēṣanni yâši	It brought me out of my house.
issu pān ḫābirīya iptarsanni yâši	It separated me from my lover,
šēpēya issakana ina qaqqar lā târīya	And set my feet toward a land from which I will not return.

The ironic pathos in Ereshkigal's complaint of love interrupted, of course, is that she has lost her lover to the realm of life, not death. Rather than mourning over a lifeless corpse, she is grieving for a vivacious lover who has abandoned her. And Ereshkigal cannot pursue her fleeing lover, as Ninlil follows Enlil even to the Netherworld, because she is imprisoned in her own dark palace (see Hutter 1985:94–98).

Amid her sorrowful gestures, Ereshkigal's plaintive speech expresses her sexual frustration at her lover's desertion. Her claim to be unsatisfied even after six days of erotic indulgence evokes the image of voracious female sexuality, insatiable once it has been aroused (Harris 2000:136). As Foster (1993:410) observes, the story of "Nergal and Ereshkigal" actually "hinges on the isolation and sexual frustration" of the Netherworld queen. According to many interpreters, Ereshkigal's erotic yearning is also employed in "Ishtar's Descent" when Ea creates an *assinnu* or *kuluʾu* named Asushunamir (*aṣûšu-namir*, "his appearance is pleasant") to flirt with the lonely queen and thus trick her into releasing Ishtar's corpse.[42] Ereshkigal will rejoice (*liḫdu*) and become cheerful (*kabtassa ippereddû*; line 96) upon seeing Asushunamir.[43] Possibly a eunuch or homosexual prostitute, the *assinnu* was a transvestite actor in the cult of Ishtar who may have charmed Ereshkigal through song and dance. A more likely explanation for Ea's ruse, however, understands a humorous sexual artifice at work in Ereshkigal's attraction to the pretty but impotent Asushunamir. Sladek (1974:91–92) argues that procreative ability is "abhorrent" and "an abomination" to Ereshkigal; he (1974:40, n. 1) writes that since "procreative sex was forbidden to the goddess of the netherworld, she could only be attracted to a sexless creature."[44] To the contrary, the myth of "Nergal and Ereshkigal" portrays the Netherworld queen's passionate desire for the virile Nergal. It seems more likely, therefore, that the sexual frustration of an enforced celibacy makes Ereshkigal an easy target for Ea's crafty manipulation in both "Nergal and Ereshkigal" and "Ishtar's Descent." Just as the two creatures created from the dirt under Ea's fingernails trick Ereshkigal by feigning sympathy with her mourning in "Inana's Descent" (Kilmer 1971; Sladek 1974:86–88, 93–99), so Nergal and Asushunamir manipulate Ereshkigal's sexual desire in order to gain an advantage in their contests. Indeed, these myths indicate the passionate nature of the Netherworld queen and demonstrate the symbolic association between grief and sexual desire.

Ereshkigal's Complaint

In response to Ereshkigal's distress, Namtar volunteers to go and retrieve Nergal for his queen.[45] She composes an urgent message to Anu, Enlil, and Ea (Uruk v 13–14) that, while frantic, incorporates a rhetorical progression from an appeal for sympathy to stringent demands and a chilling threat. Instead of a love letter to Nergal, Ereshkigal constructs her entreaty to persuade the ruling gods to act on her behalf. She is powerless to forcibly seize the object of her desire and so must rely on others to do her bidding. To be successful, Ereshkigal's argument must establish her power over the celestial gods to impel them to act in accordance with her will. Ereshkigal begins her suit with a pathetic description of her loneliness and isolation (v 2′–4′; cf. 18–20):

ultu ṣeḫrākū-ma mārtāku	Ever since I was a very little girl,
ul īdi mēlulu ša ardāti	I have never known the play of young women;
ul īdi dakāka ša ṣeḫḫerāti	I have never known the romping of little girls.

Ereshkigal seems to play upon the fact that she was sequestered to the Netherworld as a young girl and so was denied the simple joys of childhood (see Hutter 1985:94–98). More doleful than the Greek goddess Persephone, who was abducted by her uncle Hades, Ereshkigal was cloistered in the bowels of the earth to rule over the dead without a consort or husband. While the Amarna version of the myth describes Ereshkigal as a "sister" of the celestials (*aḫātīšunu*; EA, 2), the Sultantepe edition calls her the "daughter" of Anu, Enlil, and Ea (*māratkunu*; v 17′, 45′). Ereshkigal uses the inequality of their relations for her own rhetorical purpose with the predicative construction, *mārtāku*, "I was a daughter." This phrase connotes the protection and warm familial ties of fathers to daughters, yet it also conveys an implicit criticism of the ruling gods who awarded her this infernal realm as her dowry before she could enjoy the pleasures of her youth.

More significantly, in describing her pathetic life Ereshkigal implicitly compares herself with the demoness *ardat-lilî*.[46] JoAnn Scurlock (1995:1890) notes that young people who die before knowing the joys of marriage could become a special class of demons called *lilû*, *lilītu*, or *ardat-lilî*, night demons who slip "through windows into people's houses looking for victims to fill the role of the husbands and wives whom they had never had." Deprived of human love and childbirth, an *ardat-lilî* is a sexual predator who seeks erotic gratification from sleeping men, a succubus who has distilled her own sexual frustration into a "malicious vengeance" against nubile young people (Farber 1995:1897; cf. Leick 1994:228). Incantations explicitly describe an *ardat-lilî*'s origin as a dead women who did not marry and who did not bear and raise a son (see Lackenbacher 1971). The demoness was a "girl who like (normal) women did not experience sex; a girl who like (normal) women was not deflowered"; and "a girl who never had pleasure in a husband's lap."[47] Ereshkigal's complaint of having no girlhood friends is strikingly similar to the lonesome girl who becomes an *ardat-lilî*: "A girl who did not pass along the streets with other girls"; "a young woman who did not rejoice with other young women; a young woman who did not celebrate the festival of her city."[48] Since sexual hunger and loneliness are characteristics that Ereshkigal shares with malevolent underworld demons, her self-description hints at her own potential for demonic activity. Thus, Ereshkigal's grievance cleverly combines a tearful plea for compassion with a veiled threat of demonic outbreak from the Netherworld.

Ereshkigal's appeal for sympathy quickly develops into an indictment of the gods and demand for redress (v 5′–8′; cf. 21′–24′):

ilu šâšu ša tašpurānâšū-ma[49] *urtaḫḫânnī-ma littatīl ittīya*	That god whom you sent to us, he had sex with me, so now let him lie with me again!
ila šâšu šuprānâšū-ma lū ḫāmirī[50] *libīt ittīya*	Send that god to us so that he may be my lover and spend the night with me.
musukkākū-ma ul ebbēk ul adâni[51] *dīni ša ilānī rabûti*	I am defiled; I am impure. I cannot render judgment for the great gods,
ilānī rabûti ašibūt qirib Irkalla	The great gods who dwell in the midst of Irkalla.

Ereshkigal assigns all responsibility for her situation to the celestial gods who dispatched Nergal to her realm. In an adroit rhetorical maneuver, Ereshkigal avoids any culpability for summoning Nergal to her abode or seducing him. She portrays herself as the aggrieved party, sent to rule the Netherworld before experiencing the pleasures of a young woman and now taken advantage of by the gods' envoy. Having tasted the sweetness of love, however, Ereshkigal is no longer content to live the celibate life of the Netherworld. She orders the gods to return her lover with an imperative command (*šuprānâšu*; v 6′) even as she appeals to their sense of justice in explaining her right to her seducer (*urtaḫḫânnī-ma*). The celestial gods must act in order to satisfy her claim.

The significance of Ereshkigal's defilement (*musukkākū-ma ul ebbēk*; v 7′) remains obscure (Hutter 1985:98–100). *CAD* (10/2:239–40) defines *musukku* as an unclean person or one under a temporary taboo; most references seem to refer to a woman who has recently given birth or is perhaps menstruating. The commonality of vaginal bleeding allows the possibility that a recently deflowered-woman might also be included in the category (cf. *CAD* s.v. *naqābu*). Although conjectural, this interpretation fits well with the context of "Nergal and Ereshkigal." Moreover, the word *musukku* appears in a Sumerian-Akkadian bilingual edition of the Sumerian myth "Enlil and Ninlil" (lines 59–60) to describe Enlil at his banishment (Behrens 1978:8, 28; *CAD* 10/2:239). Guilty of the (statutory?) rape of the young Ninlil, Enlil is called a "violator" or "sex offender," ú.zug$_x$ in Sumerian, translated by *musukku* (see Behrens 1978:150–59). Ereshkigal thus may claim to be defiled due to a sexual violation instead of her own physical condition. Cuneiform legal tradition requires a man who seduces or rapes an unattached woman to marry his victim (see Finkelstein 1966), so perhaps Ereshkigal is alluding to this practice when she cries out that she has been undone by Nergal. Since Nergal has slept with her, he must now return to take her as his wife.[52]

Alternatively, some interpreters understand *urtaḫḫânni* (v 5′) to mean, "he has impregnated me." *CAD* (14:254) claims that the D-stem of *reḫû* specifically denotes "to impregnate," but the other four citations do not necessitate this nuance for the D-stem. Conception often follows insemination, especially among the gods, and a reference to Ereshkigal's pregnancy would be consistent with her common identification as the mother of Ninazu and other deities, as well as her description as ama-gan, "birth-giving mother," in line 230 of "Inana's Descent" (see Sladek 1974:208–9; Alster 1983:7–8). Ninazu, however, is the son of Gugalanna rather than Nergal in ancient sources. Some scholars (e.g., Leick 1994:252) assume that pregnancy would make Ereshkigal unfit for her office, but this too is conjecture since there is no Akkadian evidence that a pregnant woman is *musukkatu*. Thus, whether Ereshkigal claims to have been deflowered, inseminated, or impregnated—and exactly how that state would defile her—remains obscure. What is clear, however, is that

Ereshkigal demands that Nergal be returned to her so that she may again have sex with him.

As a further complication to this passage's interpretation, the editors of *CAD* (10/2:317) put forward an alternative reading of the beginning of v 7′: *mūtu kalû-ma ul essik*, "Or else I (Ereshkigal) will not decree death at all."[53] This interpretation excises any reference to defilement and places Ereshkigal's first threat prior to the ultimatum of v 9′. Reiner (1985:53) argues that Ereshkigal threatens to put an end to death in order to extort the celestial gods: "I will not decree death any longer." Although this reading avoids the difficulty of Ereshkigal's impurity, its use of *kalû* is grammatically peculiar. I therefore retain Gurney's reading, as do most interpreters.[54] Regardless, the second half of v 7′, "I cannot (or, will not) render judgment for the great gods" (*ul adâni dīni ša ilānī rabûti*), clearly states that Ereshkigal will cease to fulfill her responsibilities as ruler of the Netherworld. A more precise understanding of Ereshkigal's claim would aid our appreciation of her rhetorical goal, but the general idea is clear enough. Ereshkigal's cessation of her royal duties—through either inability or unwillingness—demands an immediate response from the ruling gods.

Thus far in her complaint, Ereshkigal relies upon traditional feminine images to depict herself as a victim. In so doing, she engages in what Judith Butler refers to as citationality or iterability, in which subjects are compelled to identify themselves by citing the very norms that constrain them (see Allen 1999:72, 120). The reiteration of these gender norms, however, also allows the opportunity to redefine or subvert them as an act of resistance. Ereshkigal thus cites her feminine roles as a little daughter (*ṣeḫrākū-ma mārtāku*; v 2′) and the object of Nergal's sexual activity (*urtaḫḫânni*; v 5′). Rather than contest the powerlessness of women within the patriarchal system, she will use her own agency to resist and redefine the cultural categories that repress women (see Allen 1999:72). For example, Ereshkigal describes herself as a lonely little girl, yet she will now threaten cataclysmic upheaval through her awesome powers as an authoritative queen. Likewise, she affirms the taboo of feminine impurity caused by sexual activity—surely an androcentric and patriarchal concept!—but uses the concept as a means of empowerment rather than a source of shame. That is, she claims that her impurity renders her unable to perform her royal duties on behalf of the ruling gods. Ereshkigal thus manipulates for her own rhetorical advantage the gendered categories that would traditionally constrain her power.

Dispensing entirely with her appeal for sympathy, Ereshkigal directly challenges the celestial gods with a rash ultimatum. The Netherworld queen invokes her royal authority to menace the ruling gods with her demonic powers. Playing on the trope of the emotional woman, the myth portrays Ereshkigal working herself into a rage and issuing threats of apocalyptic proportions (v 9′–12′):

šumma ila šâšu lā taltaprāšu	And if you do not send that god to me, then
kī parṣi Irkalla u erṣetim rabītu[55]	According to the ordinances of Irkalla and the wide Netherworld,
ušellē-ma mītūti ikkalū balṭūti	I will raise up the dead and they will consume the living!
el balṭūti ušamʾad mītūti	I will make the dead more numerous than the living.

Over the course of this episode, Ereshkigal is transformed from a gracious hostess inviting Nergal to eat and drink (iv 45′) to an enraged maenad offering up the living as food for the dead. Rather than the compassionate queen who receives humanity into her dark realm, Ereshkigal threatens to send forth her minions upon the earth where they will feast upon the living. As a goddess scorned, Ereshkigal's wrath is similar to Inana's fury at Shukalletuda, the gardener who raped the sleeping goddess and then fled into hiding (see Volk 1995). Inana devastates the earth and its inhabitants in her quest for vengeance against the impudent gardener. Sexually violated or not, Ereshkigal is incensed at her lover's desertion and promises to wreak havoc upon the earth if her demands are not met. In fact, the Babylonian Ishtar utters the identical threat when she commands the opening of the Netherworld gates in her descent to challenge Ereshkigal's sovereignty and again when she approaches Anu to acquire the Bull of Heaven in the Gilgamesh epic.[56] In Ishtar's mouth the words are melodramatic and hyperbolic; they represent sheer bravado from the impetuous goddess. Ereshkigal, on the other hand, actually wields the power and authority to carry through with her nefarious threat to release the dead from her realm.

The gods have awarded Ereshkigal the dubious honor of ruling the Netherworld, perhaps because they expected the young female to be a docile caretaker of the dead on their behalf. As Exum (1995:79) explains androcentric ideology, "good" women are passive; they do not involve themselves with public issues; they are dependent upon men for decisions. Most importantly, good women do not pose a threat to men or male institutions. To their consternation, the celestial gods discover that Ereshkigal acts as an autonomous ruler rather than a passive woman in "Nergal and Ereshkigal." She threatens their authority with her own sovereign rights. In fact, Ereshkigal relies solely upon her office and its legitimate powers (*parṣi Irkalla*) in menacing the ruling gods (v 9′–12′). She is empowered to act by simply accepting her own sovereignty; by exercising her royal authority, she attempts to gain power over the supernal gods to compel them to act on her behalf.

Hell hath no fury like a woman scorned, and the scorned queen of hell has particularly awesome powers to express her fury. Ereshkigal's baleful threat cleverly exploits the deep-seated fear of malevolent ghosts (*eṭemmu*) and visitations from the dead (*mītūtu*) in ancient Mesopotamia (see *CAD* s.v.v.; Scurlock 1988; 1995). Ereshkigal authorizes the opening and closing of the Netherworld gates and controls admittance to her abode. If, in a passive-aggressive stance, she merely ceases to fulfill her royal duties, not allowing the dead to enter her realm, then their ghosts will be left to roam the earth in restless exile. Furthermore, the Netherworld queen threatens to contest the gods' organization of the cosmos by releasing the inhabitants of her domain upon the earth. By abolishing the boundary between the living and dead, Ereshkigal essentially threatens the collapse of the cosmic order established by the gods. Marduk imagines a similar scene of utter chaos in "Erra and Ishum," when demons are released from the Netherworld and "the gods of hell rise up and destroy the living."[57]

Although the Mesopotamian gods have notoriously little regard for humanity at times, even they must conclude that one case of a jilted lover does not warrant such cataclysmic destruction. Ereshkigal's rash threat plays upon the ancient Near Eastern motif, identified by Jo Ann Hackett (1989:24), of a goddess's disproportionate wrath over a sexual rejection.[58] Like Inana and Shukalletuda, Ishtar in the Gilgamesh epic, and Anat in the Ugaritic epic of "Aqhat," Ereshkigal reacts to Nergal's insult with unrestrained malice to avenge her wounded pride. Hackett (1989:24) explains that the motif dramatizes the abuse of absolute power, since the offended goddess is always allowed her request in order to avert her capricious threats. "Nergal and Ereshkigal" plays upon this motif with Ereshkigal's outrageous response to Nergal's desertion of her bed.

By combining a pathetic appeal for sympathy with dire threats of boundless violence, Ereshkigal has constructed a persuasive rhetorical tool to bend the celestial gods to her will. Her complaint relies upon traditionally feminine patterns of discourse to achieve her desires, beginning with her weeping entreaty and the invocation of familial relationships to paternal males (cf. Harris 2000:137). Just as she coyly incites Nergal to act by displaying her body, Ereshkigal attempts to elicit compassion from the gods for her helplessness as a mere woman. In an example of non-violent and passive resistance, Ereshkigal claims to be unable to perform her duties because of Nergal's sexual aggression. Her feminine identity begins to take on new dimensions, however, when she invokes her royal office and its legitimate authority. In resisting the gods, she makes no threats of direct confrontation or violent attack upon those in power. Ereshkigal resorts to violence only through the indirect means of releasing the dead to ravage humanity and upset the divinely mandated order of the cosmos. In her desperation, Ereshkigal threatens the foundations of political structure even though such action will not bring about her desired goal of Nergal's return. Like a terrorist's agenda of fear and intimidation, her threats are destructive, punitive, and retaliatory. Ereshkigal is empowered to resist and destroy, but she is powerless to replace the patriarchal structures of order and control. The fact that only Ishtar and Ereshkigal threaten such catastrophic retribution evinces the gender stereotypes that undergird this motif. This scene thus portrays Ereshkigal as an especially dangerous adversary in her embodiment of a woman's spiteful fury combined with the legitimate power of sovereign authority.

Namtar obediently delivers his queen's foreboding message to the celestial gods, who again pay homage by kneeling before death's emissary (v 32′–33′). Ereshkigal commands the gods to send Nergal to her (*šuprānâšu*; v 6′, 22′),[59] but Ea responds to Namtar's recitation by saying, "Seek him out and take him" (*buʾʾīšū-ma leqâššu*; v 48′). In this subtle change of language, Ea cleverly transfers responsibility for locating Nergal from the gods to Namtar. Since Ea has transformed Nergal into an unrecognizable form, Namtar will not be able to identify him among the assembled deities. Ea's trick allows the supernal gods to passively resist Ereshkigal while appearing to comply with her demand. Namtar returns empty-handed to report to his queen, who recognizes the disfigured god as Ea's work. Ereshkigal, angered by Ea's ruse, now directly charges Namtar with singular imperatives, "Go! Seize that god and bring him to me!" (*alik ila šâšu ṣabtaššū-ma leqâ yâši*; v 39′, 46′). The gods again comply with Ereshkigal's order by allowing Namtar the freedom to accomplish his task, safe in the knowledge that Ea's trickery will again frustrate his mission.

In contrast to his usually macho and confrontational manner, the warrior Nergal quietly hides among the gods in the hope that concealment will save him from Namtar. Such inglorious passivity is uncharacteristic of a hero, but the text does not suggest any disgrace for Nergal. Much like his escape from the Netherworld by posing as a messenger (iv 23′–25′), Nergal's dissimulation seems to be a legitimate gambit in the continuing struggle for domination. The myth implies that it is fair game for Nergal to evade Ereshkigal by trickery and deception because she first tricked him with her deceptive hospitality and feminine wiles. Exum (1995:78–79) contrasts stereotypical "good" women (i.e., virgins and mothers), who are defined by their passivity in androcentric ideology, with the "wanton" woman, "who arouses in men both desire and animosity" and is blamed for enflaming male passions. Indeed, one can imagine a smug pleasure in the gods' conspiracy to harbor the fugitive from Ereshkigal's grasp. The gods stand in masculine solidarity to support their fellow—a "son of Ishtar" (iv 29′)—in a classic battle of the sexes.[60] Thus, Nergal's evasion of his lover's bonds demonstrates the cleverness of male strategies rather than an unheroic character. Cunning and strength together make the proper hero in this myth.

Unfortunately, the resolution of Namtar's third visit to heaven is unclear. The celestial gods make the unprecedented offer of a drink, a bath, and anointing oil (v 54′) to Ereshkigal's vizier after his long journey from the Netherworld. Whether their hospitality is part of a ruse to distract Namtar from his mission and how it relates to the offer of celestial hospitality in other mythological contexts remains obscure. It is possible that Namtar is recruited by the gods to support Nergal's bid for sovereignty in the Netherworld. Regardless, it seems most likely that the fragmentary lines at the beginning of column vi constitute a conversation in which either Ea or Namtar instructs Nergal on how to enter the Netherworld without being stripped of his divine powers.[61] Scholars disagree on whether Nergal's descent is voluntary or mandatory. Leick (1994:251), for example, holds that Nergal transgressed the Netherworld ordinances by having sex with Ereshkigal and so is under the authority of the infernal realm. It is equally possible that Nergal successfully avoids entrapment by Ereshkigal and is free of underworld dominion after he slips away from her bed. Since the extant text does not mention Namtar accompanying Nergal on his descent, it seems more likely that Nergal chooses to return to Ereshkigal's realm of his own volition. Having survived all of her wiles, escaped her control, and established his free agency, Nergal may return to Ereshkigal as a triumphant hero rather than a craven subordinate.

TO REIGN IN HELL

Nergal's Return

In Book 11 of the *Odyssey*, Odysseus sails across the treacherous Oceanus to the edge of death's realm to seek knowledge from the shades. There he encounters the ghost of heroic Achilles, who remains unreconciled to his underworld existence: "I would rather be plowman to a yeoman farmer on a small holding than lord Paramount in the kingdom of the dead" (11.489–91), as W. H. D. Rouse translates the warrior's forlorn complaint (1937:134). While Achilles would prefer a meager life on earth to dominion in the

Netherworld, Nergal forfeits his heavenly existence in order to reign in hell's dark caverns. What drives him to this grim decision is debated by scholars. Some think it is love for Ereshkigal that draws him back to Death's realm; others believe it is duty or a desire for power. Whatever his motivation, Nergal storms the gates of Death to win a kingdom and claim a bride in both editions of "Nergal and Ereshkigal."

In the Amarna text, Nergal is accompanied by an entourage of demonic helpers as he rushes past the gates of Irkalla to arrive in Ereshkigal's courtyard. Once there, he assaults the unprotected queen with lethal intent (EA, 77–79):

ina libbi bīti iṣṣabat Ereškigal	In the midst of the house he seized Ereshkigal
ina šartīša uqeddidaššī-ma ištu kussî	by the hair. He pulled her down from the throne
ana qaqqari qaqqassa ana nakāsi	to the ground in order to cut off her head.

Ereshkigal offers marriage and dominion over her realm to save herself from Nergal's brutal attack. Nergal's reaction to her weeping entreaty is surprisingly tender, as he kisses her and wipes away her tears (*unaššaqši dimtaša ikappar*; EA, 86). Harris (2000:133–34) asserts that Nergal's sudden change of mood represents the Mesopotamian ideal of a dominating but restrained husband. This scene thus exemplifies the passions of conflict and surrender, and the thin line between love and hate.

The Sultantepe recension dramatically reinterprets the confrontation as a reunion of estranged lovers. Nergal apparently stages a violent assault on the Netherworld, striking down (*inār*) its seven gate-keepers as he single-handedly bullies his way into Ereshkigal's courtyard, unchecked and unannounced.[62] The description of Nergal's encounter with Ereshkigal is partly broken, but the general tone is clear (vi 29–36):

ērum-ma ana palkî kisallīša	He entered her wide courtyard,

iʾīršī-ma iṣīḫ	He approached her and laughed aloud.
iṣbassī-ma ina uprîši	He seized her by her headdress,
ultu muḫḫi [*kussî* …]	From upon [her throne… he pulled her?]
iṣbassī-ma ina abbuttīša	He seized her by her tresses,
… *rāʾi*[*mūt*]*īšu* …	… his love (?) …[63]
innadrū-ma aḫāmeš kilallān	The two of them embraced one another, and
ana mayyāli šitmuriš īterbū	They went passionately off to bed.

In contrast to the Amarna text, in which grabbing Ereshkigal by the hair is in preparation for her decapitation, Nergal's grasping of Ereshkigal signals his erotic intentions in the Sultantepe edition. Nergal's laughter also carries erotic implications, as the verb *ṣiāḫu*, "to laugh," is often linked with sex in Akkadian literature (see Hirsch 1982:117–19; Hutter 1985:90–91; Harris 2000:138–39).

In their previous encounter in the Sultantepe text (col. iii), Nergal acts in accordance with Ereshkigal's treachery and covert warfare. He politely refuses her poisonous food and drink and makes no advances of his own. Just when it appears that he has been conquered by six days in Ereshkigal's bed, Nergal triumphs by slipping out of her realm and beyond her reach. In his second trip to Irkalla, however, Nergal no longer adheres to the feminine script of subtle negotiation and unacknowledged conflict. He resorts to a fierce and intimidating gesture to demonstrate his masculine power and to assert his physical dominance over the Netherworld queen. Even in jest, his aggressive assault invites her surrender to his superior strength. Nergal's laughter conveys his self-confident pleasure in the rough play as he exploits her fears of masculine violence. Ereshkigal responds to Nergal's aggressive overture with sexual passion; they hurry to bed for another week of erotic expenditure (vi 42). The myth thus eroticizes violence within the context of heterosexual relations.

Ereshkigal's amorous response plays upon the patriarchal stereotype that women want to be dominated by virile and brutal men. Niditch (1989:52–53) points out the androcentric projection that may undergird the belief that women are satisfied only when they yield themselves to a dominant male. This androcentric assumption further exploits the misogynistic depiction of feminine sexuality as voracious, animalistic, and in need of male control. The myth portrays Ereshkigal's coy seduction of Nergal as a strategic maneuver in her attempt to dominate him, yet, ironically, she is the one bound by the constraints of desire. She is polluted—perhaps impregnated—and disqualified from her sovereign office. Even so, Ereshkigal ardently yearns for her absent lover and is compelled to seek his return by any means necessary. In her frantic message to the gods, she is explicit about her libidinal motivation: "Send that god to us so that he may be my lover and spend the night with me!" (*ila šâšu šuprānâšū-ma lū ḫāmirī libīt ittīya*; v 6′). Nergal's flight from her bed, however, suggests his emotional detachment and indifference to Ereshkigal's allure. She is held in thrall by her feminine desires while Nergal is free to roam about the cosmos.

The fragmentary ending of the Sultantepe text (vi 43–53) prevents a definitive conclusion, but it seems that Ereshkigal will now share power over the Netherworld with her husband, Nergal. This arrangement is consistent with other Mesopotamian mythological sources, which present them as the Lord and Lady of Irkalla. The Amarna text makes Ereshkigal's proposal explicit (EA, 82–85):

atta lū mutī-ma anāku lū aššatka lušeṣbitka	"You be my husband and I will be your wife! Let me cause you to seize
šarrūta ina erṣeti rapašti luškun ṭuppa	kingship over the wide Netherworld. Let me place
ša nēmeqi ana qātīka atta lū bēlu	the tablet of wisdom in your hand. You be lord,
anāku lū bēltu	I will be lady!"

The Sultantepe text likely resolves its narrative with Anu's decree that Nergal and Ereshkigal will now rule over the Netherworld forever.

Gender and Power

In her important article on gender as a category of historical analysis, Joan Scott (1986:1067) notes that gender is "a primary way of signifying relationships of power." This maxim holds true for "Nergal and Ereshkigal," in which the Netherworld queen is accorded honor but not power by the celestial gods. Like the chivalrous acclaim of women as the nobler but weaker sex, Ereshkigal's honor among the gods is limited to social gestures and polite condescension. As a goddess, she stands in opposition to the hierarchical structure of patriarchal authority under the leadership Anu, Enlil, and Ea. Although Ereshkigal exercises authority within her own realm, she is a second-class citizen among the ruling deities. She is excluded from the their assembly and has no voice in their politics. Ereshkigal is effectively disenfranchised and disempowered among the ruling gods, and gender is one means of signifying this disparity. Ereshkigal attempts to exert power over the gods with her threats of cataclysmic upheaval if they do not return Nergal. The celestial gods, however, resist her coercion through male solidarity and passive resistance. They do not deny or countermand her order, but through Ea's trickery they conspire to aid the fugitive god in his concealment and impede the success of Namtar's mission. Nergal eventually combines both cunning trickery and violent aggression to form the complete masculine hero.

Allen's analytical perspective on three modalities of power (power-over, power-to, and power-with) advances the analysis of Ereshkigal's power relations in "Nergal and Ereshkigal" by distinguishing between domination, empowerment, and resistance. Ereshkigal begins the myth as an autonomous sovereign within the Netherworld. The clearest example of Ereshkigal's power-over is the authority she wields over Namtar, her fearsome vizier. She commands him to do her bidding (e.g., v 39', 46'), and he obediently follows her orders. He meekly accepts her reprimand for his apparent arrogance: "Namtar, do not aspire to ruling authority or imagine deeds of valor for yourself" (*Namtari illilūtu ē-tuba*ʾʾ*a u qarrādūta ayy-ibannâ libbukku*; Uruk iii 6′).[64] Namtar is not completely dominated by Ereshkigal, however, as he exhibits his own agency at points in the myth, such as when he volunteers to fetch Nergal for his distraught queen (iv 57′–59′; Uruk v 10–11).

Ereshkigal's complaint to the gods (v 2′–12′) demonstrates her own empowerment. After appealing for sympathy and fair treatment from the celestial gods, she claims her own authority over the subjects of her realm by threatening to release the dead upon the earth if the supernal gods do not respond to her demands for Nergal. Yet even as Ereshkigal threatens to release the dead, she does not seem to consider seriously her ability to free herself from the Netherworld's constraints.[65] At the beginning of the myth, Anu explains that the supernal gods do not descend to the Netherworld, and the infernal gods to not ascend to heaven (i 31′–34′). He says to Ereshkigal, "You do (or, may) not ascend. The whole year you do not (even once) ascend to us" (*attī-ma ul ša elî ina šattīkī-ma ul telli ana maḫrīni*; i 31′–32′). Readers often accept Anu's words as axiomatic, but a hermeneutics of suspicion must question whether one can trust Anu's proclamation that keeps Ereshkigal confined to the Netherworld.[66] By not challenging the authoritarian pronouncement with her own capacity to act, Ereshkigal collaborates with her oppressors and contributes to the limitation of her freedom. Deities do have the power to enter and exit her realm (i.e., Kakka, Namtar, Nergal, Ishtar). Apart from the political ramifications of separate "spheres of influence," there is little explanation for Anu's geographical segregation. At the least, a feminist analysis should point out the oppressive character of this patriarchal rule and how it imprisons Ereshkigal behind the locked gates of her own realm. Indeed, Ereshkigal is confined to her palace much like a wife is restricted to the domestic spaces of her husband's house in repressive patriarchal cultures.

The limits to Ereshkigal's power and authority are most clearly revealed in her interactions with Nergal. The Netherworld queen cannot simply decree Nergal's death or order his execution in either version of "Nergal and Ereshkigal." To be sure, Ereshkigal commands Namtar to afflict Ishtar with lethal diseases in "Ishtar's Descent" (lines 68–69), and in "Inana's Descent" (lines 167–71) she assembles the Anunnaki to pronounce a sentence of death over Inana. Inana-Ishtar, however, is guilty of a treasonable offense in attempting (and failing) to usurp Ereshkigal's sovereignty (see Katz

1995:227, 231–32; Sladek 1974:202, 256; cp. Penglase 1994:246–47). Ereshkigal therefore has the authority to call for her sister's death, but she must rely on another god's power to accomplish the execution. Nergal's lack of obeisance to Ereshkigal's envoy, on the other hand, is probably closer to a breach of etiquette than a capital offense in the mythological imagination, and so Ereshkigal lacks the authority to legitimately decree his death. Ereshkigal imperiously summons Nergal to her realm with murderous intentions in the Amarna edition (EA, 27, 60), but the warrior god is too powerful to be slain by Ereshkigal or her representative. On the contrary, Nergal strikes down Namtar (EA, 75) and is about to decapitate Ereshkigal (EA, 77–79) when she surrenders to him.[67] The Amarna text thus demonstrates the superiority of violent aggression over authority as a means to achieve power over another. Similarly, in the Sultantepe edition, Ereshkigal cannot decree Nergal's death and so must trick or manipulate the warrior god into residing in her realm. Nergal, however, has been empowered by Ea's counsel to retain his life and so escapes Ereshkigal's realm without submitting to her dominance.

Allen's analysis of power relations is also helpful in illuminating what Ereshkigal most lacks in her network of power relations. The Netherworld queen is completely deprived of companionship with other women, as she makes explicit in her complaint to the gods that she has never known the joys of female friendship (v 2′–4′). She is denied women's traditional social experiences and the opportunity for collective solidarity with other females. In her feminist analysis, Allen (1999:126–29) stresses the importance of feminist solidarity and coalition-building as a means to oppose oppressive structures. This mode of power relations (power-with) can affect change by collectively resisting the domination of patriarchal power and authority. Indeed, it appears that the ruling gods have purposely isolated Ereshkigal as part of a plan to more easily control her. Ereshkigal has no option for feminine collectivity or solidarity and so must stand alone in opposition to the assembly of male gods.

Ereshkigal's solitude as Queen of the Netherworld is poignantly expressed in "Ishtar's Descent," a myth that dramatizes the two goddesses' rejection of power-with in order to compete for power over the other. This misogynistic portrayal of feminine conflict denies the goddesses' ability to forge a feminine collective to resist the ruling gods. Instead, the myth depicts the two sisters as contentious adversaries. When Ereshkigal hears of Ishtar's arrival at the gates of her realm, she expresses hostility and suspicion: "What has prompted her heart (that she come) to me? What has incited her against me?" (*minâ libbaša ublanni minâ kabtassā-ma ušperdânnī-ma*; 31).[68] The two goddesses confront each other in open hostility and overt violence. Ereshkigal has Ishtar stripped at the gates, thus exercising her power over the other goddess (Katz 1995). When the naked Ishtar is brought before her, "Ereshkigal saw her and became furious at her" (*Ereškigal īmuršī-ma ina panīša irʾub*; 64). For her part, Ishtar either usurps Ereshkigal's throne as in the Sumerian version or aggressively attacks her elder sister.[69] Regardless, their conflict continues with Ereshkigal's condemnation of Ishtar, her sentence of death, and the hanging of Ishtar's corpse on a meat hook. Enki-Ea must intervene between the goddesses by sending his sexually ambiguous creature(s) to trick Ereshkigal into releasing Inana-Ishtar's corpse (see Kilmer 1971). Rather than combine their powers in feminist solidarity, the two powerful sisters confront each other as bitter rivals. While feminism teaches that "sisterhood is powerful," this androcentric myth conveys the fractious nature of women's relationships when freed from male restraints.[70]

In conclusion, "Nergal and Ereshkigal" portrays complex power relationships in which both god and goddess employ deception, passive resistance, and authoritative command. Unlike Nergal's final triumph through physical intimidation, Ereshkigal and the supernal gods prefer intrigue and manipulation over direct confrontation. Ereshkigal's attempt at persuasion by complaint and the evocation of sympathy may reflect a traditionally feminine mode of discourse, but the techniques are simply those available to the disempowered. The Netherworld queen's violent threats of cosmic upheaval demonstrate her sovereign authority within her own realm. Thus, the myth does not rely heavily upon specifically gendered categories of the exercise of power. Rather than draw a stark contrast between masculine and feminine forms of power relations, the myth simply demonstrates Ereshkigal's inferior exercise of similar modes of power. That is, Ereshkigal's exercise of power is not different from the male gods so much as it is less proficient. Like her gender, Ereshkigal's isolation is intrinsic to the plot of "Nergal and Ereshkigal." The myth conveys her inability to compete in the political contests by depicting her inability to defeat the masculine conspiracy of the heavenly gods. Rather than portray the conniving woman as a serioues threat to male rule and male autonomy, the myth demonstrates the inevitable victory of patriarchal power over feminine opposition.

CONCLUSION: DESIRE AND DEATH

In contrast to the theme of Eros become Thanatos, in which a lover is slain by the beloved's embrace (see Niditch 1989), "Nergal and Ereshkigal" presents Thanatos become Eros: the feminine embodiment of death becomes the object of the hero's desire. The Sultantepe text plays upon masculine fears of woman's sexuality before resolving the tension in a successful romance, while the Amarna version unveils the object of Nergal's tearful dread (EA, 43–45) as little more than a woman's desire. Like Shakespeare's Sonnet 147—which begins, "My love is a fever, longing still / For that which longer nurseth the disease"—the myth of "Nergal and Ereshkigal" also explains that "Desire is death" for its hero.[71] The sonnet's concluding thoughts could equally be attributed to Nergal as a literal description of his beloved Ereshkigal:

> For I have sworn thee fair, and thought thee bright,
> Who art as black as hell, as dark as night.

The myth of "Nergal and Ereshkigal" portrays the Netherworld queen as a sympathetic character with a full range of human needs and emotions. She is alternately shrewd and gullible, delighted and distraught, furiously raging and seductively alluring. Far from the frigid Queen of the Damned, Ereshkigal is a passionate character in Mesopotamian myth. She is neither an infernal demon who seeks to enlarge her domain nor a grim reaper who feeds her appetite on harvested souls. Ereshkigal mourns the souls under her care. Ravaged by her own fierce emotions, she yearns for Nergal as she laments her lost childhood. More needy than nefarious, more pathetic than terrifying, Ereshkigal suffers grievously as she benevolently rules the realm where ghosts reside. Emily Vermeule (1979:177) observes that while Greek goddesses may also grieve the dead, "they can displace some of the grief with *pothos* and *himeros* [desire], with sung lament, with the comforts of Sleep and Death, and with a love which has some power to revive the darkened mind." In the tale of their courtship, Nergal likewise provides Ereshkigal with relief from her mordant duties and somber tasks. He awakens desire within her body, lulls her to blissful sleep, and pains her with *pothos*. He eventually returns to her infernal home with "love...to revive the darkened mind." Just as Nergal's aggressive treatment of Ereshkigal eroticizes violence, the romance of Nergal and Ereshkigal eroticizes death. Instead of representing the extinction of passion, as suggested by the twelfth tablet of the Gilgamesh epic, the land of death holds the realization of desire for Ereshkigal and Nergal.

The mysterious Netherworld is the great unknown, the "dark continent" within Mesopotamian cosmic geography. The image of the dark continent was applied to Africa by Victorian writers but was then reappropriated by Freud to describe the essential mystery (to him) of female psychology (see Doane 1991:209; Doniger 1998:31, 163). The unexplored continent is exotic, dangerous, and appealing and thus served Freud as a paradigm of the feminine Other. As queen of the dead in her infernal realm, Ereshkigal embodies this dangerous, feminine Other in the androcentric myth of "Nergal and Ereshkigal." She is easily stereotyped as the hungry, clinging woman, ruled by her emotions and violent mood swings. She is the bitch, vindictive and spiteful, as well as the insatiable sex goddess of masculine fantasy. Ultimately, she is the "woman as adversary" as perceived by the male protagonist and male reader, who could appreciate the wisdom of the gods and the bravado of Nergal as they overpower the unruly queen.

"Nergal and Ereshkigal" also identifies feminine sexuality with death in a strikingly simple equation. Ereshkigal's portrayal is replete with Freudian symbolism as she sits behind locked gates in a dark cavern beneath the earth's surface. Her kingdom is powerful and mysterious, passively awaiting the entrance of (male) subjects into its dank chambers. Indeed, interpreters of various schools—Jungian, feminist, and Freudian—symbolically associate women with chthonic images of the moist earth and its hidden inner spaces (e.g., Meador 1992; Paglia 1990; Perera 1981; Torsney 1989:188). The underworld is thus an appropriate domain for female sovereignty. The feminine threat to males and their autonomy is also starkly represented in the myth. If Nergal succumbs to Ereshkigal's powerful allure then he risks becoming subject to her lethal authority. Nergal is faced with a crucible of desire in his attraction for the nude goddess. By explicitly identifying the myth's only female character and her sexuality with death, decay, and disguised poison, "Nergal and Ereshkigal" manifests a Freudian dread of women. This fear of feminine power is exorcised, however, by Nergal's dramatic conquest of death and its queen. Unlike Gilgamesh, who rejects Ishtar's advances, Nergal engages the erotic goddess and lives to tell the tale. He is virile enough to enjoy her body for a week of sexual indulgence and crafty enough to escape before it is too late. Indeed, Nergal's defeat of death is equated with his sexual conquest of Ereshkigal; he exhausts her through lovemaking to make good his escape, and he is welcomed to share her rule because of her ardent desire for him. In contrast to Paglia's (1990:20) claim that intercourse reminds men of their own mortality—"Men enter in triumph but withdraw in decrepitude"—the myth of "Nergal and Ereshkigal" celebrates a masculine libido that never tires. In perfect masculine fantasy, Nergal overcomes the mysterious woman and her dark realm through his sexual prowess.

Freud's use of the "dark continent" as a metaphor for feminine psychology further evokes the sexist and racist implications of the western colonial perspective. The celestial gods' attitude toward the dark Netherworld and its Queen seems equally sexist and colonial in "Nergal and Ereshkigal." The gods allow Ereshkigal to reign in hell as long as she does not interfere in the politics of heaven. Once she attempts to impose her will upon the ruling patriarchy, however, she loses her throne and her sovereign autonomy. As Bottéro (1992b:245) suggests, the celestial gods colonize the Netherworld by replacing the unruly woman with their own man in an effort to stabilize the political order. In analyzing this myth, Harris (2000:143) aptly notes the Akkadian proverb, "A house without a lord (is like) a woman without a husband" (*bītu ša lā bēli sinništu ša lā muti*; Lambert 1960:229). The myth of "Nergal and Ereshkigal" enacts this proverb by demonstrating the instability of both the "house" and the woman bereft of masculine control. Rather than leave the Netherworld as the inverted realm of opposites, where a woman rules dead subjects, the myth concludes with the installation of male dominion in Irkalla. This provides a normative order to the Netherworld, colonizing and annexing the territory as part of the patriarchal domain. Harris (2000:140) states that a queen as sole ruler is "intolerable and unacceptable" in Mesopotamian political ideology, as evidenced by the complete absence of autonomous queens after the legendary Ku-Bau of Kish in the third millennium. Like Tiamat's defeat by Marduk in *Enuma Elish*, Ereshkigal must cede the throne to the virile Nergal for the myth's properly androcentric resolution.

Feminist criticism should reveal "the misogyny of literary practice" (Torsney 1989:181). Accordingly, a feminist analysis of power relations in "Nergal and Ereshkigal" reveals the supernal gods' conspiracy to limit Ereshkigal's freedom and power. As an autonomous woman, Ereshkigal threatens first Nergal's life and then the entire cosmos with the release of the dead upon the earth. This dissolution of cosmic boundaries illustrates the chaos of feminine power in ancient Mesopotamian discourse. Ereshkigal is unmasked as an unfit ruler of her realm and a danger to the ordered universe. Debby Dale Jones (1993:264) concludes her feminist analysis of "Inana's Descent" by observing that "in this narrative the power granted to female characters appears to have been used as a means of ridiculing females in power, perhaps even as a means of deconstructing female power." "Nergal and Ereshkigal" similarly employs the androcentric stereotype of women as irrational, emotionally volatile, and in need of male control, a control that is envisioned in explicitly sexual terms (see Carson 1990; Walls 1992:27–38, 217–24). Indeed, the myth's resolution in divine marriage implies that Ereshkigal finds fulfillment in her subordination to Nergal's masculine control.

Finally, "Nergal and Ereshkigal" commemorates a marriage between a god who abandons heaven for an eternity among the shades and the Netherworld queen who sacrifices her autonomy to feminine desire. Rather than celebrate Ereshkigal's feminine power, the myth advocates for her voluntary subordination within an androcentric and patriarchal structure as Nergal gains control of her underworld dowry. Her dangerous powers—political and sexual—are similarly domesticated by masculine power and patriarchal institutions. The myth implies that Ereshkigal, like all unruly women, can be pacified through sex and controlled through masculine intimidation. Ereshkigal thus models women's complicity with patriarchal authority rather than resistance to masculine domination.

NOTES

[1]Recent studies of "Nergal and Ereshkigal" include Bottéro and Kramer (1989:437–64), Harris (2000:129–46), Hutter (1985), Izre'el (1997:51–61), and Reiner (1985:50–60). Short comments on the text's interpretation are also found in Izre'el (1992), Leick (1994:249–53), and Vogelzang (1992). Additional translations include Dalley (1989:163–81), Foster (1993:410–28), and Müller (1994).

[2]Harris (2000:129–46), Hutter (1985:84–100), Leick (1994:249–53), and Reiner (1985:50–60) interpret the myth as a love story or romance. Jacobsen (1976:229–30) also understands the text as a simple tale of adolescent sexual attraction, but he is uncharacteristically confused by its mythic dimensions: "...as one looks for a more ultimate meaning, it appears almost impenetrable, and we do not pretend to offer even a reasonable suggestion."

[3]Vogelzang (1992) stresses the humorous nature of the Amarna version and its openness to divergent readings (cf. Foster 1995).

[4]Previous scholars had read line 27 of the Amarna text as *ana mūtīšu* (see Izre'el 1997:57), but Izre'el's new text edition reads, *ana muḫḫīya šūbilannīšū-ma ludūkšu*, "Bring him to me so that I may kill him." The signs are not at all clear, but Izre'el reads *mu-ú-ḫi-ia* rather than *mu-ú-ti-šu* and states that the last sign is certainly not a *šu*. Regardless, the wordplay is still a clever synopsis of the myth's plot.

[5]The most recent text edition is by Izre'el (1997:51–61). See Izre'el (1992:199, n. 57; 1997:55, 60–61) on the text's Peripheral Akkadian features, and contrast Moran's (1987) statement that the text is in a purely MB dialect apart from its final phrase.

[6]Drawings of the Assyrian tablet from Sultantepe were published by Gurney and Finkelstein (1957: text 28) and Gurney and Hulin (1964: texts

113–14). The Akkadian text was edited by Gurney (1960). The late Uruk tablet was published by Hunger (1976:17–19). In an attempt to lessen the confusion between these texts, I will refer to each by the name of its find site.

[7]Foster (1993:410–28) follows Gurney's line count except in the latter half of column iii, where the restoration of a lacuna with Uruk iii requires additional lines.

[8]The term *ḫurbāšu* often means "shivers of fear" (*CAD* 6:248–49) and Izre'el (1997:60) suggests that "to cut fear" (*ḫurbāša nakāsu*) means "to overcome fear." Others have read the signs of *ḫurbāša* differently and taken the *ša* as a pronominal suffix. Dalley (1989:181) tentatively suggests *ḫuṭṭumaša*, "to seal her in." Bottéro and Kramer (1989:440) and Foster (1993:416) leave this part of the line untranslated.

[9]Nergal seizes a man by his hair (*ina abūsātīya iṣbatannī-ma*) in order to kill him in "The Underworld Vision of an Assyrian Prince" (rev. 12–14; Livingstone 1989:68–76; cf. Foster 1993:730–37). Enkidu dreams of an underworld demon grabbing him by his hair to carry him off to death in the Gilgamesh epic (VII 172). Nergal also seizes Ereshkigal by her hair in the Sultantepe text (vi 31), with much different intent. Harris (2000:133) points out the three occurrences of the verb *ṣabātu*, "to seize" in this passage (EA, 77, 82, and 86): "The iterative term is thus a key word underlining the power struggle between male and female, with the male emerging victorious." She emphasizes Nergal's aggressiveness in this text.

[10]Harris (2000:133–34) argues that this is a "posture associated with both the conquered and the old," but *CAD* (13:45) provides only two other attestations of this D-stem verb to describe people, one referring to the conquered, one referring to the aged. Jones (1993:244), on the other hand, points out the sexual implications of the image of a bent-over woman. She suggests that it is an allusion to a common visual portrayal of sexual intercourse in Mesopotamian sources (see Cooper 1975).

[11]See Izre'el (1997:60–61) on the last phrase, *adu kīnanna*. *CAD* (8:380) defines *kīnanna* (without *adu*) as "for such reason, on account of this" and "in this manner, under such circumstances." It notes this line as uncertain, perhaps a mistake for *adu inanna*. Some interpreters understand the phrase to mean that Nergal would have complied with Ereshkigal's desires long before if she had only made them known (e.g., Bottéro and Kramer 1989:441; Dalley 1989:181; Harris 2000:134; Jacobsen 1976:229; Müller 1994:769; and Vogelzang 1992:278). I would then translate, "What have you been desiring from me for many months until now?" Foster

(1993:428), Hutter (1985), Izre'el (1997:60–61), and Moran (1987), however, understand the phrase as a scribal note in a peripheral Akkadian dialect. Izre'el (1992:196–98) explains the phrase as the result of oral dictation by a teacher, who saw that there was no more room on the tablet for the rest of the text and so concluded the exercise.

[12]Harris (2000:132) argues that "Nergal and Ereshkigal" constitutes "a reflexive discourse on gender relations and male/female sexuality" from ancient Mesopotamia. On the analysis of gender in the ancient Near East, note Asher-Greve (1997; 1998), Day (1989), Frymer-Kensky (1992), Guinan (1998), Harris (2000: passim), Walls (1992), and Wyke (1998). Scott (1986) remains a very useful resource on gender as a category of historical analysis. On the feminist interpretation of ancient texts by scholars of the ancient Near East, see also Brenner and Fountaine (1997), Exum (1995), and Jones (1993:240–63), to name but a few examples.

[13]I thank Tamara Yates for guiding me through the literature on power relations and bringing Allen's recent book to my attention.

[14]In his survey of underworld gods, Lambert (1980:60–64) explains that while early Sumerian sources are inconsistent, Ereshkigal is established as the ruler of the Mesopotamian Netherworld by the end of the third millennium.

[15]For descriptions of the Mesopotamian underworld, see Horowitz (1998:268–95, 348–62). Earlier discussions of the Netherworld and afterlife include Alster (1980), Bottéro (1992b:268–86), Cassin (1987:236–57), Cooper (1991), Groneberg (1990), Katz (1993), Scurlock (1995), Spronk (1986), and Tsukimoto (1985).

[16]See George 1999:179. Sumerologists disagree on this topic. Jacobsen (1993:121, 123) states that Enki in given as a slave to Ereshkigal in the primordial distribution of rule between the three siblings Anu, Enlil, and Ereshkigal. Kramer identifies Kur as a monster instead of the Netherworld and so translates, "Once Ereshkigal had been given over to the *Kur* as a gift from them" (i.e., An and Enlil, who had "carried off" heaven and earth, respectively) (Kramer and Maier 1989:82–83). Horowitz (1998:135, n. 33) notes that sag-rig$_7$ may simply mean "gift" rather than "dowry."

[17]Jacobsen (1987a:210–11) explains Gugalanna as "the great bull of heaven," Gu(d)galanna(k); others suggest that his name originally meant "canal inspector of Anu" (e.g., Black and Green 1992:77; cf. Sladek 1974:194). He is listed as Ereshkigal's husband in god-lists, including the "canonical" MB tradition of An = Anum, while Nergal is listed in a later section with different wives (Lambert 1980:62–64). Katz (1995:230, n.

22), like Kramer (1967:111, nn. 8–9) before her, believes that Gugalanna is probably Enlil in early sources. Ninazu is the son of Ereshkigal and Gugalanna. As usual, the evidence suggests historically and geographically divergent traditions in ancient Mesopotamia.

[18]On the god Nergal, see von Weiher (1971), Lambert (1973; 1980:59–64), and Livingstone (1999), as well as the debate between Lambert (1990b; 1990c) and Steinkeller (1987; 1990). Lambert (1973:356; 1990b:52) derives his name from the Sumerian en-erigal, "Lord of the Netherworld," and reports that he is already identified with Erra, Meslamtaea and other divine names in the late third millennium (1980:62–63). Note Erra's important role in the first-millennium myth, "Erra and Ishum" (Cagni 1969; Foster 1993:771–805).

[19]Foster's (1993:775) translation is from "Erra and Ishum" (I 81) (*CAD* 17/1:100; Cagni 1969:66).

[20]On the iconography of Netherworld deities, including Nergal and Ereshkigal, see Black and Green (1992:77, 135–37, with references), Livingstone (1989:68–76), Jacobsen (1987b), and Porada (1980; 1987).

[21]Others read Gaga; see Steinkeller 1982.

[22]Meier (1988:159) suggests that the celestial gods' bowing to Namtar is evidence that the text is from Cutha, where the Netherworld gods were more cultically central than the heavenly gods (see also Hutter 1985: 78–83).

[23]The gender of the verbal forms is not clear. The second imperative may be either 2 f.s. (*dīnī*) or 2 m.s. with the "overhanging vowel" typical in middle-weak verb forms (*dīni*); *tišab* is an "alternate" form of the G-stem (or Gt-stem, with *CAD* 1/2:386) imperative of *wašābu* (Huehnergard 1997:144; *GAG* §103 h). Perhaps *tišab*, attested in both the Sultantepe (iii 51′) and Uruk (iv 6) tablets, serves as a 2 c.s. form, since the 2 f.s. form (**tišbī*) remains unattested (Huehnergard 1997:144). Gurney (1960:117, n. 47) states that these two lines are more likely Ereshkigal's response than part of Anu's message, but the Uruk text makes it clear that these are Anu's words.

[24]On the role of messengers in "Nergal and Ereshkigal," see Hutter (1985: 78–83) and Meier (1988:147–50, and passim).

[25]Erra and Nergal are equated in sources ranging from the third millennium (Lambert 1973:357–63) to the first millennium, including "Erra and Ishum" (V 39–40) (see Cagni 1969; Foster 1993:771–805).

[26]See Reiner 1985:52–53. On Ea's cunning and finesse in general, see Bottéro (1992b:232–50) and Kramer and Maier (1989).

[27]The identity and purpose of Nergal's chair remain obscure. Ea instructs Nergal on its construction before his first descent, yet the chair plays a prominent role only in his second journey, according to some interpreters, when Nergal appears to leave parts of the chair at each of the seven Netherworld gates (vi 19–27). Based upon the stripping of Ishtar as she passed through these gates on her descent, interpreters suggest that the parts of the chair are left in lieu of Nergal's clothes and powers (but contrast Dalley 1989:175, 177, n. 25). Anu's reference to "this throne" (*kussî annî*; iii 51′) in his message to Ereshkigal indicates that Nergal has taken the chair with him on his first journey, too, even though it receives no other reference in this episode. Dalley (1989:163) suggests some relation to a "ghost's chair" in lexical texts, which she identifies with the a chair in a ritual to prevent seizure by ghosts. Others suggest that the chair is a gift for Ereshkigal (Harris 2000:130), who relinquishes her sovereignty over the Netherworld when she leaves her own throne to sit on the new chair (Reiner 1985:52).

[28]For the text of "Adapa and the South Wind," see Picchioni (1981:112–42) and Izre'el (1997:43–50; 2001) (cf. Foster 1993:429–34). The numbering of lines follows Picchioni's poetic division, not the lines of the Amarna tablet (i.e., 60′–65′).

[29]This text is from Fragment D, lines 4–6. See Picchioni 1981:122; Foster 1993:433.

[30]The Sultantepe text has been restored based on Uruk ii 11′–15′. The Sultantepe text has somehow confused the vetitive and indicative verbal forms in both ii 41′–43′ and iii 55′–59′ (see Gurney 1960:129), and so I have corrected the verbs in ii 41′–43′ to correspond with Uruk ii 13′–15′. The idiom in iii 48′ has been reconstructed based on Gurney's reading (1960:114, n. 31) and the parallel in iii 63′ (cf. *CAD* 11/2:105). Note the play on the verbal root (*w*)*âru* in the Uruk text (ii 13′–15′ and iv 9–12; cf. *CAD* 1/2:319 and 11/2:93).

[31]All quotations from the SB Gilgamesh epic follow Parpola's edition (1997). OBM refers to the Old Babylonian tablet of the Gilgamesh epic published by Meissner (1902). The Akkadian text of "Ishtar's Descent to the Netherworld" is edited by Borger (1963:86–93; cf. Sladek 1974:240–62).

[32]Line 301: úr-dam nì-du$_{10}$-ge-eš nu-si-ge-me-eš (Sladek 1974:141, 176).

[33]On the shared vocabulary of loving and killing in Greek texts, see Vermeule (1979:154–77).

[34]In a nice example of intertextuality, a bilingual text cited in *CAD* (16:68) describes Nergal as he who "brings sleep to the sleepless (but) is alert even when he seems to sleep."

[35]*Ina libbi erṣetim sakāpum mādū attillam-ma kalu šanātim*; OBM i 11–12. See *CAD* 15:74; Tournay and Shaffer 1994:198, n. 7.

[36]According to Foster (1993:412), "Ereshkigal arises in a leisurely way, enjoys a bath, and calls that the rooms be freshened and breakfast served." Whether there is a ritual or magical connotation to the sprinkling of rooms is unclear (Gurney 1960:130).

[37]Literally, "he ascended his mountain." Like the English phrase "to head for the hills," the idiom *šadâ elû* expresses flight from pursuit or responsibility, desertion, or going into hiding (see *CAD* 4:124).

[38]See Harris 2000:136. Compare Sultantepe's *ultu muḫ*[*ḫi kussî*...] (vi 32) with the Amarna text, *ištu kussî ana qaqqari* (78–79).

[39]The portrait of Ereshkigal in mourning is found in the Gilgamesh epic (XII 48–49), "Gilgamesh, Enkidu and the Netherworld" (see George 1999:184), and "Inana's Descent" (230–39; see Sladek 1974; cf. Jacobsen 1987a:219–20).

[40]See Borger 1963:88–89. Ereshkigal's speech begins, "This is me! I drink water with the Anunnaki / For bread I eat clay; for beer I drink muddy water!" (*annû anāku itti Anunnaki mê ašatti / kīma aklī akkal ṭiṭṭa kīma šikari ašattâ mê dalḫūte*; lines 32–33). Some scholars, however, interpret these and the following remarks as sarcastic rhetorical questions indicative of Ereshkigal's lack of sympathy for others' sorrows (Reiner 1985:38–39).

[41]Lines 303–5, Sladek 1974:176. The Sumerian text reads (Sladek 1974:141):

dam úr-lú-ka ba-ra-an-si-il-si-il-le-eš
dumu-lú du_{10}-ub-ta ba-ra-an-zi-ge-eš
e-gi_4-a é-ušbar$_x$-ra-ka im-ta-an-è-eš-àm

[42]On the *assinnu* and *kuluʾu*, see the comments by Sladek (1974:86–93), Lambert (1992:147–53); Maul (1992); Henshaw (1993:197–201, 284–89); Leick (1994:157–69); and Nissinen (1998:28–36). Kilmer (1971:300) correctly notes *CAD*'s (8:558) error in saying that they are "neither male nor female" in "Ishtar's Descent" (cf. Sladek 1974:87, n. 2). See Katz (1995:229, n.19) on the name Asushunamir. Dalley (1989:161) whimsically calls him "Good-looks the playboy" and explains his name as a pun on an epithet of the moon god, "who like the boy could travel to and from the Underworld without being harmed." In the Sumerian "Inana's Descent," Ea creates two creatures from the dirt under his fingernails, the

gala-tur-ra and *kur-gar-ra* (see Sladek 1974:93–99). These cultic functionaries are also sexually ambiguous in cuneiform sources, but their manipulation of Ereshkigal is unrelated to her sexual frustration (see Kilmer 1971).

[43]Contra Sladek (1974:92), the phrase does not mean "inflame with passion" (see *CAD* 11/1:278–79).

[44]Sladek's argument is inconsistent. He disavows the possibility of Ereshkigal's interest in procreative sex but translates lines 230–31, "A pregnant woman, Ereshkigal by name, is lying there *in labor*(?)" (1974:171, 208–9; cp. Alster 1983:7–8). Sladek attempts to explain that sexual intercourse in "Nergal and Ereshkigal" is "not really a contradiction" to his previous statement that there can be no sex in the Netherworld because the myth is a "relatively late aetiology" (1974:67, n. 1).

[45]See iv 57'–59' and Uruk v 11; the former text is fragmentary and the latter has grammatical problems. Namtar says, "Send me!" (*šuprīnnī-ma*) and "I will seize" (either *lū ṣabtāku* or *luṣbatašsu* in proper Akkadian). One should not restore "that he may kiss you," however, as Dalley (1989:172) following Gurney (1960:120).

[46]Cassin 1987:234, n. 29. On *ardat-lilî* see Lackenbacher (1971) and Farber (1987; 1989). On the links between *ardat-lilî* and Ishtar, see Groneberg (1997:125–30).

[47]*Ardatu ša kīma sinništi lā reḫâtu ardatu ša kīma sinništi lā naqpatu* (Lackenbacher 1971:131, 139; cf. 136); *ardatu ša ina sūn mutīša kuzba lā ilputu* (Lackenbacher 1971:136, 140). The word *reḫâtu* may mean "be impregnated."

[48]*Ardatu ša itti ardāti sūqa u sulâ lā ibāʾu* (Lackenbacher 1971:136). *Ardatu ša itti ardāti lā iḫdû ardatu ša ina isinni ālīša lā innamru* (Farber 1989:15).

[49]I parse the verb as 2c.pl. with a 1c.pl. dative suffix (*nâšu* written for *nâši*) (cf. *CAD* 17/1:435). Also possible is *tašpurānaššu*, 2c.pl. with a ventive (*nam* written for *nim*) and 3m.s. accusative suffix (as Gurney 1960:130), or, less likely, *tašpurannâšu*, 2m.s. with ventive and 1c.pl. dative suffix (*CAD* 14:254). Gurney (1960:130) explains the Sultantepe scribes' preference for /a/ rather than /i/ in some contexts.

[50]I am following *CAD*'s (17/1:435) textual emendation to read *šuprānâšu* instead of a D-stem form (*šup-pu-ra-na-šu-ma*).

[51]See Gurney's (1960:130–31) comments on this difficult line. He (1960:122) mistakenly reads *ebbēk-ma* in v 7′, but the *ma* does not appear

in either v 23′ or the autograph of the tablet (Gurney and Finkelstein 1957: text 28).

[52]Edzard (1989:126–27), on the other hand, suggests that this passage is composed of rhetorical questions. Accordingly, Ereshkigal asks why Nergal should not sleep with her again: "Am I defiled? Am I impure?" The following phrase—"Do I not render judgment for the great gods?"—might then be a more ominous question, leading to the explicit threat of v 9′–12′. While this interpretation is possible, there is no suggestion of an interrogative in the grammar or cuneiform orthography of these phrases (e.g., Huehnergard 1997:425). The significance of *musukku* in this interpretation remains obscure, as well.

[53]The text of this phrase (v 7′, 23′) is not clear. Gurney (1960:122, 130–31) reads *mu-suk-ka-ku-ma ul e-bek* (*musukkākū-ma ul ebbēk*). He (1960:131) notes the "barbarous spelling" of *ebbēk(u)* and the possibility of reading *e-siq*. *CAD* (10/2:317) suggests *mu-tú ka-lu*(?)*-ma ul e-sik* (*mūtu kalû-ma ul essik*). The verb *esēḫu*, "to assign," is spelled *esēku* in Mari and NA (*CAD* 4:327–28).

[54]Bottéro and Kramer (1989:451), Dalley (1989:173), Edzard (1989:126), Foster (1993:425), Hutter (1985:98–100), Leick (1994:252–53), and Müller (1994:777) follow Gurney (1960:122, 130–31). Harris (2000:137) and Reiner (1985:53) prefer *CAD*'s (10/2:317) suggestion.

[55]The words *parṣi Irkalla* are largely restored by Gurney (1960:122), based on vi 6.

[56]Apart from a subordination marker and ventive, the threat is verbatim in the Gilgamesh epic (VI 99–100). "Ishtar's Descent" (lines 19–20) uses *imaʾʾidū* , "they will outnumber," instead of *ušamʾad*, "I will make them outnumber."

[57]*Anunnaki illûnim-ma šiknat napištim imessū* (I 177; see Cagni 1969:76; *CAD* 10/2:35; Foster 1993:780). In response (I 181–89), Erra volunteers to dispatch the demons to the Netherworld and "go down to the depths and keep the gods of hell in order" (Foster 1993: 781; Cagni 1969:78).

[58]Hackett does not include "Nergal and Ereshkigal" or "Inana and Shukalletuda" in her remarks. See Hoffner (1998:90–92) for the Hittite text cited by Hackett (1989:26–27, nn. 28, 34); see also Hollis (1989) for similar motifs.

[59]Again, amend the text to read as a G-stem rather than D-stem imperative.

[60]The gods' solidarity is not an example of power-with according to Allen's model, since they do not challenge, subvert, or overthrow "a system of domination" (1999:127). To the contrary, they are protecting their own hierarchical powers.

[61]Foster (1993:412), for example, suggests that Ea advises Nergal concerning the use of the chair he constructed earlier, while Dalley (1989:175, 177, n. 25) implies that Namtar instructs Nergal on striking down the gatekeepers.

[62]Reading *inār*, "he strikes," with Dalley (1989:177:25) rather than *īlul*, "he hangs," with Gurney (1960:125) in vi 21′. The broken line is uncertain, and either reading is possible.

[63]Gurney (1960:126) suggests *mala rāʾimūtīšu ša libbīšu*, "for the love that was in his heart," for vi 34 (cf. *CAD* 14:82; Bottéro and Kramer 1989:453), but the text remains uncertain.

[64]Her commands to Namtar to sit on the throne and judge the Netherworld (Uruk iii 7′–10′) must be sarcastic because, as Foster (1993:411) notes, they make no sense in this context if taken literally (Dalley 1989:69–70; cp. Reiner 1985:56). Ereshkigal then commands Namtar to go and fetch Nergal, which he immediately does (Uruk iii 11′–12′). Ironically, Ereshkigal will soon lose her throne to the warrior Nergal, but she will not be freed to join the celestial deities.

[65]Ereshkigal may vacate her throne (e.g., v 7′), but she does not threaten to abandon the Netherworld except in her ironic remarks in Uruk iii 7′–10′.

[66]Reiner (1985:57), for example, accepts Anu's interdiction against traveling between realms at face value. She compares the "unbridgeable chasm" with that of Luke16:26 and states that interpreters would have to infer this cosmic ordinance were it not documented in Anu's words. Even if truthful, Anu's words are ambiguous in the Akkadian and could be translated as indicatives or subjunctives (but not prohibitives or vetitives). The Akkadian text does not use the verb *leʾû*, "to be able."

[67]Many scholars read *ittakis Namtar*, "He (Nergal) cut down Namtar." Izre'el (1997:60) separates the two words and translates line 75, "He (Nergal) ordered Namtar (and) his troops," *Namtar ṣābīšu ṭēma išakkan*. In either reading, Nergal usurps authority over Namtar.

[68]See Dalley 1989:156; *CAD* 8:13; cf. *CAD* 11/1:279 (s.v. *napardû*). Foster (1993:405, 409) cites a private communication from Lambert for reading *uštamṭannī-ma* instead of *ušperdânnī-ma*, and so translates, "What has aroused bad feelings in her against me?"

[69]Line 65 (*Ištar ul immalik elēnušša ušbi*) is difficult. *CAD* (4:85) suggests, "Ištar gave the matter no thought but sat down(?) above her (i.e., in the place of honor due to Ereškigal)" (cf. Foster 1993:406, 409; Sladek 1974:256). On *šubeʾû*, see *CAD* (17/3:171) and *GAG* §109 j.

[70]See Jones (1993) for a feminist analysis of the Sumerian text. Compare the feminist and archetypal readings of Perera (1981) and Meador (1992). Grahn (1987) provides a postmodern adaptation of their struggle.

[71]Quoted by Dollimore (1998:103), with references.

References

Abusch, Tzvi

1986 Ishtar's Proposal and Gilgamesh's Refusal. *HR* 26:143–87.

1993a Gilgamesh's Request and Siduri's Denial (Part I). Pp. 1–14 in Cohen, Snell, and Weisberg.

1993b Gilgamesh's Request and Siduri's Denial. Part II: An Analysis and Interpretation of an Old Babylonian Fragment about Mourning and Celebration. *Journal of the Ancient Near Eastern Society of Columbia University, New York* 22:3–17.

1998 Ghost and God: Some Observations on a Babylonian Understanding of Human Nature. Pp. 363–83 in *Self, Soul and Body in Religious Experience*, eds. A. I. Baumgarten, J. Assmann, and G. G. Stroumsa. Studies in the History of Religions, 78. Leiden: Brill.

1999 *Eṭemmu. DDD* 309–12.

Abusch, Tzvi, John Huehnergard, and Piotr Steinkeller, eds.

1990 *Lingering Over Words: Studies in Ancient Near Eastern Literature in Honor of William L. Moran*. Harvard Semitic Studies 37. Atlanta: Scholars Press.

Alexie, Sherman

1993 *The Lone Ranger and Tonto Fistfight in Heaven*. New York: The Atlantic Monthly Press.

Allen, Amy

1999 *The Power of Feminist Theory: Domination, Resistance, Solidarity*. Boulder: Westview Press.

Alster, Bendt

1983 The Mythology of Mourning. *Acta Sumerologica* 5:1–16.

1996 Inanna Repenting: The Conclusion of Inanna's Descent. *Acta Sumerologica* 18:1–18.

Alster, Bendt , ed.

1980 *Death in Mesopotamia: papers read at the XXVIe Rencontre assyriologique internationale*. Mesopotamia 8. Copenhagen: Akademisk forlag.

Anderson, Gary A.

1991 *A Time to Mourn, A Time to Dance: The Expression of Grief and Joy in Israelite Religion*. University Park, PA: Pennsylvania State University Press.

Asher-Greve, Julia M.

1997 Feminist Research and Ancient Mesopotamia: Problems and Prospects. Pp. 218–37 in Brenner and Fontaine.

1998 The Essential Body: Mesopotamian Conceptions of the Gendered Body. Pp. 8–37 in Wyke.

Atkins, G. Douglas, and Laura Morrow, eds.

1989 *Contemporary Literary Theory*. Amherst: University of Massachusetts Press.

Bailey, John A.

1970 Initiation and the Primal Woman in Gilgamesh and Genesis 2–3. *JBL* 89:137–49.

1976 Male, Female and the Pursuit of Immortality in the Gilgamesh Epic. *La Parola del Passato* 17:433–57.

Baines, John

1991 Egyptian Myth and Discourse: Myth, Gods, and the Early Written and Iconographic Record. *JNES* 50: 81–105.

1996 Myth and literature. Pp. 361–77 in Loprieno.

Barks, Coleman, and Michael Green

1997 *The Illuminated Rumi*. New York: Broadway Books.

Bataille, Georges

1987 *Eroticism: Death and Sensuality*. Trans. Mary Dalwood. San Francisco: City Lights Books.

1991 *The Accursed Share. Volume II*. Trans. Robert Hurley. New York: Zone Books.

Beard, Mary, and John Henderson

1998 With This Body I Thee Worship: Sacred Prostitution in Antiquity. Pp. 56–79 in Wyke.

Behrens, Hermann

1978 *Enlil und Ninlil: Ein sumerischer Mythos aus Nippur*. Studia Pohl 8. Rome: Biblical Institute Press.

Behrens, Hermann, Darlene Loding, and Martha T. Roth, eds.

1989 *Dumu-e$_2$-dub-ba-a: Studies in Honor of Åke W. Sjöberg*. Occasional Papers of the Samuel Noah Kramer Fund, 11. Philadelphia: University Museum.

Behrmann, Almuth

1989 *Das Nilpferd in der Vorstellungswelt der alten Ägypter*. Frankfurt am Main and New York: P. Lang.

Bell, Shannon

1994 *Reading, Writing, and Rewriting the Prostitute Body*. Bloomington and Indianapolis: Indiana University Press.

Biggs, Robert D.
1967 *ŠÀ.ZI.GA: Ancient Mesopotamian Potency Incantations*. Texts from Cuneiform Sources, 2. Locust Valley, NY: Augustin Publisher.

Blanc, Yannick.
1991 *Enquête sur la Mort de Gilgamesh*. Paris: Éditions du Félin.

Bleeker, C. J.
1973 *Hathor and Thoth*. Leiden: E. J. Brill.
1988 Isis and Hathor: Two Ancient Egyptian Goddesses. Pp. 29–48 in *The Book of the Goddess Past and Present*, ed. Carl Olsen. New York: Crossroad.

Bloch, Maurice
1982 Death, Women and Power. Pp. 211–30 in *Death and the Regeneration of Life*, eds. Maurice Bloch and Jonathan Parry. New York: Cambridge University Press.

Borger, Riekele
1963 *Babylonisch-assyrische Lesestücke*. Analecta Orientalia 54. Rome: Pontificium Institutum Biblicum.

Bottéro, Jean
1982 Les inscriptions cunéiformes funéraires. Pp. 373–406 in *La Mort, les morts dans les sociétés anciennes*, eds. G. Gnoli and J. P. Vernant. Cambridge: Cambridge University Press.
1992a *L'Épopée de Gilgameš. Le grand homme qui ne voulait pas mourir*. Paris: Gallimard.
1992b *Mesopotamia: Writing, Reasoning, and the Gods*. Trans. Zainab Bahrani and Marc Van De Mieroop. Chicago: University of Chicago.

Bottéro, Jean, and Samuel Noah Kramer
1989 *Lorsque les dieux faisaient l'homme: Mythologie mésopotamienne*. Paris: Gallimard.

Bottéro, Jean, and H. Petschow
1975 Homosexualität. *RlA* 4:459–68.

Brenner, Athalya, and Carole Fontaine, eds.
1997 *A Feminist Companion to Reading the Bible: Approaches, Methods and Strategies*. Sheffield: Sheffield Academic Press.

Broze, M.
1996 *Mythe et Roman en Égypte ancienne. Les aventures d'Horus et Seth dans le Papyrus Chester Beatty I*. Orientalia lovaniensia analecta 76. Leuven: Uitgeverij Peeters.

Brunner-Traut, Emma
1986 *Altägyptische Marchen*. 7th ed. Cologne: Eugen Diederichs Verlag.

1988 *Gelebte Mythen. Beiträge zum altägyptischen Mythos.* 3rd ed. Darmstadt: Wissenschaftliche Buchgesellschaft.

Butler, S. A. L.
1998 *Mesopotamian Conceptions of Dreams and Dream Rituals.* Münster: Ugarit-Verlag.

Bynum, Caroline Walker
1986 Introduction: The Complexity of Symbols. Pp. 1–20 in *Gender and Religion: On the Complexity of Symbols*, eds. Caroline Walker Bynum, Stevan Harrell, and Paula Richman. Boston: Beacon.

Cagni, Luigi
1969 *L'epopea di Erra.* Studi Semitici 23. Rome: Instituto di Studi del Vicino Oriente.

Cassin, Elena
1987 *Le semblable et le différent: symbolismes du pouvoir dans le proche-orient ancien.* Paris: Éditions la découverte.

Caldwell, Richard
1989 *The Origin of the Gods: A Psychoanalytic Study of Greek Theogonic Myth.* Oxford and New York: Oxford University Press.
1990 The Psychoanalytic Interpretation of Greek Myth. Pp. 344–89 in Edmunds.

Carson, Anne
1990 Putting Her in Her Place: Woman, Dirt, and Desire. Pp. 135–69 in Halperin, Winkler, and Zeitlin.

Clair, Jean
1989 *Méduse: contribution à une anthropologie des arts du visuel.* Paris: Gallimard.

Cohen, Percy S.
1969 Theories of Myth. *Man* 4:337–53.

Cohen, Mark E., Daniel C. Snell, and David B. Weisberg, eds.
1993 *The Tablet and the Scroll: Near Eastern Studies in Honor of W. W. Hallo.* Bethesda, MD: CDL Press.

Comstock, Gary David
1992 Love, Power and Competition Among Men in Hebrew Scripture: Jonathan as Unconventional Nurturer. Pp. 9–29 in *Religion, Homosexuality and Literature*, eds. Michael L. Stemmeler and José Ignatio Caberón. Las Colinas: Monument Press.

Cooper, Jerrold S.
1975 Heilige Hochzeit. B. Archäologisch. *RlA* 4:259–69.

1977 Gilgamesh Dreams of Enkidu: The Evolution and Dilation of Narrative. Pp. 39–44 in *Essays on the Ancient Near East in Memory of Jacob Joel Finketstein*, ed. M. de Jong Ellis. Memoirs of the Connecticut Academy of Sciences 19. Hamden, CT: Archon Books.

1980 Review of Behrens 1978. *JCS* 32:175–88.

1989 Enki's Member: Eros and Irrigation in Sumerian Mythology. Pp. 87–89 in Behrens, Loding, and Roth.

1991 The Fate of Mankind: Death and Afterlife in Ancient Mesopotamia. Pp. 19–33 in *Death and Afterlife: Perspectives of World Religions*, ed. H. Obayashi. Contributions to the Study of Religion, 33. New York: Greenwood Press

1993 Sacred Marriage and Popular Cult in Early Mesopotamia. Pp. 81–96 in *Official Cult and Popular Religion in the Ancient Near East*, ed. E. Matsushima. Heidelberg: Universitätsverlag C. Winter.

1996 Magic and M(is)use: Poetic Promiscuity in Mesopotamian Ritual. Pp. 47–57 in Vogelzang and Vanstiphout.

1997 Gendered Sexuality in Sumerian Love Poetry. Pp. 85–97 in *Sumerian Gods and Their Representations*, eds. I. L. Finkel and M. J. Geller. Cuneiform Monographs 7. Groningen: Styx Publications.

Day, Peggy, ed.

1989 *Gender and Difference in Ancient Israel*. Minneapolis: Fortess.

Detienne, Marcel

1979 *Dionysos Slain*. Trans. M. Muellner and L. Muellner. Baltimore: Johns Hopkins University Press.

Devereux, George

1983 *Baubo, le vulve mythique*. Paris: Jean-Cyrille Godefroy.

van Dijk, Jacobus

1986 ʿAnat, Seth and the Seed of Preʿ. Pp. 31–51 in *Scripta Signa Vocis*, ed. H. Vanstiphout et al. Groningen: Egbert Forsten.

Dillard, Annie

1989 *The Writing Life*. New York: HarperCollins.

Dittmar, Johanna

1986 *Blumen und Blumenstrausse als Opfergabe im alten Ägypten*. Munich: Deutscher Kunstverlag.

Doane, Mary Ann

1991 *Femmes Fatales: Feminism, Film Theory, Psychoanalysis*. New York and London: Routledge.

Dollimore, Jonathan

1998 *Death, Desire and Loss in Western Culture*. New York: Routledge.

Doniger, Wendy

1998 *The Implied Spider: Politics and Theology in Myth*. New York: Columbia University Press.

Doty, William G.

1986 *Mythography: The Study of Myths and Rituals*. Birmingham: University of Alabama Press.

1993 *Myths of Masculinity*. New York: Crossroad.

Drenkhahn, R.

1977 "Hirtengeschichte." *LÄ* II:1223.

van Driel, G., et al., eds.

1982 *Zikir Šumim. Studies presented to F. R. Kraus*. Leiden: Brill.

Dubuisson, Daniel

1993 *Mythologies du XXe siècle*. Lille: Presses universitaires de Lille.

Dundes, Alan

1980 *Interpreting Folklore*. Bloomington: Indiana University.

1987 The Psychoanalytic Study of Folklore. Pp. 3–46 in *Parsing Through Customs: Essays by a Freudian Folklorist*. Madison: University of Wisconsin Press. Originally in *Annals of Scholarship* 3/3 (1985) 1–42.

1989 The Psychoanalytic Study of the Grimms' Tales: "The Maiden Without Hands" (AT 706). Pp. 112–50 in *Folklore Matters*. Knoxville: University of Tennessee.

1996 Madness in Method Plus a Plea for Projective Inversion in Myth. Pp. 147–59 in Patton and Doniger.

DuQuesne, Terence

1994 The Raw And The Half-Baked: approaches to Egyptian religion. *Discussions in Egyptology* 30:29–35.

Dux, Gunter

1992 *Liebe und Tod im Gilgamesch-Epos: Geschichte als Weg zum Selbstbewusstsein des Menschen*. Wien: Passagen Verlag.

Dynes, Wayne R. and Stephen Donaldson, eds.

1992 *Homosexual themes in literary studies*. Studies in homosexuality, v. 8. New York: Garland.

Edmunds, Lowell, ed.

1990 *Approaches to Greek Myth*. Baltimore: Johns Hopkins University Press.

Edzard, D. O.
1989 Review of Hutter 1985. *ZA* 79:124–27.

Eilberg-Schwartz, H., and W. Doniger, eds.
1995 *Off with Her Head! The Denial of Women's Identity in Myth, Religion, and Culture*. Berkeley: University of California Press.

Eisner, Robert
1987 *The Road to Daulis: Psychoanalysis, Psychology, and Classical Mythology*. Syracuse: Syracuse University Press.

Exum, Cheryl
1995 Feminist Criticism: Whose Interests Are Being Served? Pp. 65–90 in *Judges and Method: New Approaches in Biblical Studies*, ed. Gale A. Yee. Minneapolis: Fortress Press.

Farber, Walter
1987 Lilû, Lilītu, Ardat-lilî. A. Philologisch. *RlA* 7:23–24.
1989 (W)ardat-lilî(m). *ZA* 79:14–35.
1995 Witchcraft, Magic, and Divination in Ancient Mesopotamia. *CANE* 3:1895–1909.

Faulkner, R. O.
1969 *The Ancient Egyptian Pyramid Texts*. London: Oxford University Press.
1990 *The Ancient Egyptian Book of the Dead*, ed. Carol Andrews. Austin: University of Texas Press.

Finkelstein, J. J.
1966 Sex Offenses in Sumerian Laws. *Journal of the American Oriental Society* 86:355–72.

Fontaine, Carole
1988 The Deceptive Goddess in Ancient Near Eastern Myth: Inanna and Inaraš. *Reasoning with the Foxes: Female Wit in a World of Male Power*, eds. J. Cheryl Exum and Johanna W. H. Bos. *Semeia* 42:84–102.

Foster, Benjamin
1987 Gilgamesh: Sex, Love, and the Ascent of Knowledge. Pp. 21–42 in *Love & Death in the Ancient Near East: Essays in Honor of Marvin H. Pope*, eds. John Marks and Robert M. Good. Guilford, CT: Four Quarters.
1993 *Before the Muses: An Anthology of Akkadian Literature*. 2 vols. Bethesda, MD: CDL Press.
1995 Humor and Wit in the Ancient Near East. *CANE* 4:2459–69.

Foucault, Michel
1978 *The History of Sexuality: An Introduction*. Trans. Robert Hurley. New York: Random House.

Frantzen, Allen J.
1998 *Before the Closet: Same-Sex Love from* Beowulf *to* Angels in America. Chicago and London: The University of Chicago Press.

Frymer-Kensky, Tikva
1992 *In the Wake of the Goddesses: Women, Culture and the Biblical Transformation of Pagan Myth.* New York: Free Press.

Furlani, Giuseppe
1977 Das Gilgamesch-Epos als Hymnus auf die Freundschaft. Pp. 219–36 in *Das Gilgamesch-Epos*, ed. K. Oberhuber. Darmstadt.

Gardiner, Alan
1931 *The Library of A. Chester Beatty.... The Chester Beatty Papyri, No. I.* London: Oxford University Press.
1935 *Chester Beatty Gift.* 2 vols. *Hieratic Papyri in the British Museum*, vol. 3. London: British Museum.

Gardner, John, and John Maier
1984 *Gilgamesh: Translated from the Sîn-leqi-unninnī version.* New York: Knopf.

Geertz, Clifford
1966 Religion as a Cultural System. Pp. 1–46 in *Anthropological Approaches to the Study of Religion*, ed. Miachel Banton. London and New York: Tavistock.

George, Andrew
1999 *The Epic of Gilgamesh: The Babylonian Epic Poem and Other Texts in Akkadian and Sumerian.* New York: Barnes & Noble.

Gilligan, Carol
1982 *In a Different Voice: Psychological Theory and Women's Development.* Cambridge and London: Harvard University Press.

Gleason, Maud W.
1990 The Semiotics of Gender: Physiognomy and Self-Fashioning in the Second Century C.E. Pp. 389–415 in Halperin, Winkler, and Zeitlin.

Goedicke, Hans
1970 The Story of the Herdsman. *Chronique d'Égypte* 45:244–66.

Grahn, Judy
1987 *The Queen of Swords.* Boston: Bracon Press.

Gray, John
1985 *Near Eastern Mythology.* New York: Peter Bedrick.

Greenberg, David F.
1988 *The Construction of Homosexuality.* Chicago: University of Chicago Press.

Griffiths, John Gwyn
1960 *The Conflict of Horus and Seth from Egyptian and Classical Sources*. Liverpool: Liverpool University Press.
1970 *Pluratch's "De Iside et Osiride"*. Cambridge: University of Wales Press.

Groneberg, Brigitte
1990 Zu den mesopotamischen Unterweltsvorstellungen: Das Jenseit als Fortsetzung des Diesseits. *Altorientalische Forschungen* 17:244–61.
1997 *Lob der Ištar: Gebet und Ritual an die altbabylonische Venus Göttin* Tanatti Ištar. Cuneiform Monographs 8. Groningen: Styx Publications.

Guinan, Ann Kessler
1998 Auguries of Hegemony: The Sex Omens of Mesopotamia. Pp. 38–55 in Wyke.

Gurney, Oliver R.
1960 The Sultantepe Tablets VII. The Myth of Nergal and Ereshkigal. *Anatolian Studies* 10:105–31.

Gurney, Oliver R., and J. J. Finkelstein
1957 *The Sultantepe Tablets I*. London: British Institute of Archaeology at Ankara.

Gurney, Oliver R., and P. Hulin
1964 *The Sultantepe Tablets II*. London: British Institute of Archaeology at Ankara.

Haas, Volkert, ed.
1992 *Aussenseiter und Randgruppen. Beiträge zu einer Sozialgeschichte des Alten Orients*. Xenia 32. Constance: Universitätsverlag Konstanz.

Hackett, Jo Ann
1989 Rehabilitating Hagar: Fragments of an Epic Pattern. Pp. 12–27 in Day.

Hallissy, Margaret
1987 *Venomous Woman: Fear of the Female in Literature*. New York: Greenwood Press.

Halperin, David M.
1990 *One Hundred Years of Greek Homosexuality: And Other Essays on Greek Love*. New York and London: Routledge.

Halperin, David M., John J. Winkler, and Froma I. Zeitlin, eds.
1990 *Before Sexuality: The Construction of Erotic Experience in the Ancient Greek World*. Princeton: Princeton University Press.

Hammond, Dorothy, and Alta Jablow

1987 Gilgamesh and the Sundance Kid: The Myth of Male Friendship. Pp. 241–58 in *The Making of Masculinities: The New Men's Studies*, ed. Harry Brod. Boston: Allen & Unwin.

Hardman, Paul D.

1993 *Homoaffectionalism: male bonding from Gilgamesh to the present*. San Francisco: NF Division, GLB Publishers.

Harris, Rivkah

1990 Images of Women in the *Gilgamesh Epic*. Pp. 219–29 in Abusch, Huehnergard, and Steinkeller. Reprinted in Harris 2000:119–28.

1991 Inanna-Ishtar as Paradox and Coincidence of Opposites. *HR* 30:261–78. Reprinted in Harris 2000:158–71.

2000 *Gender and Aging in Mesopotamia: The Gilgamesh Epic and Other Ancient Literature*. Norman: University of Oklahoma Press.

Healey, J. F.

1999 Mot. *DDD* 598–603.

Hecker, K.

1994 Das akkadische Gilgamesch-Epos. *TUAT* III/4:646–744.

Held, George F.

1983 Parallels between *The Gilgamesh Epic* and Plato's *Symposium*. *JNES* 42:133–41.

Henderson, Jeffrey

1988 Greek Attitudes to Sex. *Civilizations of the Ancient Mediterranean*, eds. Michael Grant and Rachel Kitzinger. II:1249–63. New York: Charles Scribner's Sons.

Henshaw, Richard A.

1993 *Female and Male: The Cultic Personnel—The Bible and the Rest of the Ancient Near East*. Allison Park, PA: Pickwick Press.

Hirsch, H.

1982 Über das Lachen der Götter. Pp. 110–20 in van Driel et al.

Hollis, Susan Tower

1989 The Woman in Ancient Examples of the Potiphar's Wife Motif, K2111. Pp. 29–42 in Day.

1990 *The Ancient Egyptian "Tale of Two Brothers": The Oldest Fairy Tale in the World*. Norman: University of Oklahoma Press.

Hollis, Susan Tower, Linda Pershing, and M. Jane Young, eds.

1993 *Feminist Theory and the Study of Folklore*. Urbana and Chicago: University of Illinois Press.

Hornung, Erik

1975 Seth. Geschichte und Bedeutung eines ägyptischen Gottes. *Symbolon* N.F. 2:49–63.

1983 *Conceptions of God in Ancient Egypt: The One and the Many.* Trans. John Baines. Ithaca: Cornell University Press.

1986 The Discovery of the Unconscious in Ancient Egypt. Pp. 16–28 in *Spring: An Annual of Archetypal Psychology and Jungian Thought.* Dallas: Spring Publications.

1992 *Idea into Image: Essays on Ancient Egyptian Thought.* Trans. E. Bredeck. Princeton: Timken Publishers.

Huehnergard, John

1997 *A Grammar of Akkadian.* Harvard Semitic Studies 45. Atlanta: Scholars Press.

Hunger, H.

1976 *Spätbabylonische Texte aus Uruk I.* Berlin: Mann.

Hutter, Manfred

1985 *Altorientalische Vorstellungen von der Unterwelt: Literar- und religionsgeschichtlische Überlegung zu "Nergal und Ereškigal".* OBO 63. Freiburg: Universitätsverlag; Göttingen: Vandenhoeck & Ruprecht.

Izre'el, Shlomo

1992 The Study of Oral Poetry: Reflections of a Neophyte. Pp. 155–225 Vogelzang and Vanstiphout.

1997 *The Amarna Scholarly Tablets.* Cuneiform Monographs 9. Groningen: Styx.

2001 *Adapa and the South Wind: Language Has Power of Life and Death.* Mesopotamian Civilizations 10. Winona Lake, IN: Eisenbrauns.

Jackson, W. T. H.

1982 *The Hero and the King: An Epic Theme.* New York: Columbia University Press.

Jacobsen, Thorkild

1930 How Did Gilgameš Oppress Uruk? *Acta Orientalia* 8:62–74.

1976 *The Treasures of Darkness: A History of Mesopotamian Religion.* New Haven: Yale University Press.

1987a *The Harps That Once...: Sumerian Poetry in Translation.* New Haven and London: Yale University Press.

1987b Pictures and Pictoral Language (The Burney Relief). Pp. 1–11 in Mindlin, Geller, and Wansbrough.

1990 The Gilgamesh Epic: Romantic and Tragic Vision. Pp. 231–49 in Abusch, Huehnergard, and Steinkeller.

1993 The Descent of Enki. Pp. 120–23 in Cohen, Snell, and Weisberg.

Jagose, Annamarie

1996 *Queer Theory: An Introduction*. Washington Square, NY: New York University Press.

Jones, Debby Dale

1993 *She Spoke to Them with a Stormy Heart: The Politics of Reading Ancient (or Other) Narrative*. Ph.D. Dissertation, University of Minnesota.

Junge, Friedrich

1995 Die Erzählung vom Streit der Götter Horus und Seth um die Herrschaft. *TUAT* 3/5:930–50.

Katz, Dina

1993 The Concept of Death and Netherworld in Mesopotamia According to the Sumerian Sources. Unpublished Ph. D. dissertation, Tel-Aviv University. (In Hebrew)

1995 Inanna's Descent and Undressing the Dead as a Divine Law. *ZA* 85:221–33.

Kilmer, Anne Draffkorn

1971 How Was Queen Ereshkigal Tricked? A New Interpretation of the Descent of Ishtar. *UF* 3:299–309.

1982 A Note on an overlooked Word-Play in the Akkadian Gilgamesh. Pp. 128–32 in van Driel et al.

Kirk, G. S.

1970 *Myth: Its Meaning and Functions in Ancient and Other Cultures*. Berkeley and Los Angeles: University of California Press.

1974 *The Nature of Greek Myths*. London and New York: Penguin Books.

Kluger, Rivkah Scharf

1991 *The Archetypal Significance of Gilgamesh*. Einsiedeln, Switzerland: Daimon Verlag.

Kovacs, Maureen Gallery

1989 *The Epic of Gilgamesh*. Stanford: Stanford University Press.

Kramer, Samuel Noah

1967 The Death of Ur-Nammu and His Descent to the Netherworld. *JCS* 21:104–22.

1991 The Death of Ur-Nammu. Pp. 193–214 in *Near Eastern Studies Dedicated to H. I. H. Prince Takahito Mikasa on the Occasion of His Seventy-Fifth Birthday*, eds. M. Mori, H. Ogawa, and M. Yoshikawa. Wiesbaden: Harrassowitz.

Kramer, Samuel Noah, and John Maier
1989 *Myths of Enki, the Crafty God*. New York and Oxford: Oxford University Press.

Kroll, Josef
1932 *Gott und Hölle: Der Mythos vom Descensuskampfe*. Leipzig and Berlin: B. G. Teubner.

Lackenbacher, Sylvie
1971 Note sure l'*ardat-lilî*. *Revue d'assyriologie* 65:119–54.

Lambert, Wilfred G.
1960 *Babylonian Wisdom Literature*. Oxford: Oxford University Press.
1973 Studies in Nergal. *Bibliotheca Orientalis* 30:355–63.
1980 The Theology of Death. Pp. 53–66 in Alster.
1982 The Hymn to the Queen of Nippur. Pp. 173–218 in van Driel et al.
1987a Gilgamesh in Literature and Art: the Second and First Millennia. Pp. 37–52 in *Monsters and Demons in the Ancient and Medieval Worlds*, eds. A. Farkas, P. Harper, and E. Harrison. Mainz on Rhine: Verlag Philipp von Zabern.
1987b Devotion: The Languages of Religion and Love. Pp. 25–39 in Mindlin, Geller, and Wansbrough.
1990a A New Babylonian Descent to the Netherworld. Pp. 289–300 in Abusch, Huehnergard, and Steinkeller.
1990b The Name of Nergal Again. *ZA* 80:40–52.
1990c Surrejoinder to P. Steinkeller. *ZA* 80:220–22.
1992 Prostitution. Pp. 127–57 in Haas.

Lamott, Anne
1999 *Traveling Mercies: Some Thoughts on Faith*. New York: Anchor Books.

Leach, Edmund
1976 The Mother's Brother in Ancient Egypt. *Royal Anthropological Institute News*15 (August):19–21.

Lederer, Wolfgang
1968 *The Fear of Women*. New York and London: Grune & Stratton.

Leick, Gwendolyn
1994 *Sex and Eroticism in Mesopotamian Literature*. London and New York: Routledge.
1998 The Challenge of Chance: An Anthropological View of Mesopotamian Mental Strategies for the Dealing with the Unpredictable. Pp. 195–98 in Prosecký.

Lewis, Theodore J.
1989 *Cults of the Dead in Ancient Israel and Ugarit*. HSM 39. Atlanta: Scholars Press.

Lichtheim, Mariam
1976 *Ancient Egyptian Literature. Volume II: The New Kingdom*. Berkeley and Los Angeles: University of California.

Lilly, Mark
1993 *Gay Men's Literature in the Twentieth Century*. Washington Square: New York University Press.

Littleton, C. Scott
1982 *The New Comparative Mythology*. 3rd ed. Berkeley and Los Angeles: University of California Press.

Livingstone, Alasdair
1989 *Court Poetry and Literary Miscellanea*. State Archives of Assyria III. Helsinki: Helsinki University Press.
1999 Nergal. *DDD* 621–22.

Longman, Tremper, III
1991 *Fictional Akkadian Autobiography: A Generic and Comparative Study*. Winona Lake, IN: Eisenbrauns.

Loprieno, Antonio (ed.)
1996a *Ancient Egyptian Literature: History and Forms*. Probleme der Ägyptologie 10. Leiden: E. J. Brill.
1996b Defining Egyptian Literature: Ancient Texts and Modern Literary Theory. Pp. 209–32 in *The Study of the Ancient Near East in the Twenty-First Century: The William Foxwell Albright Centennial Conference*, eds. Jerrold S. Cooper and Glenn M. Schwartz. Winona Lake, IN: Eisenbrauns.

Loraux, Nicole
1990 Herakles: The Super-Male and the Feminine. Pp. 21–52 in Halperin, Winkler, and Zeitlin.

Lubell, Winifred Milius
1994 *The Metamorphosis of Baubo: Myths of Woman's Sexual Energy*. Nashville and London: Vanderbilt University Press.

McClelland, David C.
1975 *Power: The Inner Experience*. New York: Irvington.

Maier, John
1984 Introduction: The One Who Saw the Abyss. Pp. 3–54 in Gardner and Maier.

Maier, John, ed.
1997 *Gilgamesh: A Reader*. Wauconda, IL: Bolchazy-Carducci.

Manniche, Lise

1987 *Sexual Life in Ancient Egypt*. London and New York: KPI.

Maul, Stefan M.

1992 *kurgarrû* und *assinnu* und ihr Stand in der babylonischen Gesellschaft. Pp. 159–71 in Haas.

Meador, Betty De Shong

1992 *Uncursing the Dark: treasures from the underworld*. Wilmette, Ill.: Chiron.

Meier, Samuel A.

1988 *The Messenger in the Ancient Semitic World*. HSM 45. Atlanta: Scholars Press.

Meissner, B.

1902 Ein altbabylonisches Fragment des Gilgamosepos. *Mitteilungen des Vorderasiatischen Gesellschaft* 7/1:1–16 and pl. I–II.

Michalowski, Piotr

1990 Presence at the Creation. Pp. 381–96 in Abusch, Huehnergard, and Steinkeller.

1996 Sailing to Babylon, Reading the Dark Side of the Moon. Pp. 177–93 in *The Study of the Ancient Near East in the Twenty-First Century: The William Foxwell Albright Centennial Conference*, eds. Jerrold S. Cooper and Glenn M. Schwartz. Winona Lake, IN: Eisenbrauns.

Mindlin, M., M. J. Geller, and J. E. Wansbrough, eds.

1987 *Figurative Language in the Ancient Near East*. London: School of Oriental and African Studies.

Miller, D. Gary, and P. Wheeler

1981 Mother Goddess and Consort as Literary Motif Sequence in the Gilgamesh Epic. *Acta Antiqua* 29:81–108.

Mobley, Gregory

1997 The Wild Man in the Bible and the Ancient Near East. *JBL* 116:217–33.

Moran, William L.

1987 Review of Hutter 1985. *Catholic Biblical Quarterly* 49:114–15.

1991 Ovid's *Blanda Voluptas* and the Humanization of Enkidu. *JNES* 90:121–27.

1995 The Gilgamesh Epic: A Masterpiece from Ancient Mesopotamia. *CANE* 4:2327–36.

Morson, Gary Saul, and Caryl Emerson

1990 *Mikhail Bakhtin: Creation of a Prosaics*. Standford: Stanford University Press.

Müller, Gerfrid G. W.
1994 Akkadische Unterweltsmythen. *TUAT* III/4:760–80.

Nissinen, Martti
1998 *Homoeroticism in the Biblical World*. Minneapolis: Fortress.

Oden, Robert A., Jr.
1979 "The Contendings of Horus and Seth" (Chester Beatty Papyrus No. 1): A Structural Interpretation. *HR* 18:352–69.
1987 *The Bible Without Theology*. New York: Harper and Row.
1992 Myth and Mythology. *ABD* 4:946–56.

O'Flaherty, Wendy Doniger
1980 *Women, Androgynes, and Other Mythical Beasts*. Chicago: University of Chicago.

Olender, Maurice
1990 Aspects of Baubo: Ancient Texts and Contexts. Pp. 83–113 in Halperin, Winkler, and Zeitlin. Abbreviated translation by Robert Lamberton of Aspects de Baubô: Textes et contextes antiques. *Revue de l'histoire des religions* 202 (1985) 3–55.

Oppenheim, A. Leo
1956 *The Interpretation of Dreams in the Ancient Near East with a Translation of an Assyrian Dream-Book*. Transactions of the American Philosophical Society NS 46/3.

Paglia, Camille
1990 *Sexual Personae: Art and Decadence from Nefertiti to Emily Dickinson*. London and New Haven: Yale University Press.

Parkinson, R. B.
1995 'Homosexual' Desire and Middle Kingdom Literature. *JEA* 81:57–76.

Parpola, Simo
1993 The Assryian Tree of Life: Tracing the Origins of Jewish Monotheism and Greek Philosophy. *JNES* 52:161–208.
1997 *The Standard Babylonian Epic of Gilgamesh: Cuneiform Text, Transliteration, Glossary, Indices and Sign List*. State Archives of Assyria Cuneiform Texts 1. Helsinki: The Neo-Assyrian Text Corpus Project.
1998 The Esoteric Meaning of the Name of Gilgamesh. Pp. 315–29 in Prosecký.

Patton, Laurie L., and Wendy Doniger, eds.
1996 *Myth and Method*. Charlottesville: University Press of Virginia.

Paul, Robert A.
1996 *Moses and Civilization: The Meaning Behind Freud's Myth*. New Haven and London: Yale University Press.

Penglase, Charles.
1994 *Greek Myths and Mesopotamia: Parallels and Influence in the Homeric Hymns and Hesiod.* London and New York: Routledge.

Perera, Sylvia Brinton
1981 *Descent of the Goddess: A Way of Initiation for Women.* Toronto: Inner City Books.

Picchioni, S. A.
1981 *Il poemetto di Adapa.* Assyriologia 6. Budapest.

Porada, Edith
1980 The Iconography of Death in Mesopotamia in the Early Second Millennium B.C. Pp. 259–70 in Alster.
1987 Lilû, Lilītu, Ardat-lilî. B. Archäologisch. *RlA* 7:24–25.

Prosecký, Jiří, ed.
1998 *Intellectual Life of the Ancient Near East. Papers Presented at the 43rd Rencontre assyriologique internationale Prague, July 1–5, 1996.* Prague: Oriental Institute.

Rank, Otto
1990 The Myth of the Birth of the Hero. Pp. 3–86 in *In Quest of the Hero*, ed. Robert A. Segal. Princeton: Princeton University Press. Originally *The Myth of the Birth of the Hero.* Trans. F. Robbins and Smith Ely Jelliffe. New York: Journal of Nervous and Mental Disease Publishing, 1914; German original, 1909.

Ray, Benjamin C.
1996 The Gilgamesh Epic: Myth and Meaning. Pp. 300–26 in Patton and Doniger.

Reiner, Erica
1985 *Your Thwarts in Pieces, Your Mooring Rope Cut. Poetry from Babylonia and Assyria.* Michigan Studies in the Humanities 5. Ann Arbor: University of Michigan.

Richlin, Amy
1993 Not Before Homosexuality. *Journal of the History of Sexuality* 3:523–72.

Ricoeur, Paul
1969 *The Symbolism of Evil.* Trans. Emerson Buchanan. Boston: Beacon Press.
1974 *The Conflict of Interpretations: Essays in Hermeneutics*, ed. Don Ihde. Evanston: Northwestern University Press.

Ritner, Robert K.
1993 *The Mechanics of Ancient Egyptian Magical Practice.* Studies

in Ancient Oriental Civilization 54. Chicago: Oriental Institute.

Robins, Gay
1979 The Relationships specified by Egyptian Kinship Terms of the Middle and New Kingdoms. *Chronique d'Égypte* 54, no. 108:197–217.

Rogerson, J. W.
1974 *Myth in Old Testament Research.* Berlin: Walter de Gruyter.

Róheim, Géza
1972 Aphrodite, or the Woman with a Penis. Pp. 169–205 in *The Panic of the Gods and Other Essays*, ed. and intro. by W. Muensterberger. New York: Harper Torchbooks. Originally published in *The Psychoanalytic Quarterly* 14, no. 13 (July 1945) 350–90.
1992 *Fire in the Dragon and Other Psychoanalytic Essays on Folklore*, ed. and intro. by Alan Dundes. Princeton: Princeton University Press.

Rouse, W. H. D., trans.
1937 *The Odyssey: The Story of Odysseus.* New York: New American Library.

Säve-Söderbergh, T.
1953 *On Egyptian Representations of Hippopotamus Hunting as a Religious Motive.* Horae Soederblomienae III. Uppsala; Lund: C. W. K. Gleerup.

Scott, Joan W,
1986 Gender: A Useful Category of Historical Analysis. *American Historical Review* 91:1053–75.

Scurlock, JoAnn
1988 *Magical Means of Dealing with Ghosts in Ancient Mesopotamia.* Ph.D. Dissertation, University of Chicago. Ann Arbor: UMI Dissertation Services.
1995 Death and the Afterlife in Ancient Mesopotamian Thought. *CANE* 3:1883–93.

Sedgwick, Eve Kosofsky
1985 *Between Men: English Literature and Male Homosocial Desire.* New York: Columbia University Press.

Sedgwick, Eve Kosofsky, ed.
1997 *Novel Gazing: Queer Readings in Fiction.* Durham and London: Duke University Press.

Segal, Robert A.
1980 In Defense of Mythology: The History of Modern Theories of

Myth. *Annals of Scholarship* 1:3–49.

1990 *In Quest of the Hero*, ed. and intro. Robert A. Segal. Princeton: Princeton University Press.

1999 *Theorizing about Myth*. Amherst: University of Massachusetts Press.

Shaffer, Aaron

1963 *Sumerian Sources of Tablet XII of the Epic of Gilgamesh*. Ph.D. dissertation, University of Pennsylvania.

Sladek, William R.

1974 *Inanna's Descent to the Netherworld*. Ph.D. Dissertation, Johns Hopkins University.

Slater, Philip E.

1968 *The Glory of Hera: Greek Mythology and the Greek Family*. Boston: Beacon.

Smith, Mark S.

1997 The Baal Cycle. Pp. 81–180 in *Ugaritic Narrative Poetry*, ed. Simon B. Parker. Atlanta: Scholars Press.

Sperber, Dan

1975 *Rethinking Symbolism*. Trans. Alice L. Morton. Cambridge: Cambridge University Press.

Spronk, Klaas

1986 *Beatific Afterlife in Ancient Israel and in the Ancient Near East*. AOAT 219. Neukirchen-Vluyn: Neukirchener Verlag; Kevelaer: Butzon & Bercker.

Staten, Henry

1995 *Eros in Mourning: Homer to Lacan*. Baltimore: Johns Hopkins University Press.

Steinkeller, Piotr

1982 The Mesopotamian God Kakka. *JNES* 41:289–94.

1987 The Name of Nergal. *ZA* 77:161–68.

1990 More on the Name of Nergal and Related Matters. *ZA* 80:53–59.

Sternberg, Heike

1985 *Mythische Motive und Mythenbildung in den ägyptischen Tempeln und Papyri der griechisch-romischen Zeit*. Gottinger Orientforschungen IV, 14. Wiesbaden: Harrassowitz.

Strenski, Ivan

1987 *Four Theories of Myth in Twentieth-Century History: Cassirer, Eliade, Lévi-Strauss, and Malinowski*. Iowa City: University of Iowa Press.

Taylor, Martin, ed.
1989 *Lads. Love Poetry of the Trenches*. London: Constable.

Thompson, R. Campbell
1930 *The Epic of Gilgamesh: Text, Transliteration, and Notes*. Oxford: Clarendon Press.

Tigay, Jeffrey H.
1982 *The Evolution of the Gilgamesh Epic*. Philadelphia: University of Pennsylvania.

Torsney, Cheryl B.
1989 The Critical Quilt: Alternative Authority in Feminist Criticism. Pp. 180–99 in Atkins and Morrow.

Tournay, Raymond Jacques, and Aaron Shaffer
1994 *L'Épopée de Gilgamesh. Introduction, Traduction et Notes*. Paris: Les Éditions du Cerf.

Tsukimoto, Akio
1985 *Untersuchungen zur Totenpflege im alten Mesopotamien*. AOAT 216. Neukirchen-Vluyn: Neukirchener Verlag; Kevelaer: Butzon & Bercker.

Van Nortwick, Thomas
1992 *Somewhere I Have Never Travelled: The Second Self and the Hero's Journey in Ancient Epic*. New York: Oxford University Press.

Vanstiphout, H. L. J.
1990 The Crafsmanship of Sin-leqi-unninni. *Orientalia Lovaniensia Periodica* 21:45–79.

te Velde, H.
1977 *Seth, God of Confusion*. 2nd. ed. Leiden: E. J. Brill.

Veldhuis, Niek
1991 *A Cow of Sîn*. Library of Oriental Texts, 2. Groningen: Styx Publications.

Vermeule, Emily
1979 *Aspects of Death in Early Greek Art and Poetry*. Berkeley and Los Angeles: University of California Press.

Vernant, Jean-Pierre
1990 One…Two…Three: *Erōs*. Pp. 465–78 in Halperin, Winkler, and Zeitlin.
1991 *Mortals and Immortals: Collected Essays*, ed. Froma I. Zeitlin. Princeton: Princeton University Press.

Vice, Sue
1997 *Introducing Bakhtin*. Manchester and New York: Manchester University Press.

Vogelzang, Marianna E.
1998 Some Aspects of Oral and Written Tradition in Akkadian. Pp. 265–78 in Vogelzang and Vanstiphout.
Vogelzang, Marianna E., and Herman L. J. Vanstiphout, eds.
1992 *Mesopotamian Epic Literature: Oral or Aural?* Lewiston: Edwin Mellen Press.
1996 *Mesopotamian Poetic Language: Sumerian and Akkadian.* Cuneiform Monographs 6. Groningen: Styx Publications.
Volk, Konrad
1995 *Inanna und Šukaletuda: Zur historisch-politischen Deutung eines sumerischen Literaturwerkes.* Wiesbaden: Harrasowitz.
Walls, Neal H.
1992 *The Goddess Anat in Ugaritic Myth.* Society of Biblical Literature Dissertation Series 135. Atlanta: Scholars Press.
Watanabe, Chikako Esther
1998 Symbolism of the Royal Lion Hunt in Assyria. Pp. 439–50 in Prosecký.
von Weiher, Egbert
1971 *Der babylonische Gott Nergal.* AOAT 11. Neukirchen-Vluyn: Neukirchener Verlag; Kevelaer: Butzon & Bercker.
1980 Gilgameš und Enkidu—Die Idee einer Freundschaft. *Baghdader Mitteilungen* 11:106–19.
Weller, Barry
1997 Wizards, Warriors, and the Beast: Glatisant in Love. Pp. 227–48 in Sedgwick.
Wendte, Edward F.
1973 The Contendings of Horus and Seth. Pp. 108–26 in *The Literature of Ancient Egypt*, ed. William Kelly Simpson. New Haven: Yale University Press.
1979 Response to Robert A. Oden's "The Contendings of Horus and Seth" (Chester Beatty Papyrus No. 1): A Structural Interpretation. *HR* 18:370–72.
Westenholz, Joan Goodnick
1992 Metaphorical Language in the Poetry of Love in the Ancient Near East. Pp. 381–87 in *La circulation des biens, des personnes et des idées dans le Proche-Orient ancien. Actes de la XXXVIIIe Rencontre Assyriologique Internationale (Paris, 8–10 juillet 1991)*, eds. D. Charpin and F. Joannès. Paris: Éditions Recherche sur les Civilisations.
1995 Love Lyrics from the Ancient Near East. *CANE* 4:2471–84.

Whiting, Robert M.
1985 An Old Babylonian Incantation from Tell Asmar. *ZA* 75:179–87.

Wilcke, Claus
1985 Liebesbeschwörungen aus Isin. *ZA* 75:188–209.

Willbern, David
1989 Reading after Freud. Pp. 158–79 in Atkins and Morrow.

Winkler, John J.
1990 *The Constraints of Desire: The Anthropology of Sex and Gender in Ancient Greece*. New York: Routledge.

Winter, Irene J.
1996 Sex, Rhetoric, and the Public Monument: The Alluring Body of Naram-Sîn of Agade. Pp. 11–26 in *Sexuality in Ancient Art*, ed. Natalie Boymel Kampen. Cambridge and New York: Cambridge University Press.

Wyke, Maria, ed.
1999 *Gender and the Body in the Ancient Mediterranean*. Oxford: Blackwell Publishers.

Subject Index

Text Index

OTHER TITLES IN THIS SERIES

1 Larry G. Herr with Warren C. Trenchard
Published Pottery of Palestine

2 Itamar Singer
*Muwatalli's Prayer to the Assembly of Gods through the Storm-God of Lightning (*CTH *381)*

3 Tomis Kapitan (ed.)
Archaeology, History and Culture in Palestine and the Near East: Essays in Memory of Albert E. Glock

4 Stephen L. Cook and S. C. Winter (eds.)
On the Way to Nineveh: Studies in Honor of George M. Landes

5 Samuel Wolff (ed.)
Studies in the Archaeology of Israel and Neighboring Lands in Memory of Douglas L. Esse (published jointly with The Oriental Institute of the University of Chicago)

6 Burton MacDonald
"East of the Jordan": Territories and Sites of the Hebrew Scriptures

7 Beth Alpert Nakhai
Archaeology and the Religions of Canaan and Israel